# SECRET
# MUSEUMS

# SECRET MUSEUMS

The Films of Arthur Lipsett

**STEPHEN BROOMER**

WILFRID LAURIER
UNIVERSITY PRESS

This book has been published with the help of a grant from the Federation for the Humanities and Social Sciences, through the Awards to Scholarly Publications Program, using funds provided by the Social Sciences and Humanities Research Council of Canada. Wilfrid Laurier University Press acknowledges the support of the Canada Council for the Arts for our publishing program. We acknowledge the financial support of the Government of Canada through the Canada Book Fund for our publishing activities. Funding provided by the Government of Ontario and the Ontario Arts Council. This work was supported by the Research Support Fund.

**Library and Archives Canada Cataloguing in Publication**

Title: Secret museums : the films of Arthur Lipsett / Stephen Broomer.

Other titles: Films of Arthur Lipsett

Names: Broomer, Stephen, author

Description: Includes bibliographical references and index.

Identifiers: Canadiana (print) 20240462807 | Canadiana (ebook) 20240462831 | ISBN 9781771126878 (hardcover) | ISBN 9781771126908 (PDF) | ISBN 9781771126892 (EPUB)

Subjects: LCSH: Lipsett, Arthur, 1936-1986—Criticism and interpretation. | LCSH: Motion picture producers and directors—Canada—Biography. | LCSH: Motion pictures—Canada—History. | LCGFT: Biographies.

Classification: LCC PN1998.3.L57 B76 2025 | DDC 791.4302/33092—dc23

Cover and interior design by John van der Woude, JVDW Designs

Front cover image: Arthur Lipsett, Montreal, circa 1964. Copyright Judith Sandiford. Reproduced with permission of Judith Sandiford.

© 2026 Wilfrid Laurier University Press
Waterloo, Ontario, Canada
www.wlupress.wlu.ca

 This book is printed on FSC® certified paper. It contains recycled materials and other controlled sources, is processed chlorine-free, and is manufactured using biogas energy.

Printed in Canada

Every reasonable effort has been made to acquire permission for copyrighted material used in this text, and to acknowledge all such indebtedness accurately. Any errors and omissions called to the publisher's attention will be corrected in future printings.

No part of this publication may be reproduced, stored in a retrieval system, or transmitted, in any form or by any means, without the prior written consent of the publisher or a licence from the Canadian Copyright Licensing Agency (Access Copyright). For an Access Copyright licence, visit http://www.accesscopyright.ca or call toll-free to 1-800-893-5777.

*Wilfrid Laurier University Press is located on the Haldimand Tract, part of the traditional territories of the Haudenosaunee, Anishnaabe, and Neutral Peoples. This land is part of the Dish with One Spoon Treaty between the Haudenosaunee and Anishnaabe Peoples and symbolizes the agreement to share, to protect our resources, and not to engage in conflict. We are grateful to the Indigenous Peoples who continue to care for and remain interconnected with this land. Through the work we publish in partnership with our authors, we seek to honour our local and larger community relationships, and to engage with the diversity of collective knowledge integral to responsible scholarly and cultural exchange.*

# CONTENTS

List of Illustrations / **ix**
Acknowledgements / **xi**

Introduction / **1**
One  The Stranger / **7**
Two  Revelation / **25**
Three  A Personal Vision / **41**
Four  Processional / **55**
Five  The Green Fuse / **71**
Six  Time-Capsule / **87**
Seven  Print-Out / **107**
Eight  Landscapes / **127**
Nine  Messages from Space / **153**
Ten  The 10,000 Things / **181**

Notes / **195**
Filmography / **225**
Archival Sources / **227**
Bibliography / **229**
Index / **235**

# LIST OF ILLUSTRATIONS

1.1 *Anything Can Happen on Channel 6* (Arthur Lipsett, NFB, 1960) / **21**
2.1 Arthur Lipsett contorts his face for a self-portrait in *Very Nice, Very Nice* (Arthur Lipsett, NFB, 1962) / **33**
2.2 *Very Nice, Very Nice* (Arthur Lipsett, NFB, 1962) / **33**
4.1 *21-87* (Arthur Lipsett, NFB, 1964) / **64**
4.2 John Max offers a Buddhist prayer in *21-87* (Arthur Lipsett, NFB, 1964) / **66**
5.1 Arthur Lipsett, self-portrait, in *Free Fall* (Arthur Lipsett, NFB, 1964) / **77**
5.2 Martin Lavut and Judith Sandiford in *Free Fall* (Arthur Lipsett, NFB, 1964) / **81**
6.1 *A Trip Down Memory Lane* (Arthur Lipsett, NFB, 1965) / **93**
6.2 *A Trip Down Memory Lane* (Arthur Lipsett, NFB, 1965) / **96**
7.1 *Fluxes* (Arthur Lipsett, NFB, 1968) / **118**
7.2 *Fluxes* (Arthur Lipsett, NFB, 1968) / **122**
8.1 Arthur Lipsett poses with his Secret Museum in *N-Zone* (Arthur Lipsett, NFB 1970) / **132**
8.2 *N-Zone* (Arthur Lipsett, NFB, 1970) / 139
9.1 Arthur Lipsett as The Mongolian in *Strange Codes* (Arthur Lipsett, 1975) / **168**
9.2 Arthur Lipsett as The Monkey King in *Strange Codes* (Arthur Lipsett, 1975) / **171**

# ACKNOWLEDGEMENTS

I first encountered Arthur Lipsett's films, as many of my generation did, on Canadian television. His films had continued to flourish in broadcast, decades after his death, shown interstitially to a country that valued the arts and for whom such a complex, sardonic vision of humanity might yet be met with knowing laughter. The barrage of image, that style with which Lipsett is most closely associated, had come to permeate the aesthetics of broadcasting, and yet it still seemed new and alive for its wit and its deep allusions—eternally vital in its absurd constitution. I came to know Lipsett's struggles through the shorthand and inaccurate explanations that circulate in film schools: there his rhythms could be celebrated and taught, but the comic overtones of his films—a trait less easy to recognize, let alone imitate—were rarely acknowledged. This book celebrates not only Lipsett's art and technique, but his humanity, which was restless, funny, and wise.

My studies in the films of Arthur Lipsett began informally at York University's Department of Film and Video in the early 2000s. My mentors in that department, Seth Feldman, Janine Marchessault, and the late Peter Morris, played instrumental roles in developing my passion for Canadian and experimental cinema. I came late to the study of Arthur Lipsett, and my work is indebted to those who came before, among them Lois Siegel, William Wees, and Brett Kashmere, whose research, scholarship, and interviews have proven invaluable. Special mention must be made of the makers of the three most comprehensive studies of Lipsett's work preceding mine, Amelia Does, Michael Dancsok, and the late Martin Lavut. Their projects—a book, a master's thesis, and a documentary, respectively—served as essential resources for my own project, and also as curatives to the flawed, casual, and reductive narratives of Lipsett's life and work that were taking root elsewhere.

Judith Sandiford was generous and patient with my questions and illuminated aspects of Arthur's life and personality that have long been misreported and misunderstood. My thanks to her and her husband, Ronald Weihs, for their time and insights. Interest in Lipsett's work has been maintained in the four decades since his passing thanks to the efforts of his many friends and former colleagues, some of whom did a great deal to support and care for him in his anguished later years. Tanya Tree, Terry Ryan, Fortner Anderson, John Max, and Christopher Nutter made selfless efforts to secure and protect the legacy of Lipsett's creative work, and it is thanks to their efforts that so many of Lipsett's charts and notebooks survived. Knowledge of Lipsett's early life is also strongly informed by his sister Marian Arnold and her willingness to give testimony to the challenges of their family life, as related to Amelia Does and Martin Lavut.

Materials related to Lipsett's life and career are held at both the archives of the National Film Board of Canada (NFB) and the Cinémathèque québécoise (CQ), and both organizations were generous in their support of this research. My thanks to André D'Ulisse and Steven Woloshen of the NFB, and to Guillaume Lafleur, Jean Gagnon, Lorraine LeBlanc, and Sylvie Brouillette of the CQ. The archives and curatorial staff at CQ were essential collaborators throughout this project, from Jean's collaboration in my restoration of Lipsett's *Strange Codes* in 2016, to Sylvie's research facilitation during the COVID-19 pandemic. Clint Enns, who conducted research on my behalf at the Cinémathèque, served this study not only through his meticulous documentation of Lipsett's charts and notebooks, but through his thoughtful interpretations of that material. Illuminating judgment has long been a hallmark of Clint's own creative and critical work, and his support for this research and our conversations about our findings informed my own response to the puzzle of the secret museum.

Siobhan McMenemy, Anne Brackenbury, and Murray Tong of Wilfrid Laurier University Press have championed this manuscript with immense patience and generous enthusiasm, and I am grateful for their trust as they stewarded this project from proposal to draft to bound book. My collaboration with Siobhan, which for this project began in 2017 but reaches back to my days as a graduate student, has been one of the rich rewards of my professional life, and her wise counsel and compassionate interest in the topics of my work have served as great encouragement, as has her practical, visionary, and egalitarian sensibilities for scholarly publishing. The staff and board of WLUP have been invaluable supporters of this project, as were the peer reviewers whose thoughtful advice improved and refined the text. My thanks to copy editor Ren Baron and designer John van der Woude for their considerable efforts.

This project developed through many animated conversations with friends and colleagues. For the encouragement, support, and fine company, I thank Izabella Pruska-Oldenhof, Jim Shedden, R. Bruce and Kathryn Elder, Kier-La Janisse, Guy Maddin, Michael Zryd, Eva Kolcze and Spencer Barclay, John Creson and Adam Rosen, Richard Kerr, Dave Spittle, Justine McCloskey, Daniel McIntyre, Madi Piller, Bruce Posner, Daniel Adams, José Sarmiento Hinojosa, Irene Bindi, Jim Anderson, Rick Hancox, and Christine Lucy Latimer. The side of my research that deals in technical analysis has been facilitated by the Liaison of Independent Filmmakers of Toronto, its board, and its staff, Karl Reinsalu, Renata Mohamed, Chris Kennedy, Noah Henderson, and Robin Riad. Image reproductions were made with the advice of Mark Loeser, whose comprehensive knowledge of experimental film has been a vital asset in the development of this project. This project has benefitted a great deal from the generosity of my colleagues at University of Toronto's Innis College, James Cahill, Bart Testa, Alberto Zambenedetti, and Charlie Keil. Under the direction of librarian Kate Johnson, the Innis College Library was a magnificent refuge where the final draft of this book was undertaken.

*Secret Museums* was developed in part while I was serving as the Fulbright Visiting Scholar at University of California Santa Cruz and the Prelinger Library, an experience that deepened my interest in collage and compilation filmmaking at an integral crossroads in my scholarly and creative practice, and which afforded me some long and pleasant car rides with friend and fellow Lipsett scholar Brett Kashmere. My thanks to Rick and Megan Prelinger, the faculty and staff of UC Santa

Cruz, and the Fulbright Foundation. A subsequent postdoctoral fellowship, sponsored by the International Council for Canadian Studies and held at the Centre for Canadian Studies at Brock University under the supervision of Gregory Betts, afforded me focused time to study the Canadian experimental tradition. My early research into Arthur Lipsett resulted in an article, "The Success and Failure of Arthur Lipsett," that was published by *Found Footage Magazine* in 2016, thanks to publishers César Ustarroz and Cristina Martínez. That essay was reprinted with revisions in *Moments of Perception: Experimental Film in Canada*, edited by Jim Shedden and Barbara Sternberg.

I have been able to persist in my critical work thanks to the support of my family: my parents, Cherie and Stuart Broomer, whose own interests in art and culture inspired my strange passions and who have always encouraged me to pursue my interests within a framework of love and justice; my brother, Geoffrey Broomer, who taught me how to watch movies and how to edit video and who continues to be my mentor in matters of world cinema and history; and my partner, Emmalyne Laurin, who has spent countless hours watching these films with me, patiently reading and listening to drafts of the work as it developed, and inspiring me always to persist.

I dedicate this book to Cameron Moneo, my scholarly and creative collaborator of almost two decades. Together we have borne strange witness to thousands of hours of films, strange to most for our celebration of the outsider and the misfit, stranger still for our creative digestion of all we have encountered. Cameron has long influenced my approach to writing on experimental cinema by his own wisdom, comic disposition, and wit. This study springs in part from the assiduous research and findings of his doctoral dissertation, on comedy and the avant-garde, and has benefitted immensely from his thoughtful responses to early drafts of the manuscript. I have never in my life laughed harder than I have with Cameron—strangling tides of laughter that came to comfort us in terrible hours and that taught us what Mark Twain and Arthur Lipsett knew: that "against the assault of Laughter, nothing can stand."

# INTRODUCTION

BETWEEN 1960 AND 1975, ARTHUR LIPSETT MADE EIGHT films, the bulk of which can be broadly characterized as collages, a mix of original and appropriated images, set to soundtracks that proffer warnings, platitudes, and hysterical testimonies. His films were often concerned with the place of spiritual experience in a civilization matured on science, war, and the mass media of Western Atomic Age society, but they are also informed by the loneliness of the crowd, an absence of meaning felt by the long faces captured in his street photography. The films were not declarations of the tragedy of a godless world, or the failure of mass movements, or the terror of the crowd, or the promise of the bomb: they were experiences, often riotously comic, that placed irreconcilable ideals in contrast. They confounded viewers and critics, as well as the government agency that had commissioned them. Most of Lipsett's films were made for the National Film Board of Canada (NFB), a federal communications arm whose mission was to represent what constituted good citizenship. His inability to adapt to that work culture or, conversely, the inability of the agency to accommodate him, resulted in a schism that slowly ended his career as a filmmaker. When he took his own life in 1986, he had not completed a film in eleven years and was living in solitude with schizophrenia.[1]

The NFB was formed out of the passage of the National Film Act in 1938, an effort on the part of the government to aide in the coordination of government film activities.[2] With Canada's entrance into the Second

World War, the NFB became a state instrument for mass communication. By the late 1950s, when Lipsett joined, it had transformed into a utility for the dissemination of Canadian culture. Personal filmmaking had not found purchase there; while American art cinema was experiencing its first soundings of an organized experimental film movement in the 1940s, the newly founded Film Board was breaking ground in stylistic approaches to cinema as mass communication, establishing conventions through its own conservative experimentation with film form. While it would continue to evolve in new directions, the NFB never abandoned its root mission, an inflexible conceptualization of cinema as an art of communication. Lipsett's films, fractured modernist treatments of mid-century life, were unprecedented in the experience of his colleagues, and they supported them, for a time and insofar as they could define them within the goals of the institution.

Lipsett's approach was specialized in the broader context of experimental filmmaking, wherein absurdist themes had been overshadowed by the earnest suffering of the trance film and, later, by impulses to cast intimacies, abstractions, and psychedelia. Absurdist humour was seldom proclaimed as a foundational value of experimental cinema, yet it remains, as a component of Surrealism, at the very root of that cinema. An absurdist impulse in American experimental filmmaking flourished in small pockets in the 1940s and 1950s—for instance, in the work of Sidney Peterson, James Broughton, and Christopher Maclaine—but it became more dominant in the late 1950s, following on the influences of Dada and Surrealist cinema, the American screwball comedy, the growing circulation of absurdist literature and theatre, and the emergence of the Neo-Dada movement.[3] It was in these years that filmmaker Ron Rice wrote a mock manifesto for Absurdist film before his untimely death, and among his contemporaries, filmmakers like Jack Smith, Richard Bartlett, and Carl Linder made films distinctively indebted to the Theatre of the Absurd.[4]

Film has a unique capacity for animating the aesthetics of modern literary Absurdism, an inheritance of nonsense from the likes of Alfred Jarry, Franz Kafka, Samuel Beckett, Eugene Ionesco, and Albert Camus, benefitting from cinema's ability to place images in immediate contrast to one another, to juxtapose, to operate in time, to declare continuities of action and space, all traits that are ready-made for creative subversion. Further to this, the experimental collage film is distinctively attuned to absurdism for its inevitable undermining of the images that it pilfers and the attitudes, narratives, histories, and archives that those images represent.[5] Like Camus, Lipsett located the absurd in the divorce between ideological convictions and in a recognition that progress was a futile illusion. Like Beckett, Lipsett's humour became a form of heroism in the desolate sunset of the twentieth century—and like the protagonist of a Kafka novel drowned by the maddening insouciance of bureaucracy, or a character in an Ionesco play who convinces themselves of a lie through cunning but wrong deductions, Lipsett lived in a fog of trivialities. Absurdism was a natural extension of his affect, his resilient, if mordant, sense of humour. At the National Film Board, he became something of a 'pataphysical artist after Jarry, in the sense that his work appeared to speak in an elegant way about serious things, concealing his embrace of illogic in an illogical world and even, from some viewers, his bemusement at the futility of it all.[6] Lipsett was an absurdist in an era of double-talk, exhausting consumerism, and mass movements. He explored these themes through flaneurism, sifting the tortured and jocular faces in the crowd, following in the immediate wake of Robert Frank in capturing the dispossession and aimlessness of the modern Western face. To some, the stream of consciousness effected in Lipsett's montage was just this: madness and nonsense and the heights of the absurd. To others, straining to pin down an elusive, didactic meaning, the films were reduced to clear and stable commands: resist consumerism, love humanity, find God.

Lipsett's films endorsed the premise of the Theatre of the Absurd, which had rejected the search for a model "through which to discover fundamental ethical or philosophical certainties about life and the world."[7] His films could embrace ambiguity and still serve as a jeremiad on the corruption of man. Steeled against ready interpretation, they feature images that provoke rage and compassion without occupying those emotions, even forcing a contradictory tone through the buoyancy of his sound design. He maintained this resistance to ready meaning even as his approach transformed with each new film, an urgent and restless series of transitions, each building on the last. While his films are commonly remembered for a few narrow strategies, no two are perfectly alike. The trajectory of Lipsett's work bears a continuous evolution; rather than rest on his laurels, he departed quickly from his early success to develop challenging approaches, to break new ground.

Lipsett was not merely an heir to the absurdist streak of the twentieth century's literary avant-garde; he was also an aspiring mystic, absorbing the syncretic, Omnist take on Buddhism popularized by Alan Watts and Walter Evans-Wentz, as well as the spiritual roots music and avant-garde art music that he encountered through the Folkways record label. Between his tragicomic relationship with the Atomic Age and his pantheistic tour of ancient knowledge and ritual, Lipsett shared common ground with the Beats. In his decade making films, Lipsett's arcane fascinations grew to drown out the social comment of his work, and his colleagues found the results incomprehensible. Lipsett's spiritual contemplations were matched in his films with themes of technological progress, provoking reflection of the history and future of humankind, guided by a steady interest in cybernetics and the philosophies of Warren McCulloch. His spiritual and historical interests were neither clinical nor dogmatic, and a clue to how Lipsett saw himself and his work in relation to the whole of the human project—that is, against a backdrop of the great ontological and theological questions—is revealed by his fascination with the time charts of John B. Sparks. Published by Rand McNally as "Histomaps," Sparks's time charts were oversized vertical timelines that graph the chronological progression of vast topics: world history (1931), evolution (1931), and world religions (1947).[8] The Histomap represents an impossible task of containing all of humanity's conflicts and progress. Its density mirrors Lipsett's profuse, rapid montage. As Lipsett's work evolved towards a greater and more ambiguous density, he returned again and again to a recorded interview that he had saved and transcribed, between cybernetics philosopher Warren McCulloch and Lipsett's NFB colleague Roman Kroitor, in which McCulloch describes the concept of anastomotic knowledge, knowledge fed by many strands of data, a philosophy of information that is tied to the image of a river fed by many branching paths. By the end of the 1960s, the search for an anastomotic method in art became the seed for Lipsett's conception of the collage film and of artmaking in general.

In their day, Lipsett's films were considered funny. The NFB promoted them as "wryly amusing," their ad copy noting that the films have "humorous aspects." In the years since his tragic death, they have been regarded in a different light, and, as such, the nature of his humour has seldom been addressed.[9] It begins in a comedy of fast, mechanical rhythms, to the end of perceptual impossibilities, its images passing at a greater speed than the mind can readily grasp or relate. Like the piano rolls of Conlon Nancarrow, punched to perform what human hands cannot, Lipsett allows the projector to see in ways that eyes cannot.[10] Lipsett's humour assumes a growing sense of sardonic juxtaposition, as, with each passing film, his rhythms even out and the filmmaker spends more time meditating on the ridiculousness of life on Earth. His comedy tends to lie in a disparity between sound and image, which begins with contrasting and truncated rhythms and later becomes a puckish vertical montage of motivated disagreement between elements. Nowhere is this clearer than in *Fluxes*, in which the testimony of Adolf Eichmann, on trial in his glass booth, is replaced with the sounds of sitcoms and gameshows. However, another absurdist aspect of Lipsett's work lies in his ability to condense a rapidly changing inventory of information and affect into the relative miniature of the short film. His films become, to use Robert S. Dupree's term, a "copious inventory," one that, like the attempts of literary moderns of the early twentieth century, attempts to contain all the world in a work or, in the spirit of comic failure, whatever will fit.[11] The copious inventory acts inversely to Stephane Mallarmé's concept of the "the Book to end all books," which tends to imagine an infinite container, the impossible promise of an eternal spine.[12] The copious inventory finds its humour and its meaning in the hard limit of its container and, accordingly, its inevitable failure.

This book considers Arthur Lipsett as an absurdist filmmaker whose astonishing resilience is reflected in the tragicomic gestures of his films. In charting his life and work, I seek to correct the narratives that dominate how Arthur Lipsett is remembered, often sentimentalized as a victim of society, a portrayal that obscures the worth and pleasure of the work itself. This portrayal of Lipsett has been advanced by critics writing in the wake of his suicide and, in recent decades, by the NFB itself. My account considers his last films as major, deliberated works of intention, against the grain of a discourse that cannot separate them from the circumstances of his resignation or of his death.[13] Lipsett's story is that of the universal homelessness of the poet in the twentieth century, in the avaricious, murderous climate of contemporary Western society. As the details of Lipsett's life and tragic end are widely known by those who would encounter his films, the films demand a separation of the work from their maker in order to see them clearly. Those who seek out a crushing sadness in Lipsett's films will find it; those who seek out laughter will find that as well. This is the strength of their ambiguity. Without prejudice, without foreknowledge of the artist's illness and death, seeing these films as viewers first saw them, one finds a laughter that isn't quite joyful and a reprehension that isn't quite personal. In the films of Arthur Lipsett, even the redemption of laughter can't be trusted. At the same time, this book does not disavow his life as a context for his work: Lipsett was immersed in an environment of social criticism, and, in his departure from the security of the NFB and the decline of his final years, he comes to reflect Artaud's conception of the artist "suicided by society."[14]

With this book, I provide a key to the copious inventories of Lipsett's images, to whatever degree is possible. Lipsett's sources, what they represent, and how he uses them, are brought into dialogue with what can be gleaned of his motives from memoranda, proposals, and charts, what he began late in his career to refer to as his "secret museum," a label that is itself a strange and obscure joke. I deliberated on Lipsett's interest in the Histomap as a structural template, beginning in 1966—again, that copious inventory, the attempt to harness in miniature a totality of experience. However, the power of these films is, in the end, a result of his instinct, his rhythm, his will to totality, his sense of humour, his desire to play the Holy Fool to a straight world. These traits that give his films a lingering power also cast what can be known of his elusive sources, his motives, and his life into relative triviality. The dust of life is stripped away, and only the work remains, the victory of an uncompromising mystic.

ONE

# THE STRANGER

I N THE FINAL DAYS OF APRIL 1986, DR. NANCY CARPENTER, A psychologist stationed at the Jewish General Hospital in Montreal, paid a visit to the apartment of a patient. It was a wellness check, done out of concern for the middle-aged man, recently discharged, who had often reported hearing voices and who had a history of attempting suicide. She found him inside, dead, hanging by a rope. Arthur Lipsett had killed himself two weeks short of his fiftieth birthday.

At the time of his death, Lipsett had been Carpenter's patient for three years.[1] He had reported to her the nature of his interior voices, conversations he would have with himself that, at times, gave him comfort but that, at other times, tormented him with virulent antisemitic doubts about himself. He had also intimated to her that suicide was a necessary path for him because he had lost his creativity.[2] Creative action had given Lipsett's life a sense of direction in a society that he recognized as being on the wrong side of a devilish bargain; the world around him was one in which faith, commerce, technology, and rhetoric were so sorely muddled as to drown the sensitive—a world of mixed-up confusion. He had contested this melancholy paradigm through his own creative work, with films that met the horror and despair of the Atomic Age with joyous rhythms, raucous humour, and absurdist convictions. But much of that had come to an end by the late 1970s, when his struggles with mental illness and poverty had overtaken him.

Arthur Harold Lipsett was born in Montreal, Quebec, on May 13, 1936, to Solomon and Norma Lipsett.[3] Three years later, his sister, Marian, was born. Their mother Norma, née Goldberg, was of Jewish-Polish extraction; she had emigrated to Winnipeg with her family at age seventeen. Solomon Lipsett had received his Ph.D. in Chemistry from McGill University in Montreal and, prior to that, had lived in Winnipeg, where the Lipschitz family had emigrated from England, and, before that, from Russia. Solomon and Norma Lipsett married in Montreal on September 22, 1931, and lived for a number of years in apartments in the Queen Mary Road and Rue Lemieux area in Westmount. With his background in chemistry, Solomon Lipsett assumed a position as an analytical chemist at J.T. Donald and Company, a firm of geological assayists.[4] By the time of her son's birth, Norma Lipsett's mother had died, and she was far from her remaining family in Winnipeg and in Europe. Shortly after Marian's birth in 1939, the family moved into a unit in a quadruplex at 5106 Lacombe Avenue, but their home during much of Lipsett's childhood was 4970 Hingston Avenue in Montreal's Notre-Dame-de-Grâce district, far from the impoverished Jewish community of the Main.[5]

The Montreal in which Arthur Lipsett grew up was deeply divided along lines of language and race. A small Jewish community had been fostered in Canada from the 1760s onward, with Quebec acting as a major landing point for Jews migrating from Europe. The community remained small until the late nineteenth century brought a tide of Eastern European, Yiddish-speaking Jewish immigrants. This unanticipated growth of the Jewish community led to the creation of more synagogues and distinctive social systems, clinics, and cultural organizations. From the early 1900s to the 1930s, the number of Jewish Canadians living in Montreal ballooned from a few thousand to more than 60,000, many of them poor, seeking better opportunities in the "New World," and fleeing from growing antisemitism in Europe. Montreal became an iconically Jewish city through this cultural influx, a distinction that sat poorly with those Anglophone Protestants and Quebecois Catholics who feared that Jewish immigration was transforming the traditionally

Christian character of the country. For the Quebecois, there was also, beyond mere xenophobia, a fear that the massive influx of Jewish children into the Anglophone school system would contribute to a decline in the use of French. From the 1920s onward, these fears manifested in a racist othering of the Jews of Montreal.[6]

It was in the interwar period that Quebecois antisemitism became most visible, primarily in resort regions surrounding Montreal, where a Jewish presence came with the seasons. Montreal Jews visiting in the summer to regions like the Laurentian mountains would discover forbidding shops with signs reading "Jews Not Allowed."[7] In 1935, the year before Lipsett was born, a synagogue filled with worshippers was set on fire in Val David, a few hours northwest of Montreal. Victimhood was becoming woven into the Jewish Canadian identity as a result of such terrorism, largely through the work of the agitator Adrien Arcand, whose fascistic pamphleteering had advocated a racist ideology, one that unified antisemites and anti-communists, commanding them to deal, by violent means, with the "Jewish problem."[8] Arcand's diatribes imagine a world in which Jews were the source of all evil, pursuing secret and malicious rituals with a goal of domination over the good and the innocent. The sickness of Arcand's beliefs found an audience so absolute in their racist convictions that the Royal Canadian Mounted Police, which until then had focused their investigations of national threats on leftist suspects, began to investigate Arcand's people as a potential danger to the crown. By the end of the 1930s, with Canada's entry into the war effort, Arcand's Parti de l'Unité Nationale, a fascist political platform, had six thousand members and had gained attention in Canada and the United States.

The Montreal that Arthur Lipsett was born into was a city of culture and social safety that the Jewish Canadian community had done much to build in the preceding decades. However, it was also Arcand's Montreal, where student demonstrators focused their rage against communists and Jews, marching down Sainte-Catherine Street sporting antisemitic slogans. It was Arcand's Montreal where the agitator's zealots marched on Boulevard Saint-Laurent, picking fights with Jewish youths and smashing the windows of Jewish shops.[9] On some level, the goal of such a movement, no matter how fringe it was, no matter how hysterical its advocates were, had always been to convince the Jewish children of Montreal that they were less than human. These demonstrations had continued even after Arcand's arrest in 1940 for "plotting to overthrow the state" and his placement in an internment camp, where he would remain, declaring himself "the Canadian führer," spouting his antisemitic diatribes to his fellow prisoners until the end of the war.[10] He had been the architect of an infectious form of Canadian fascism, and even his imprisonment failed to deter his followers. Arcand spent many years comparing others to cockroaches and bugs, but perhaps it was a voice something like his that had crept into Arthur Lipsett's ear during his illness, hiding in his walls, belittling the artist for being born a Jew.

At age eight, Lipsett was identified by his teachers as possessing special creative gifts. At their recommendation, he was placed in Saturday art classes at the Art Association of Montreal.[11] Lipsett's pre-adolescent foundations in drawing and sculpting were reportedly a cause of conflict in the family. His father's devotion to hard science was anchored in a rejection of the imagination. As a geophysically focused chemist, Solomon Lipsett was responsible for identifying and measuring the compositional makeup of bedrock, of interpreting the most fundamental materials of the Earth. To an empiricist like Solomon, the imagining of things into being was incompatible with his own pursuits of quantifying and contemplating measurable phenomena. This lack of common ground between Lipsett and his father emerged so early in Lipsett's life as to form a lasting rift in their relationship.[12]

According to Lipsett's sister, Marian Arnold (née Lipsett), their mother Norma had lived with manic depression, now commonly known as bipolar disorder. Norma Lipsett's struggles with this disorder were compounded by her having been informed after the war ended that members of her family near Kiev had been executed in the Babi Yar massacre in September 1941.[13] This news had thrown her into a deep despair from which she would not recover. On January 8, 1947, Norma killed herself at age forty-four by ingesting a household cleaner. Accounts place her son Arthur, then age ten, as a witness to this horrific suicide.[14] The Lipsett family held a traditional Jewish funeral for Norma, complete with its religious rites: sitting shiva, covering mirrors in black cloth, and sitting on stools. After the funeral, traditional Jewish religious customs went unobserved in the home. Marian would later recall that they did not observe religious holidays or traditional rites of passage—for example, daughters being taught to prepare the Sabbath meal.[15] Lipsett was never given a bar mitzvah; the denial of this rite is symbolic of his arrested development in his father's eyes, but it may also have simply been the result of Solomon's indifference to tradition rather than willful inattention to his son. The absence of Norma ushered in a more secular lifestyle for the family, one that was suited to Solomon's empirical convictions.

In the years following Norma's death, her children would spend summers at Camp Maccabee, a Jewish sleepaway camp. That ended with Solomon's second marriage in 1952, to Renée Kramer, which brought Kramer and her daughter Eva into the family. Renée and Eva were Hungarian Jews who had survived thirteen months in Auschwitz; Renée's first husband, Zoltan Kramer, had died in Dachau in 1944, the same year that her mother, father, and brother had died in Auschwitz-Birkenau. The presence of Renée and Eva drew the Lipsett household into an even more direct confrontation with the suffering of Jews in the Holocaust. Renée Lipsett was haunted by terrible nightmares that would wake the household. For Marian, these new relationships were difficult; she found that her stepmother was unable or uninterested in mothering or in bonding with Solomon's children. Arthur was less impacted by the change and would later give his partner Judith Sandiford the impression that Renée Lipsett had served as a calming presence in a volatile household, acting as a buffer between the children and Solomon and strongly encouraging Arthur's creativity.[16] Renée worked with a resettlement organization in Montreal for survivors of the Holocaust, and between her personal trauma and her ongoing activism for those in similar straits, her preoccupation with the suffering she had witnessed and experienced became an inextricable facet of her step-children's experience. Although they lived a secular lifestyle in the aftermath of their mother's death, largely divorced from the rituals and community of Judaism, their stepmother's presence would serve as an inevitable reminder of the suffering of their people.

Lipsett attended West Hill High School, graduating in 1954. Following the path set out for him from his childhood art classes, he returned to pursue post-secondary studies at the School of Art and Design at the Art Association of Montreal, which had been renamed in

1949 as the Musée des beaux-arts de Montréal.[17] During the program, his focus narrowed to sculpture and collage. The school was led by Arthur Lismer, then a major figure in Canadian landscape painting. Lismer's lessons would have a profound impact on Lipsett; in particular, it was the senior artist's quasi-mystical philosophies of the relationship between the artist and the course of human progress, and the purpose of the artist in an uncertain age, that would find continuity in much of Lipsett's own mature work. The overarching pedagogy of the school was also designed by Lismer, and thus his beliefs in art education and, in particular, the nurturing of natural creative faculties, would have been experienced by Lipsett from his childhood classes to his post-secondary studies.

Lismer had already been established as a commercial artist in Britain prior to his move to Canada in 1911, where, in Toronto, he connected with a community of other young painters: Franklin Carmichael, J.E.H. MacDonald, and Tom Thomson. It was during the 1910s that he began to paint the Canadian wilderness, and, soon after, he received a government commission as a war painter, documenting the return of troopships in Halifax Harbour. Lismer's wartime paintings demonstrate dramatic contrasts of colour that reinforce geometric relations between subject and setting—for instance, *Olympic with Returned Soldiers* (1919), the ship a brilliant blue triangle splintering through the pallor of a snowy dock, icy waters, and clouded sky, a sign of the potential for modernist abstraction in suggesting an awakening of the land. A cofounder of the Group of Seven, Lismer joined the others on painting trips throughout the 1920s, and, through much of this time, he taught at the Art Gallery of Toronto and elsewhere.[18]

Prior to his appointment at the Art Association of Montreal in 1940, Lismer had made considerable contributions to the field of art education, giving workshops for teachers internationally, espousing the philosophies that creative energies were universal and at their freest in child art and that art-making is a form of reflection that supports emotional and intellectual development. Lismer's method, to celebrate the child's autonomy and freedom, was radical for its time, held in relief against the pretenses of commercial–industrial art training programs.[19] His methods for adult learners would follow from this philosophy: to preserve the creative impulses of childhood and to enhance those impulses with learned technique. He believed scholastic conventions of testing and systematizing art education would compromise the value of art education, privileging mimetic "school art" over the fount of unbridled energies found in art that was authentic and original.[20] Lismer would later be remembered by Northrop Frye as "one of those rare people who can persuade others to release whatever is creative within them—the quality that made Socrates call himself a midwife."[21] Like many twentieth-century painters influenced by a post-impressionist style, Lismer was devoted to the idea of material dominance in the canvas, to privilege the presence of the paint over the illusion of objects. Lismer's lessons in modernism were lessons for eternity, offering that the artist "must weave, carve and mold upon the story of human progress the living truths that masking creates as well as destroys."[22]

From the first years that Arthur Lipsett attended the School of Art and Design as a child, Lismer had been leading the school; the school's emphasis on child art education, and the fact that Lipsett's teachers knew to recommend it for him, are to the credit of Lismer and his efforts at public education and public outreach. Lismer's role at the school was one of comprehensive stewardship; the school had seen mass enrolment from veterans in the aftermath of the Second World War, but that had declined by the 1950s. In the years that Lipsett attended the School of Art and Design, Lismer was implementing a number of pedagogical plans: one was an ongoing series of visiting artist appearances called "Artists in Action," in which the visitor would demonstrate their approach by creating a work with students and members of the public observing; another of Lismer's projects was to draw in public crowds for open classes, putting into action his belief in universal creativity. For all of Lismer's symbolic and mysterious philosophies of art itself, this demonstrates his commitment to pedagogy as a process of revealing and demystifying.[23]

This balance of generosity and vision is evidenced in Lismer's lectures, many of which were part of the public record as his engagements included radio and television appearances. In a lecture, "Art in the Atomic Age," given as part of a series for Radio-Canada in 1953, Lismer spoke of the vital importance of art for the present era, declaring that "the new function of art is not to beautify but to transform life," a claim that twins the transformative power of art to that of new atomic knowledge.[24] For students such as Lipsett, Lismer represented a path that reinforced such creative acts of transformation and the idea that to transform also means to disassemble.

While at the School of Art and Design, Lipsett developed his versatility. Course offerings covered not only the traditional techniques of painting and life drawing, but also commercial skills like graphic design and lettering, mercantile fields of commercial art that Lismer, like many painters of his generation, had himself come through. Lipsett excelled: in his first year, he achieved the highest standing and was awarded the Burland scholarship, sponsored by a major Montreal lithographic company.[25] He won scholarships in each of his three years at the school. When he completed his Honours diploma in 1957, he received a Lauterman scholarship, endowed by the sister of the late Montreal sculptor Dinah Lauterman; by that time, Lipsett had begun to specialize in sculpture.[26] Although Lipsett pursued this work seriously and, according to friends, even entertained purchase offers from Lismer himself, his passion for sculpture would be postponed. Lipsett's first work opportunities would come through the Canadian government by way of the National Film Board of Canada.

Two decades earlier, in 1938, John Grierson had been invited by the Canadian government to study the Canadian film sector, generating a report that led to a further invitation for Grierson to establish a national film commission. Grierson, a lifelong student of propaganda, had been instrumental in promoting the documentary film as an emerging form in the 1920s. By the 1930s, he had a long and storied career as a social critic and communications bureaucrat, making documentaries with government agencies, which had led to his appointment as a public relations officer—essentially a film commissioner—for Britain's General Post Office (GPO) film unit. His masterful coordination of the GPO film unit demonstrated his confidence in a broad and accommodating film form, supporting emerging rhetorical systems for the poetic documentary (in films by Basil Wright and Alberto Cavalcanti) and abstract animation (in films by Len Lye and Norman McLaren). Grierson's flexible sense of film form allowed for new directions in informational filmmaking, embracing a principle of experimentation with the goal of improving communication. It is in this spirit, and not out of conviction for artistic freedom, that so institutionalized a civil servant as Grierson could support artists as vanguard as Lye.

When he came to Canada, Grierson recognized a need to strengthen and centralize government film production. He devised a plan for a federal filmmaking body that emphasized collective destiny and good citizenship. While an existing government agency, the Canadian Government Motion Picture Bureau, had used the natural beauty of the Canadian landscape as a lure to attract tourism, Grierson proposed a social model that would take movies out of the theatres and into classrooms, churches, and trade union halls. He replaced the existing capital fundraising model with one of social optimism. His vision of a "non-theatrical revolution" speaks to his belief in community activation, that nationally produced Canadian films would contribute to a sense of belonging and national pride, boost public morale with examples of a thriving economy and healthy civilization, and, in their wartime coverage, provoke shared outrage.[27] Grierson channelled the optimism of wartime propaganda into a corporatist vision of government and information that his successors would inherit and distinguish with their own variations. Grierson tried for several years to resign his post, finally doing so in 1945 shortly before being implicated by a whisper campaign in the Gouzenko Affair, rumours that also mischaracterized the NFB as a Soviet spy ring.[28]

Grierson's approach to advancing rhetorical form in non-fiction filmmaking was founded on the principle of experimenting within parameters, much as D.W. Griffith had advanced film form at the beginning of the century by expanding the vocabulary for the rhetorical systems of visual storytelling. Grierson observed the melding of actuality and storytelling in an evolving documentary film form, as in the films of Pare Lorentz and Robert Flaherty. As an information officer, he believed in cinema as a medium for communication: to engage the viewer and, while doing so, to deliver information. Cinema was the righteous messenger, a process and a method for communication. His understanding of non-fiction cinema as an art form was clear by the early 1930s, when he began to argue in favour of "the creative treatment of actuality" and the necessity of scenes "taken from the raw" of daily life as the most ready and authentic means by which to represent the modern world.[29] The bureaucratic systems he built adhered rigidly to the communicative potential of the medium, and, by the end of his time shepherding the National Film Board through the tensions of the Second World War, Grierson had reportedly become expeditious, adopting the ethos, "bang them out and no misses."[30] The demands of wartime had prioritized release dates over aesthetic exploration.

By the late 1940s, with his absence, the culture of the Board had changed. Grierson had brought a number of filmmakers to the NFB from his prior post at the GPO—among them, animator Norman McLaren and filmmaker Stuart Legg.[31] Among the first Canadians to be recruited were animator Evelyn Lambart and editor Tom Daly. The end of Grierson's era saw widespread and successful recruitment of new staff. Norman McLaren requested that candidates be sought through art colleges. Colin Low joined the animation department as a result of an NFB letter-writing campaign that reached his art teacher in Calgary; Wolf Koenig was hired for his engineering curiosity while working on a farm in southern Ontario, and he was later joined at the NFB by his brother Joseph; Roman Kroitor joined in 1949 for an internship and stayed. By the beginning of the 1950s, a contingent had formed of quick learners with diverse skills, and this group would reinvigorate Grierson's legacy of pragmatic experimentation, often while assuming multiple administrative and creative roles. With the National Film Act of 1950, the Board gained new operational policies, updating the definition of the Board and its responsibilities to the government and foregrounding its mandate to make "films designed to interpret Canada to Canadians and to other nations." The Board became more autonomous as a result.[32] The NFB underwent a massive reorganization effort, out of the ashes of which came the unit system: four units, designated A through D, each of which was responsible for a separate branch of the NFB's operations and each handling separate portfolios, including military, agricultural, sponsored, animated, feature-length, and art films.[33]

Unit B produced "cultural" films, animations, classroom and science films, sponsored work such as public notices from government ministries, and series like *The Candid Eye* that served to advance a positive image of Canadian citizenship. Unit B was primarily concerned with aesthetics and was more collaborative than the other units, given its relative lack of bureaucratic structure. For a filmmaker like Norman

McLaren, Unit B afforded him a greater autonomy in the kind of work that he could produce, leading to his shift from purely abstract animations to the message-driven pixilation film *Neighbours* (1952).[34] For those like Low and Daly, with their enthusiasm for the poetic documentary, the formation of Unit B coincided with technological shifts, including an embrace of smaller, more portable formats in production. This came in concert with the influence of French photographer Henri Cartier-Bresson, whose conception of the decisive moment and whose style of candid still photography, made possible by the portable and discreet Leica 35mm rangefinder camera, would influence the unit's approach to observational documentary. Further to all of this, Unit B was also breaking ground in terms of composition, editing, and the integration of animation techniques.

The formation of Unit B created the conditions necessary for a creative renaissance at the National Film Board. In 1956, in an ultimate gesture at the end of a decade of courting Francophone interests, the NFB had relocated their headquarters from the federal capital of Ottawa to Montreal. A move so dramatic brought with it a further push for recruitment. According to a biographical profile written by staff at the NFB for their files, Lipsett met the wife of a producer in a drawing class at the School of Art and Design. She told Lipsett that the animation department needed people, and that led to his being hired there in 1957.[35] Colin Low recalls it differently: he had visited Arthur Lismer with the purpose of recruiting students from the School of Art and Design, and he suspected Lipsett had been urged to apply personally by Lismer. When Low interviewed Arthur Lipsett, Lipsett brought a portfolio of drawings, as well as some of his wooden sculptures. He had no animation experience, but then, many of the artists in Unit B had come from non-cinematic backgrounds, including Low himself, whose training, like Lipsett's, was in fine art.

Low had a positive impression of Lipsett's strange modern sculptures and collages, but, more than that, of the enthusiasm with which he explained them.[36] Like other art college graduates, Lipsett's application was successful largely on the basis of his skills in commercial art. He was brought in to develop graphics, with the expectation that he would pick up filmmaking skills on the job. Lipsett would be tasked with service work, graphics, and titling on films and public service advisories. He would later describe it as "doing mattes, animated arrows."[37] Norman McLaren's films, often deceptively simple geometric abstractions, typified in his early success *Hen Hop* (1942), had laid the foundation for the NFB's animation films, and by the late 1950s when Lipsett joined, animation was an esteemed strength of the institution. Grierson had envisioned animation as having two pathways: one lay in the service work of graphics to support documentary films, and the other was light fare, like Norman McLaren's dancing abstractions. The NFB became known for an especially rhythmic form of animation, owing to McLaren's habit of synchronizing movement and music, and further indebted to the punctuative, leading aspect of cartoon sound. As with commercial cartoons, subtle music cues, unexpected substitutions, and violent truncations of sound dictate the velocity and emphasis of the animated image.

A survey of Lipsett's colleagues at Unit B offers some insight into his retraining and the tailoring of his existing skills in collage to the rhythmic, temporal values of filmmaking. Many of the techniques that he would soon make his own were learned from his colleagues, who were among those responsible for the NFB's growing reputation for research and innovation. For example, Colin Low's *The Jolifou Inn* (1955) was the first film for which Low employed his trademark technique of animating still images by moving them beneath a rostrum camera; in this case, his subjects were the paintings of Cornelius Krieghoff, loaned to the National Film Board by the National Gallery of Canada. This forms the visual basis for a chronicle of Krieghoff's time painting the Canadian landscape. The technique of *The Jolifou Inn* would be expanded upon by Low and collaborator Wolf Koenig when they made *City of Gold* (1957) two years later, an adaptation of a memoir excerpted from Canadian cultural history Pierre Berton's *The Klondike Fever: The Life and Death of the Last Great Gold Rush*, which the author would publish the year following the film's production, in 1958.[38] The film is a chronicle of the Yukon Gold Rush and the pilgrimage to Dawson City in the late nineteenth century, with Low applying his animation techniques to large-format glass negatives of the period.[39] This strategy, of animating still images through simple camera manipulation, anticipates Lipsett's own engagement with the still image. It is evidence that, within Unit B, sensibilities were open about what animation could be.

Lipsett brought to the NFB his own set of esoteric interests and his own principles for visual organization. When he joined the Film Board, he was living in the Clifton Arms at 4360 Côte-des-Neiges, on the edge of a highway overpass and overlooking a cemetery, away from Montreal's bohemian neighborhoods. Lipsett would tell his colleagues that it was like "living at the YMCA without the charm."[40] Lacking in consumer comforts, Lipsett's room at the Clifton Arms was, by some descriptions, a monastic sanctum, in itself a sign of his independence from the lifestyle that the Film Board's bohemian civil servants might enjoy in areas of Montreal like the Plateau. He wallpapered his apartment in paper cutout collages, charts, and storyboards, which gave him a reputation among his colleagues for being a restless collector.[41]

Lipsett's first credit on a National Film Board production came in 1960, when he provided animation for David Bairstow's *Men Against the Ice*, a film on the history of explorers navigating the Northwest Passage.[42] That same year, Lipsett was one of six animators whose work was featured in the omnibus *Hors-d'oeuvre*, a broadcast assembled for CBMT, Montreal's English-language CBC station. The broadcast contained twelve short TV spots produced for the Information Services divisions of the CBC and NFB and for the Department of Labour. Five filmmakers were featured alongside Lipsett: Gerald Potterton, Robert Verrall, Derek Lamb, Jeff Hale, and Kaj Pindal. The spots were a mix of policy and public service announcements and advertisements. Lipsett's contribution, while not credited to him on screen, was the final sequence, *Anything Can Happen on Channel 6*, which he would colloquially refer to as the "feet clip," in which cut-out photographs of a pair of bare feet march along to the comic ragtime "piano massacre" of Crazy Otto playing Glenn Miller's "In the Mood," punctuated by the percussive clicks of footsteps.[43] Throughout, a series of still photographs provides a tour of the offerings of CBC TV's channel 6, cultural programming from entertainment to sports.

*Anything Can Happen on Channel 6* is an early glimpse of Lipsett's playful rhythms and his absurdist repurposing of found images, bridging the idols of postwar Western culture with those of antiquity. As it begins, a pair of feet, cut from a still image, are set to march by basic animation, each ankle alternating, one moving up, one down, raising and lowering over the course of three successive frames and held for two frames before switching. These are unconventionally short intervals, and the rough impact demonstrates that Lipsett, as early as 1960, was exploring uncommon shot lengths. This rapid, impatient march sets reeling a series of cutouts defined by their alienation from space: first, solid black and solid white backgrounds alternate against a cutout of a rocket as it rises in an act of shaky, uneven animation, as if to indulge our disbelief. A solid second of a tight close-up on Dwight Eisenhower, finger to his brow in contemplation, is followed by rapid two-frame alternations of images, taken from different angles, of Glenn Gould at his piano. This alternation animates Gould to suggest that it is he who is performing Crazy Otto's detuned rag on the soundtrack.[44]

After this, a rapid series of still images shows a range of crooners, dancers, football players, even a Mountie; among these faces are shots of jazz trumpeter Roy Eldridge and Montreal Canadiens hockey icon Jean Béliveau in action. Most are cut-out photographs posed against white or black backgrounds. Each image holds on screen for roughly half a second; the exception to this comes at the midway point, when text announces that "anything can happen on channel 6," by which point sculptures and antiquities, some totemic, others realistic, begin to dominate the image: the looming dot eyes and semi-circular face of Jacques Lipchitz's primitivist *Figure* (1926–30) follow a tightly cropped pair of images, of the eyes and ears of a man, which are themselves intercut with text declaring "new sights" and "new sounds," implying by the impact of the cut that the new sights and sounds of channel 6 will transform the viewer into a modern icon. In a final exchange, scenes of sports, starting with Béliveau at the net and transitioning to football players passing a pigskin in quick succession, are matched by symbols of antiquity: the pillars of the Parthenon, Giambologna's *The Abduction of a Sabine Woman* (1581–83), and the third-century bronze face of the Antikythera Philosopher, its eerie, pale irises glowing at the viewer. This final turn towards classical civilization reveals Lipsett's sense of absurdity, with sport serving as a bridge between the ancient world and modern telecommunications, giving uniformity to icons while tripping through and shearing away their meaning. Lipsett's humour was as coarse as it was clever: Giambologna's howling, defeated old man, cowering from the muscular buttocks of the rapist, is transformed into a flatulent gag. The angle obscures the woman, such that the figure's pained expression seems to be a response to the bare ass in his face.

FIGURE I.I: *Anything Can Happen on Channel 6* (Arthur Lipsett, National Film Board, 1960)

There is an earlier segment in *Hors-d'oeuvre* that also resonates with Lipsett's handiwork: the first sequence, a Radio-Canada CBC advertisement that likewise uses impactful, fractional picture cutting. *Hors-d'oeuvre* serves as a declaration of the collective mentality of the Unit B animation division, featuring a mix of talents, from cartooning to cutouts to optical animations, often operating in tandem, suggesting that, while these artists may each have led projects, they were likely collaborating on many, if not all, of the sponsored clips. What makes the final sequence stand apart is the strangeness of its comedy, a trait that would soon define much of Lipsett's work at the NFB.

By the early 1960s, Lipsett's role in the institution was evolving. His animation contributions included a pair of minute-long public service announcements, *Don't Give Fire a Place to Start* (or, *Clean Up for Spring*) and *Fire Prevention Week*, and he completed a trailer for the 1960 Montreal International Film Festival, cutting it to Baby Dodds's melodic drum improvisations.[45] He continued to provide animations, for two episodes of Jacques Bobet's series *The Women Among Us*, on female emancipation, and for James Beveridge's *The Rough Road to Freedom*, an episode of Beveridge's series *The Crossroads of the World: A Study of North Africa and the Middle East*, focusing on the evolution of Arab nationalism.[46] He also worked on Pierre Patry's *Collèges classiques*, on the unique classical college system in Quebec, contributing an opening photomontage, made with Robert Verrall, a rapid sequence of still images that contextualize the contemporary spaces of education in a lineage of inquiry reaching back to the Greek forum. Lipsett was credited as an assistant to Norman McLaren on *Opening Speech*, a comedy in which McLaren's attempts to give a speech are foiled by a microphone that moves in opposition to him, of its own volition, a sight gag achieved by way of McLaren's trademark pixilation; McLaren is finally able to offer his greetings only after he jumps into a screen: on impact, the filmmaker's body becomes animated text in many languages, multilingual text being a trait common to McLaren's films.[47] Lipsett's skills as a photographer, taking candid pictures of street life in Montreal with a Leica 35mm camera, were employed in Hubert Aquin's *September Five at Saint-Henri* (1962), a record of the faces and diurnal rhythms of Montreal's Saint-Henri, which was historically known as "Les Tanneries" for its association with tanning and leatherworking. It was, at the time when Aquin's film was made, a working-class district. The flexibility of Lipsett's training in the commercial arts was proving useful, even as it simultaneously allowed him a forum to develop his particular sense of composition and rhythm.

Where the School of Art and Design had opened Lipsett to a broad range of possibilities for creative expression, the National Film Board introduced him to the utility of the commercial arts and gave him access and mentorship. His training was not irreconcilable with the Film Board, for both arose from an inalienable optimism in the social good of making things. When Arthur Lismer had advocated for artists to enjoy the same freedom and autonomy as children, his lessons were nonetheless tied to the idea that an artist evolves with skill and hard-wrought technique; the commercial arts forums that Lismer anticipated for students like Lipsett might be typified in the clearly defined tasks and bounded purposes of sponsored filmmaking. Further, the National

Film Board of the late 1950s offered a humanistic, just, and welcoming portrait of a healthy society; it remained a propaganda institution, but the society it was interested in shaping would be the antithesis of Arcand's hate-fuelled vision of eternal racial competition. It was still, even a decade after Grierson's departure, guided by its founder's optimism. The job gave Lipsett a sense of mature purpose. From accounts of Lipsett's difficult family life, and the Montreal he grew up in, it is easy to picture a fracturing, lessening, tearing apart of the self, despite the shy charm and good humour with which he met the world. Lipsett came to understand, first from Lismer and then from the process of filmmaking itself, that things must be broken down before they can reveal their nature, much as an analytical chemist like Solomon Lipsett might break down sediment to reveal its geophysical properties.

In his first years of working at the NFB, Arthur Lipsett had proven himself to be a reliable asset to the sponsored projects of Unit B. In 1960, Lipsett would begin to put together a film of his own. In his initial proposal, he made a prescient statement of his own perceptions: "life is like a journey—a continuous shifting, whispering thing, full of strange meanings and impulses."[48] The project that he proposed would assume all of the style that he had been cultivating in his animation and would draw from his playful sense of ambiguity, in an absurdist treatment of the end of the 1950s, all in a wild, dancing rhythm. Lipsett understood that things must be cut out, broken down, alienated from context, before they can be put together to assume some new form. By truncating and defamiliarizing pictures and sounds, Arthur Lipsett was putting himself together.

TWO

# REVELATION

IN 1960, ARTHUR LIPSETT BEGAN TO SPEND HIS EVENINGS IN the National Film Board's sound department. In keeping these hours, he could have the space to himself, combing through outtakes and trims of magnetic sound and salvaging anything he found interesting. What he liked, he would wind up and tape into little rolls. He set them aside in 35mm film cans, like platters of hors d'oeuvres, which he would open and present to his colleagues, joking that the sounds were delicious.[1] Whatever Lipsett's interests in collage had been while in school, they found new traction in the modular construction of cinema. The process of making a film from component strands of sound and picture appealed to Lipsett's instinct to break things down, and the notion of appropriating existing material into a new form was a natural extension of the labour of putting films together in a studio environment, surrounded by trims and scraps and fragments.[2] In borrowing material, Lipsett had plenty of precedents to draw from even within the conservative venue of the NFB: beyond the use of appropriated images in Unit B's sponsored work, the repurposing of media was a widespread phenomenon and a part of the culture at the NFB, evident as early as their first propaganda films, such as in Stuart Legg's management of the *Canada Carries On* series, much of which was assembled from newsreel footage in the tradition of compilation filmmaking.[3] While Lipsett would be aware of such precedents, his nightly visits to the sound department stemmed from fascination: he wanted to make sound collages.

"It was initially a sound experiment," Lipsett would later say, "purely for the love of placing one sound after another."[4] By one account, what had brought Lipsett into the sound department was an errand, to complete an assignment for a sound editing workshop, sponsored as a part of his training.[5] Lipsett began to edit sound together into a fragmentary montage of truncated or rambling speech, sound effects, music, and atmosphere, an approach that resonates with the acousmatic collage compositions of Pierre Schaeffer and the musique concrète movement.[6] Where the formal school of musique concrète, beginning with Schaeffer's Studio d'Essai in the early 1940s, prized the radiophonic translation of sound to emphasize its tonal, rhythmic, or sonic values, Lipsett's approach to sound collage was less abstract. Cutting quarter-inch magnetic tape, without a form of intermediary synthesis, the voice of a narrator could be interrupted by a car horn, from there giving way to rambling or hysterical or insightful speech, modern jazz, or elliptical sound effects.[7] In this, Lipsett's technique was nearer to that of Schaeffer's precursor, Walther Ruttmann, who, like Lipsett, was a film animator. In 1930, Ruttmann made *Weekend*, a sound composition recorded using a film optical soundtrack of fluidly collaged sounds that unambiguously suggest the aural landscape of a weekend in Berlin. Ruttmann, unlike Schaeffer, had a more documental approach to sound collage, one in which the source material was not intended to be abstract but to provoke a programmatic framework. After hours, Lipsett, in the nocturne of the building, followed a similar method, struck by material that traced a thematic thread, drawing from mutterings, clichés, doubletalk, half-constructed utterances, and comic bursts of music and sounds.[8] A major distinction between musique concrète and what Lipsett was doing lies in his use of comprehensible speech, employed for its content regardless of its sonic properties. Rather than embrace abstraction, Lipsett instead moves against expectation, interrupting coherent speech with sounds, a gesture of unambiguous intention that signals the maker's wit.

Lipsett shared what he was doing with two senior members of Unit B, Wolf Koenig and Robert Verrall, who found it riotously funny and powerful. He was encouraged by their response to continue the work and came to the conclusion that he would like to illustrate the sound in a way that extended the forms he'd already explored in *Anything Can Happen on Channel 6*, but at greater length and with a greater degree of authorial control. Lipsett's intentions in making such a film are suggested by his first film proposal for the NFB. *Fly Little Bird*, proposed circa June 1960, was to be a five-minute film shot in 35mm black and white with a soundtrack consisting of "music and possibly short voice patterns."[9] The proposal for *Fly Little Bird* coincides with his sound experiments, and the form he describes is similar to his advertisements: "the shooting will consist of stills, some of which would have camera movements. Possibly live action might be used in parts."[10] Lipsett claimed to be guided by ponderous, open questions: "what is this world we live in and why am I here and what am I supposed to do with my life?"[11] In this proposal, Lipsett defines the film as bearing "currents of feeling," which he sources from two ideas: the journey of life and the search for meaning in life. Lipsett's "currents of feeling" give way to related aspects in his process: flowlines and arcs of energy, abstract means by which distinct images and sounds become entangled and implicated in the cohesion of a film.[12]

Lipsett had bought a Leica camera and, while travelling in the summers after his graduation, had developed a talent for spontaneous composition. When he approached Tom Daly and Colin Low about making a film, he did so with a modest request: a budget line to purchase 35mm still film in order to take photographs to illustrate the soundtrack. The producers arranged for Lipsett to be assigned a production number in order to fund his request, with the working title *Strangely Elated*. *Strangely Elated* is a phrase that connects Lipsett's project to an immediate forerunner at the NFB, Low's *City of Gold*, in which narrator Pierre Berton concludes that the men who came to the Yukon in the gold rush were rewarded with a "strange elation" of fellowship with one another, whatever fair-weather fortune they had gained. At the NFB, a working title could coexist with a proposed title, with Lipsett's proposed title being *Revelation*.[13] Lipsett wanted to develop a revelatory experience, in the sense of the *Book of Revelations*, an eschatological work, a rapturous stripping-away of masks. Another possible source for this title is Siegfried Kracauer's *Theory of Film: The Redemption of Physical Reality*, published that same year, a book with which Lipsett was fascinated. Kracauer argues that the revelatory function of cinema engages with three categories of things normally unseen: it serves the utilitarian role of portraying "small and big things," those things that escape everyday perception by their scale; it foregrounds transient details of experience that become evanescent and haunting; and, most tellingly, it exposes "blind spots of the mind," those unseen phenomena that cinema can introduce to the viewer by challenging their perceptual habits.[14] It is this final category that speaks to Lipsett's process, as Kracauer's blind spots include both exceptional confrontations with refuse and transformational encounters with the familiar.

Making this film was also Lipsett's first occasion to present his ideas to his colleagues in an unconventional style, as a diagram that charted the emotional arc of the film. Such charts, which bewildered his colleagues, would become a staple of Lipsett's proposals. The chart for *Strangely Elated* is an arc with eight bends in it, in which a series of nineteen arrows chart the evolution of the film from an empty world of "city street scenes, sky scraper signs, shop windows," an empty world populated only with department store dummies, to scenes of "lonely isolated people in street - just looking." As the arc bends higher still, it goes through a series of scenes suggesting layers of society: "an area of depression" with "'no exit' signs"; a "leap of greatest intensity," involving the "beat" element of society; "mad" chases of children and adults in colleague Kaj Pindal's garden; and big close-ups of adults "becoming involved in excitement." The scenes become increasingly excited and expressive until finally reaching "a great acceleration of expression and the end of the film."[15] The chart follows this current of feeling into a state of bliss.

Lipsett's chart anticipates a film that is in keeping with the ingenuous whimsy of Norman McLaren's films: the tired and frustrated adult world is freed and reinvigorated, returning to the joy of childhood. It was also in keeping with Lipsett's proposal for *Fly Little Bird*, which had concluded that the search for meaning is something that follows us from childhood to old age, where "all [we are] left to do is wonder—sometimes in shock or amazement, or in just plain bewilderment at this phenomenon around us."[16] Like his mentor Arthur Lismer, who recognized an evolutionary mission in the encouragement of creativity in children, Lipsett was focused on broad questions of self-reflection and insight around the life cycle. Implied throughout is a nostalgia for childhood, not as a flight from responsibility—for Lipsett imagines a child full of precocious questions—but as a station of insight.[17]

These aspects of search and discovery suggest a utopian optimism, but they also obscure a reckoning with pain by leaving unspoken the impossible scale of Lipsett's questions, as well as a broader context still: the clenched fist of a world in conflict. Lipsett was already a disciple of the absurd, sheltering in dark, ridiculous humour. His world was much as Albert Camus had judged it, one of banalities and broken communication, where the damnation of Sisyphus offered a ready metaphor for the futility of all humanity. Lipsett's approach to that world was closer to that of Samuel Beckett, the Irish playwright whose tableaux of strange miseries were full of comedy. In Beckett, humour is a form of heroism, a redemption against futility. Lipsett's film would manifest the laughter and pleasure of a world alight with energy as it bolted toward a great exultation. In the summer of 1961, Lipsett took a leave of absence and travelled with his Leica camera to New York, London, and Paris, where he took many photographs of tired and frustrated faces in clubs, in shops, at protests, and in the streets.[18] With his soundtrack as a template, the film would develop rapidly through the course of the fall, as Lipsett expanded on the promise of *Anything Can Happen on Channel 6*, working to a length of seven minutes that allowed him to explore more varied rhythms.

The film was finished and released in the waning days of 1961 under its final title, *Very Nice, Very Nice*. Its structure differed considerably from what Lipsett had charted. He had mapped out an evolving spell of enthusiasm, a waking of the world from the slumber of misery, but he instead delivered a survey of good and evil, a reflection on the alienation of urban life and the aggression of consumerism. The spell evolved, but in a radically different spirit than had been promised. Where the proposal for *Fly Little Bird* had cohered around the perspective of a naif questioning the world and its meaning, *Very Nice, Very Nice* found its meaning in a mushroom cloud. On the soundtrack, rehearsed speech is interrupted, narrators fumble, and interviewees ramble and become incoherent. Other speakers offer folksy platitudes or shallow observations. A monastic chant, heard at sunrise and sunset, is met with showbiz affectation, the facile praise that gives the film its title, rapid applause followed with, "Bravo! Very nice, very nice."

All but a few of the film's images are 35mm stills. As he had done with the feet clip, Lipsett would animate the still images primarily through hard cuts, the images rapidly giving way in parallel to the rhythms of the soundtrack. Intermittent sections find the images cut rapidly to the pulse of Crazy Otto's ragtime piano, others to the roll of a military drum. These whirlwind passages serve to separate episodes that play out in a steadier rhythm. Lipsett's own street photography is mixed with images from mass culture—among them, portraits of celebrities and politicians, biological diagrams, and advertisements. Only four images "move": a clip of the hydrogen bomb test and its resultant mushroom cloud; a clip of a rocket taking off and shedding its boosters in the atmosphere; an image of a man's face, distorted through animation; and a collage of female nudes from classical paintings, piled in a mountainous orgy, panned across with a rostrum camera.[19]

*Very Nice, Very Nice* begins with scenes of dense high-rise buildings, sounds of street noise, and passing cars playing under them. Street signs direct the viewer forward with an arrow reading "one way," a moment of material self-consciousness along the unbroken path of the film reel. Stanley Jackson, primary narrator for the NFB in the late 1950s, begins to introduce the Salvation Army in outtakes from the soundtrack to Terence Macartney-Filgate's *Blood and Fire* (1958): "in this city marches an army whose motto is...." An interrupting car horn is met on screen with a close-up of the word "NO" written on a curb. An upturned car follows, then a rooftop billboard stripped to its bones, its marquee reading "BUY," the only word remaining. The first sign of humanity arrives in a pair of mannequins, dressed as servers, another dramatically dehumanizing symptom of capitalism. Candid photographs of faces, seen in close-up, are accompanied by an interviewee who rambles about competition until he is distracted into asking that someone answer a ringing phone. The face of a man in monster makeup, taken at a protest rally, gives way to a rapid montage of action shots of football and Ike Eisenhower, Eisenhower movement signs, and those marching on behalf of Stuart Symington for the 1960 American Democratic presidential candidacy. In a matter of seconds, this rapid montage surveys American imperialism and modern war, empty cities and highways, the graves of soldiers, ending with a series of faces with their mouths agape. Beneath this, a military drum dictates the undulating rhythm with which the images pass.

Canadian literary critic Northrop Frye speaks, describing the futile experience of average people living in a "dissolving phantasmagoria of a world," where "a politician can promise them anything and they will not remember later what he has promised." In complement to this, a series of faces, captured with a slow shutter and dissolving, one into the next, serves as a literal illustration of Frye's choice of words. Eventually, Lipsett's own face appears, posing over a lamp, grotesquely distorted by a slow shutter and by his own grimacing contortions. This self-portrait introduces a series of magazine photos of professional wrestling, contrasting looming goliaths Bruno Sammartino and Killer Kowalski with the "midget wrestler" Little Beaver while a commentator casually ranks his preferences of sports, a stammering catalogue that culminates just as an animated collage of painted female nudes overtakes the screen, macho competition dissolving into male fantasy. Lipsett had been a part of the production crew for *La lutte* (1961), the NFB's adaptation of Roland Barthes's "The World of Wrestling," in which Barthes described the practice as "the great spectacle of Suffering, Defeat, and Justice," a performance of the symbolic codes of good and evil.[20] Lipsett's role on *La lutte* is unspecified and likely marginal, but it may have been this experience that inspired him to integrate images from professional wrestling, a gesture to the world of masks and one in which exaggerations of symbol and ironic contrasts are rampant, the absurd heart of twentieth-century theatre.

An ominous drum beats under more candid faces. A facile commentator declares with optimistic bravura that "whatever's gonna happen, you feel well in a way," while a mushroom cloud blooms on a flickering horizon. Crazy Otto's "In the Mood" accompanies scenes of Lipsett's colleague Kaj Pindal's young family playing in a garden. Their colliding bodies give way to a series of close-ups on the faces and eyes of commercial photography, fashion models, a bare breast, Louis Armstrong as seen from a low angle, Indigenous tribal members in traditional face paint, modern dancers, ending with a repeat burst of the blooming mushroom cloud. It is a survey of many cultures at play, provoked by a child's energy. As the picture slows down and returns to the street, a narrator speaks: "warmth and brightness will return... and renewal of the hopes of men." Lipsett assembled this line from two separate lines spoken by the narrator for the NFB's *The Days Before Christmas* (1958). Voices respond "no" and "yes," a playful show of disagreement. The sound gives way to lulling jazz in the West Coast style, a combination of guitar, vibraphone, trombone, and bass, taken from Eldon Rathburn's score to Terence Macartney-Filgate's *Police* (1958).[21] In the image, children look to the camera, their innocence contrasted with the distrusting faces of old men and the blank expression of a mannequin dressed as a fashionable woman. Lipsett's juxtaposition—between curious, receptive human faces and guarded, defensive social masks—ends with the vacuity of the mannequin, a disavowal of presence. Narrator George Whalley's fragmentary, repeated outtake, "like birds on the side of a cliff," is held against aerial photos of Manhattan, painting the Family of Man as a family of lemmings.[22] A rapid montage, cut in time to the roll of a military drum, shows a beauty pageant, a crying clown, and a grotesque effigy, in doing so building a tragic agreement. The march continues, pausing only momentarily to linger on the face of a slack-jawed man that is subsequently distorted, twisting and bent by way of re-photography. On the soundtrack, a man is asked for his name, and a voice responds with retching.

Ordinary faces give way to a variety of "fantasy" soldiers in uniform: a gladiator, a monk, a Black man in a Klan hood, a woman with an exaggerated grin in a soda advertisement. A medical expert speaks about the importance of increasing circulation while diagrams of the human body appear, a tacit acknowledgement of the film's themes of malaise, the dysfunctional body becoming a mirror image of a sick world; but his specific statement, on increasing circulation, also serves as a metaphor for the arrested world borne witness, wherein Lipsett's subjects circulate neither among one another nor within themselves, trapped in the stasis of the decisive moment. As beat comedian Lenny Bruce complains at the reluctance of individuals "to become involved in anything," scenes of shoppers demonstrate consumerism as a form of self-involvement. A man dressed as Santa Claus gives way to the corpse of a soldier caked in mud, another strange parallel between an icon of Christian charity and the reality of blood in dirt. Scenes of

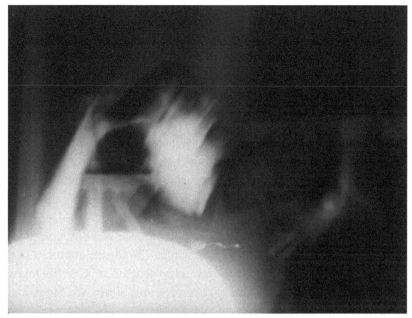

FIGURE 2.1: Arthur Lipsett contorts his face for a self-portrait in *Very Nice, Very Nice* (Arthur Lipsett, National Film Board, 1962)

FIGURE 2.2: *Very Nice, Very Nice* (Arthur Lipsett, National Film Board, 1962)

doomsday marches (with placards declaring the end near) are paired with discussions of consumerism, building an unmistakable relation. Crosstalk, music, and traffic combine under scenes of protest. A papier-mâché skull on a pike, held aloft at a protest, gives way to Julia Margaret Cameron's 1867 photograph of polymath John Herschel. Herschel's stare is met by a voice asking, "what is the meaning of life? What is good, what is of value?"—as if answers could come from the suspended wisdom of the photograph. Instead, a lone voice responds with a monastic Om, chanted over a sunrise, met by a spurious clap and a voice that says "Bravo! Very nice, very nice." The Om sounds again beneath a photograph of a sunset over the East River in Manhattan, and, again, the voice says, "Bravo! Very nice, very nice."[23]

A rocket takes off, its ascent interrupted by aerial photography of the Great Pyramids, the Roman Colosseum, Trafalgar Square, Padua, and the Arc de Triomphe.[24] As the soundtrack again shifts to the relaxing sounds of Eldon Rathburn's *Police* ensemble, a rocket's departure, moving in time, frames scenes of political figures—among them, King George VI, Richard Nixon, Dwight D. Eisenhower, John F. Kennedy, George Washington, and Abraham Lincoln. This sequence, highly suggestive of American imperialist policy and its roots in European monarchy, climaxes with Albert Bierstadt's *The Last of the Buffalo* (1888), an iconic painting in the Western imagination that signals the transition from a fantasized ideal of the American plains into the modern West; the sequence's denouement comes when the edits finally slow on an image of US Air Force planes piled up in a heap, a portrait of warmongering excess, and the picture cuts back to the rocket as its boosters detach. Soviet Chairman Nikita Khrushchev's face, in an alternating dance with the face of Ike Eisenhower, mixes with portraits of Jack LaLanne and Marilyn Monroe and advertisements for toothpaste, film, cereal, and dog treats. As with the feet clip, magazine advertisements are cut out and placed against pure black or pure white backgrounds, creating another level of visual tension. Khrushchev appears to watch them through binoculars, his mouth agape in wonder, as if the Khrushchev thaw was a sign that the Cold War could be won through American commercial culture. A wailing horn erupts as a saxophone player appears and draws the picture back to a montage of faces. The faces begin to dissolve again, that literal demonstration of Frye's dissolving phantasmagoria. As the music crescendos, the narrator again intones that "warmth and brightness will return...and renewal of the hopes of men." This cues the spurious clap: "Bravo! Very nice, very nice."

The density of Lipsett's montage is conceived to be perceptually strenuous, his images flitting past at too great a speed to be readily perceived. In those sequences in which images are held for only a few frames, their velocity undermines their comprehensibility, a condensation of imagery that places the viewer in the midst of the disoriented crowd. It is an act of copious inventory, straining the boundaries of the seven-minute container of the film.[25] His abundant contents, and their fractional presence, serve as a formal mirror to the consumer-society inertia glimpsed on screen and heard in Lipsett's sound collage. The filmmaker's attempt at filling this modest container with materials that are both plenty in number and irreducibly potent in meaning is an act of futility. Lipsett's copious inventory is a cultural scrapbook, pushed to a rapturous extremity. The phenomena become exhausting for their inexhaustibility, and where Lipsett creates circuits of repetition, of his own images and of his found materials, these only serve to reinforce the sense that his inventory results from careful strategy. The density of *Very Nice, Very Nice* allows it to embody contraries: exhausting and invigorating, effervescent and melancholy, a sanguine death knell.

Lipsett's street photography, while indebted to the observational aesthetics of Cartier-Bresson, is distinctively contemporary in its vision, more reminiscent of Robert Frank's *The Americans* (1958) in its choice of subjects, primarily working class people, and its compositions, primarily medium close-ups. The faces of working people are placed in grotesque relief to the elegant speech of the commentators, and not only by contrast to the trained voiceovers of Lipsett's colleagues: when Lenny Bruce speaks about the lack of commitment among people, placed in relation to the suffering and exhausted masses, his idealism becomes condescension; likewise, when Northrop Frye describes the dissolving phantasmagoria of ordinary people, his remarks become crueler in company of these faces. Crowding and overpopulation are a feature of much of Lipsett's photography, broadcast strongly in those images that deal with scenes of protest, but also in the dense visual fields of everyday life: the natural collage of mid-century visual culture is displayed in his images taken in stores and newsstands, where a mirror frames the face of a middle-aged woman shopping amidst various other mirrored and metallic surfaces, as if her face, too, is for sale; a man is seen in profile in front of a newsstand where issues of the *Northern Miner* and the tabloid *Midnight* crowd the frame; a woman with a stern expression and a guarded posture stands in front of another newsstand, plastered with French photo magazines and tabloids. That same density, which suggests both consumerism and fakery, is on display in an image of three women standing together in front of a poster for *Ocean's 11* (Lewis Milestone, 1960) featuring the faces of the Rat Pack. The celebrities, compartmentalized in a series of rectangles, occupy a rigid stylization of the "police lineup," and the women standing before the billboard indicate the porous boundaries between iconography and anonymous urban life. Frank's photography, like Lipsett's, has a sense of urgency in its vision of inequitable society, but Lipsett's images deflect social concern by their cinematic translation into that staggering, percussive rhythm—and Lipsett's rhythm, while often a source of comedy, is not always comic. The soundtrack broadcasts its inbuilt tensions, as Lipsett inserts fragments of Rathburn's jazz ensemble, in the relaxed West Coast style, music so calming that its truncation is felt more sharply than all the mumbled, half-felt platitudes that surround it.

Lipsett would declare his sympathy with the Beat movement but disavow any affiliation between his work and theirs, owing, in his words, to having come up in "a respectable middle class home."[26] For a man with his anarchic sense of humour, any declaration of respectability could be taken as a wry joke. From Lipsett's chart that indicates "the beat element of society" as a source of energy, to the palpable influence of Robert Frank's portraiture on his photography, Lipsett's work shares a common energy with the Beats. More than that, Lipsett's place in the world was much like that of the Beats, as Lawrence Lipton would describe them: "all the misfits of the world...All the broken, the doomed, the drunk and the disillusioned—herding together for a little human warmth, where a one-room kitchenette is an apartment and the naked electric bulb hangs suspended from the ceiling like an exposed nerve."[27] Lipton's Beat setting sounds like Lipsett's Clifton Arms apartment. While Lipsett's film form was unprecedented at the NFB, its precedents were known to him. By the time that Lipsett was making *Very*

*Nice, Very Nice*, he would have seen Alfred Leslie and Robert Frank's *Pull My Daisy* (1959), in which Jack Kerouac's asynchronous narration has a staccato comedy to it that resonates in Lipsett's truncated clips.[28] More pointedly, Lipsett would have seen, through the collection of Montreal cinephile and Film Board filmmaker Guy L. Coté, Jane Conger Belson's *Odds & Ends* (1959), a film in which sound artist Henry Jacob, under the anagrammatic pseudonym Rheny Bojac, offers posturing comic double-talk narration on the relationship between poetry and jazz, in a scathing parody of the beat sensibility, while the images, culled from travel documentaries and the artist's previous film *Logos* (1957), are cut in fractions of a second, a style that Lipsett mastered through the rapid montages of *Very Nice, Very Nice*.

In various ways, *Very Nice, Very Nice* declares itself to be about spectatorship: looking and being looked at, the experience endemic in cities of being perpetually on display. Mass culture images demand to be looked at; interesting times demand to be looked at; the man in the street wants only to fade into the crowd, as is his custom. When Lipsett presents an image of moviegoers in 3D glasses, that audience is at once concealing its identity, watching a movie, and looking out, from Lipsett's movie, at his viewers. The image aligns almost perfectly with that which precedes it: a banquet where attendees each wear a paper cutout, all of the same face, a grand conformity. The strain of public life is one more reason for mass disengagement, but against this, Lipsett poses no alternative. Like his subjects, he simply bears witness.

*Very Nice, Very Nice*, like the feet clip before it, acted against the evolutionary perspective of the NFB. Through Unit B, the National Film Board had evolved towards the neutral, open countenance of an observational style. Peter Harcourt refers to this period of Unit B's work as bearing "a quality of suspended judgment, of something left open at the end, of something undecided...detached from the immediate pressures of existence."[29] Despite this departure from the overt didacticism found in earlier Film Board productions, the films of Unit B were still rationalized within the needs and machinations of the state: *Paul Tomkowicz: Street-railway Switchman* (Roman Kroitor, 1954) is, despite any ambiguity it may bear, about the value of Canadian citizenship, just as *City of Gold*, with its veneer of nostalgia, commemorates the past with an eye to universal fellowship. The films are, per

Harcourt's interpretation, hesitant in their own messages, but they maintain a commitment to the search for meaning, to values of citizenship, fellowship, and communication. These films were ambiguous by the standards of mainstream non-fiction filmmaking of the era, but they remained didactic in comparison to the messy, absurd, anarchic edges of underground cinema. *Very Nice, Very Nice* was confident in its pessimism and, rather than embrace the lingering didacticism of the institution, was a work of negative capability, offering more questions than answers. This negative capability runs through the film from its embrace of broken statements to its enigmatic contrasts around Cold War–era politics, mass movements, and consumerism. The English Romantic poet John Keats wrote of negative capability as an ability on the part of the artist to receive the world in fascination with its phenomenal being, "when a man is capable of being in uncertainties, mysteries, doubts, without any irritable reaching after fact and reason."[30] Keats's conception of negative capability is a surrender to uncertainty, but it is also the permission of modern art to defy rationalism and didacticism, to resist the assignation of meaning. It represents a rejection of a systemic vision of the world, or of systematized philosophizing about the world, and, in the case of Lipsett's film, it is a resistance to progressive evolutionary platitudes. This refusal within the film to align itself with any particular meaning placed Lipsett in opposition to the Film Board, which, despite the ambiguous nature of the observational form, maintained its devotion to purposeful messaging. Colin Low would later remember his own role on the project as that of providing cautionary advice to Lipsett against the depressing tone of the material, a quality that, for a message-oriented filmmaker like Low, was twinned to ambiguity. Lipsett's colleague Robert Verrall, who, like Low, felt that the film was too gloomy, encouraged Lipsett to restate the line that "warmth and brightness will return" to give the film an optimistic conclusion.[31] If anything, the repetition of this phrase emphasizes the film's absurdity, as a statement of unqualified optimism in the face of mutually assured destruction. Mass movements present themselves as a shadow of the past when collectivity has become impossible. The circus, the wrestling ring, and the theatres of fashion, celebrity, and politics are ready metaphors for the quieter toils and cruelties of everyday life. At their best, they become bizarre distractions, like a rocket in flight or a doomsday preacher, out in the street where progress is merely the bravado of a petrified humanity. This existential terror is met with the strange humour of exuberant, mechanical rhythms and of the knowing way in which the tuned expression of establishment culture condemns itself.

A review of an early screening of *Very Nice, Very Nice* at the Tours Festival in France reported it as "a virtually indescribable reel of anarchy."[32] Lipsett's colleagues had seen it in much the same terms, a film so anarchic, so far from the mission of the institution, that they could not imagine how to place it in their non-theatrical distribution machine. The film received its North American premiere in New York on March 19, 1962, at the Paris Theatre in midtown Manhattan, as the short accompaniment to Luis Buñuel's *Viridiana* (1961).[33] The venue was appropriate to the material, given the emphasis Lipsett had placed on Manhattan in the film, as part of a quartet of modern urban centres surveyed alongside London, Montreal, and Paris. It began to win awards, first in its initial screenings in European film festivals, and then in the United States. Critical appraisals among cineastes at the time were generally positive. Donald Richie, then an American expatriate publishing on art cinema in Japan, recognized it as a "mordant, sarcastic, and extremely funny evaluation of western society."[34] Commentators either located social meaning in Lipsett's work or found it chaotic, a reception that reinforced the filmmaker's own commitment to ambiguity. Lipsett's devotion to participatory meaning was clear as early as his proposal for *Fly Little Bird*, in which he wrote: "[Q]uestions are implied but not boldly stated."[35]

The success of the film resulted in Lipsett's nomination for an Academy Award in the category of Best Live Action Short Subject at the 34th Academy Awards in Los Angeles. The other nominees included Robert McCarty's *Rooftops of New York* (1961); Jean Dasque's *Ballon Vole* (1960); and *The Face of Jesus* (1961), by sculptor Merrell Gage. The award went to Hilary Harris for *Seawards the Great Ships* (1961).[36] Lipsett attended the ceremony in March 1962, and when he returned to Montreal, his estimation in the eyes of his colleagues had risen. Oscar nominations were not uncommon at the NFB, but Lipsett's youth, his relative independence, and the foreignness of his work to his colleagues marked his shift from crew member to filmmaker as a curious and unexpected transit. For his independence, he had achieved something akin to the celebrity of Norman McLaren, and while many of his colleagues considered themselves artists, the isolation in which Lipsett made his work was closer to that of a poet. It helped his case that he had attracted international admirers—among them, Stanley Kubrick, then having recently established himself as one of Hollywood's leading filmmakers with *Spartacus* (1960). Kubrick wrote Lipsett a brief note declaring the film "one of the most imaginative and brilliant uses of the movie screen and sound track I have ever seen."[37] Such success placed Lipsett between two spheres in a tenuous Venn diagram of cinema: the establishment film culture in which he worked, and which finds its ideal in the glitz of Hollywood, and the underground cinema for which he had become an ambassador, if not on the broader circuit then to his colleagues and employers.

Another admirer that *Very Nice, Very Nice* had attracted was American satirical cartoonist Robert Osborn, who wrote to the NFB to purchase a personal print of the film. Lipsett would subsequently go on a road trip with Robert Verrall to visit Osborn in Connecticut, the two men having been tasked with gathering large drawings from Osborne for use in a Unit B film. On their way back, they stopped in Plattsburgh, New York, to eat. "While I was washing my hands, I was stopped by the FBI," Verrall would recount, speculating that Lipsett's beatnik appearance had provoked the agents' suspicion.[38] Lipsett's response to the arrest was to holler with joy that the FBI was arresting them, delighted, without a sense of danger, declaring to passersby, "they think we're Communist spies." Verrall recalled, "Arthur couldn't take it seriously, which made the FBI guys furious…Arthur was in high spirits the whole time. He enjoyed the insanity of being temporarily arrested."[39] The experience, and Lipsett's behaviour, mortified Verrall, but this anecdote is further evidence of Lipsett's resilience, his ability to find humour in a crisis.

## THREE

# A PERSONAL VISION

As American independent art cinema shifted from the trance films of the 1940s into a new era of abstraction and materialist challenge, those critics for whom cinema strictly represented a storytelling medium were frustrated and provoked by what they saw. Jonas Mekas, in his columns for the *Village Voice*, had sermonized a utopian vision of personal cinema, encouraging filmmakers to make modern films that were rough-hewn, spontaneous, poetic expressions against the grain of realism. Others, like Ernest Callenbach, found only an invitation to rage. Callenbach, then editor of *Film Quarterly*, used it as a bully pulpit with a screed against American filmmaker Stan Brakhage. Brakhage had, by then, assumed something of a messianic position in American personal cinema that invited confrontation. Callenbach charged, "Mr. Brakhage's films are awful," and he condemned them further as "pretentious home movies" in an attack emblematic of the reactionary stance of critics against the new.[1] Canadian critics were even less acclimated to the underground because of how rarely such films circulated north of the 49th parallel.

Experimental filmmaking was alive and well in America when Arthur Lipsett first started at the National Film Board, and as a young man with a dedication to new movements in the arts and a curiosity about the possibilities of the medium in which he was training, he kept abreast of it. His colleagues at the NFB had more conservative tastes, and the stance of the institution was that formal innovation must always explore the communicative potential of cinema. The closest to an experimental filmmaker among Lipsett's colleagues was Norman McLaren, whose abstract animations could pass for light entertainment. McLaren was not an underground filmmaker but a maker of films that prized technique above all else. In this sense, McLaren fit neatly into Grierson's corporatist conception of the Film Board, as a maker of, among other things, technique-driven entertainment. Underground filmmaking fell too far from the communicative mission of the NFB to ever take root there. It occupied a different definition of film art, a less conservative, freer disposition: freer to depict intimacy, freer to depict experiences that parted from the mainstream, freer to express doubts about the direction of human progress, as Lipsett's film had done. There is no sharper demonstration of the divide between these perspectives than in how each perceived poetry: for the NFB, poetic devices were political shorthand, rhetoric deployed to stir hearts to the mission at hand, while for Mekas and others in the American underground film movement, poetry was celebration and salvation, an ecstatic communion with eternity.

In the early 1960s, there were few forums in Canada for experiencing personal filmmaking.[2] However, only a few hours south of Montreal was its epicentre, Greenwich Village in Manhattan, where Mekas lived and worked and where, in 1962, he founded the Filmmakers Cooperative to distribute what he called the "New American Cinema."[3] In Lipsett's travels, which by 1962 included a trip to California for the Academy Awards, he had encountered experimental films in cities where underground art communities were thriving. Canada had no formal distribution service for artistic films; until 1967, the closest Canada had to a centralized distribution service was the National Film Board itself, which distributed only its own films.[4] In Montreal, Lipsett had one ready means of watching experimental films: the collection of Guy L. Coté, a cinephile who had founded the Canadian Federation of Film Clubs and who would go on to establish the Cinémathèque canadienne, later renamed the Cinémathèque québécoise.[5] As a film collector who had taken it upon himself to organize newsletters for nationwide film clubs, Coté had been able to circulate his personal prints of experimental films to those who wished to exhibit them on that modest circuit, acting as an informal distributor. In a July 1960 catalogue for his collection, Coté notes that, through his circulation of their films, "artists such as Carmen d'Avino, Stan Brakhage, Frank Stauffacher and Shirley Clarke have been given a Canadian public."[6] Through the actions of Coté, the film culture of Montreal was rich with a diversity that transcended the square, utilitarian temperament of the Film Board. One just had to know where to look.

In the few years that he had spent as a government employee, Lipsett had gone from a period of training and mentorship to a position of authorial prestige, and, for his success, he could plan for a future at the NFB where he was not merely relegated to service work. However, as a maker of experimental films, he was still an outsider among his colleagues, in the sense that he was without peers. When the opportunity came for Lipsett to collaborate with his colleague David Millar on a thirty-minute current affairs broadcast about experimental movies, the two wrote an outline. Tom Daly would produce, Lipsett would direct and edit, and Millar would serve as his assistant director. Millar, like Lipsett, lived in the Clifton Arms, and the two would travel to and from work together.[7] The program would be made by the NFB for broadcast as part of the CBC's culture series. *Lively Arts* had started airing in October 1961 with a mission to seek out critical perspectives on contemporary art. Lipsett and Millar's episode, as it was proposed in July 1962, was to be titled *Experimental Film-Makers—A Personal Vision*. Once aired, it would drop the subtitle, circulating as *The Experimental Film*.

The title was not the only thing that would change as the project evolved. It was originally planned as a showcase for the burgeoning field of underground movies, employing the newsmagazine format to allow for a balance of critical commentary, artist statements, and the films themselves. In his proposal, Lipsett charted six sequences: the show would begin with Norman McLaren's *Blinkity Blank* (1955), shown in an unconventional style, holding one frame at a time and gradually setting it into motion so as to reveal McLaren's technique. This would be followed by a second sequence of McLaren himself describing "his approach and the development of his own experiments in film."[8] McLaren would then introduce a third sequence, of *Very Nice, Very Nice*, which would stream into a fourth sequence of "a group of critics in a bull session, discussing…the film-maker and his role in society…new developments in film [and] the effects on the general public and its reactions."[9] This would be followed by a fifth sequence, containing two more films, each paired with interviews with their makers (Lipsett's choices had been Stan VanDerBeek, Bruce Conner, and an unnamed Polish filmmaker, possibly Jan Lenica who would appear in the finished project).[10] The broadcast would end with a final sixth sequence, featuring *The Wardrobe* (1958), a relatively conventional animated film by George Dunning, Stan Hayward, and Dick Williams.

Lipsett and Millar's proposal suggests that the "bull session" with critics would focus specifically on *Very Nice, Very Nice* and would be isolated from the other sequences in which artists would speak of their processes in dialogue with their own films. In other words, Lipsett intended for only his own film to be exposed to the slings and arrows of critics, which, given the provocative pessimism of his film, might be anticipated to lead to the kinds of generalizations that had crowded his sound collage. The proposal thus laid an ingenious trap for those who would dismiss "pretentious home movies."

The completed film, as it was broadcast, retains some of these planned elements and acts as a subtle showcase for Lipsett's intercut, punctuative editing style. It featured works and remarks by filmmakers Robert Breer, George Dunning, Jan Lenica, and Norman McLaren. However, the bulk of the commentary is provided not by makers but by experts: in this case, a roundtable of film historian Herman G. Weinberg, *Toronto Telegram* critic Clyde Gilmour, journalist and public intellectual Fernand Cadieux, and NFB producer Guy Glover. The resulting comedy is that, in a field so confrontational, so flagrantly against interpretation and logic, expertise itself is put on trial. Weinberg, whose work as a prolific translator of European art cinema predated his public career as a historian, is seeking communication, and what does not communicate to him, he condemns as trash. Gilmour, likewise reluctant, opens the program by declaring most experimental works to be "complete idiocy, meaningless infantilism," an excerpt placed for comic effect, as if to disgrace the whole endeavour. Glover and Cadieux provide a contrast, with Cadieux defending the possibilities of new expressions and new audiences, and Glover condemning critics for writing off experimental filmmaking and not doing the hard work of separating the wheat from the chaff.

The examples used in *The Experimental Film* demonstrate the diversity of perspectives happening in the field, but the focus is, for the most part, on animation. It begins with Robert Breer's *Blazes* (1960), in which abstract illustrations, changing with each frame, disrupt any expectation of continuity. When Breer first speaks, his statement is posed as a response to Gilmour's charge of infantilism, claiming that any reaction, even hostility and dismissal, is evidence that an experimental film is effective. Breer regards the idea of definitive meaning and the purported value of communication with ambivalence, in contrast to George Dunning, who, in a subsequent interview, gives a statement that supports the Griersonian model: films should communicate. Dunning, a Canadian expatriate in England, had made *The Wardrobe* in collaboration with Dick Williams and Stan Hayward. It was a cartoon in which one figure frustrates another through the use of a box (the titular wardrobe) that defies the laws of physics. It is, in every sense, a conventional cartoon, no different in its depiction of a flexible world than a Chuck Jones cartoon. The contrast between Dunning and Breer's perspectives is confirmed as the film returns to Breer, describing his own work as a search for new kinds of continuity. Breer's film, *A Man and His Dog Out for Air* (1957), demonstrates this relationship to continuity more literally than the rapid truncation of *Blazes*, as abstract forms morph yet maintain continuity, the same spare lines assuming a number of different forms as one might encounter on a daily walk. In placing Dunning and Breer in contrast, Lipsett makes a case for the complexity of perception in cinema and the mission of those, like Breer, who act against convention, a gesture that also acts against the easy communication of the comic strip. Further to that, Lipsett has also created a dialectical structure in which he is the arbiter, arranging statements and works for contrast, such that the viewer is guided towards an appreciation for Breer's formalism.

To this, Lipsett adds a new sequence, focused on the climax to Walerian Borowczyk and Jan Lenica's *Dom* (1958). *Dom* was a celebrated work of European art cinema made by an accomplished animation team and with significant debts to the trance films of Maya Deren. In the excerpt shown, a woman admires and passionately kisses a sculptural bust of a man. Lenica, in an interview, states that their film is about the multitude of possibilities presented by filmmaking and that the film is a series of loose sequences representing "the girl's restless thoughts." Lipsett returns to *Dom*, to find the bust arranged like an altar, with flowers adorning it as the face rots away in stop motion. However subversive their work was, Borowczyk and Lenica represent the establishment of a European art cinema movement. For Lipsett, Borowczyk and Lenica could serve as a contemporary parallel for both the European Surrealists, whose movement, though still influential, was a thing of the past, and the American trance filmmakers, whose movement was subsiding. *Dom* typifies a style of filmmaking that seeks, through realistic figuration, to explore interiority and torment.

Lipsett had planned a critic's bull session, and it arrives in full force, Weinberg initiating the discussion by decrying the failure of experimental filmmakers to present a positive image of life. He offers springtime and falling in love as two themes he claims are absent from experimental filmmaking, and, in his words, "its absence depresses me." In a series of rapid interruptions, Gilmour suggests they watch *Very Nice, Very Nice*, praising its "satirical treatment of the cliché," a comment placed by Lipsett in such proximity to Weinberg's complaint as to be accusatory. *Very Nice, Very Nice* plays in full, but the discussion that follows does not deal with it. Instead, there is a debate, with Weinberg and Gilmour siding against experimental film, and Glover and Cadieux speaking supportively of the field and its audience. The discussion becomes focused around the use of intellectual language, which Weinberg and Gilmour resent Cadieux and others for using, as if it is a sign of superiority or, as Weinberg claims, an act of rationalizing films in such a way as to obscure the experience of them, an experience that, in this case, offers him nothing. Various eruptions occur among Weinberg, Gilmour, and Cadieux, with Cadieux offering a rousing defence of the potential for open meanings in films like Breer's. The arguments wind down as Glover speaks, confronting Gilmour, arguing that there is a lack of informed criticism, that critics have reneged on the job and cannot speak with authority on this work, and that any complaints about the quality of experimental films ultimately lies with the dispassionate mishandling of this cinema by critics. When Gilmour deflects the challenge by claiming that critics don't often get to see experimental film, Weinberg demands to know "where are the film poets today?" This leads Weinberg to comment that Norman McLaren is an "authentic film poet," a means of introducing the final segment.

Norman McLaren, working at his Moviola, provides an explanation of his methods for creating electronic soundtracks by etching in the optical soundtrack area of a 35mm filmstrip.[11] Lipsett's portrayal of McLaren is an admiring portrait of a colleague, filming over his shoulder as his images flit by in the viewing window of the console. McLaren's "authenticity" as a singular film poet in the era of Jonas Mekas and Stan Brakhage is open to question, but Weinberg knows to hold McLaren in esteem because of the campaign on the part of the National Film Board to champion McLaren for his formal inventions and his technological precision. Early in the roundtable, Guy Glover offers his opinion of the state of experimental film as featuring a mix of work by master technicians and those who are learning their craft—Glover condescends that they are "learning their ABCs"—and this attitude, that those filmmakers who are disinterested in progressive evolutionary forms of technological awe are inferior, was an attitude easily shared between the NFB and establishment critics. To be engaged by McLaren's explanations of his hand-plotted electronic soundtracks does not demand an openness to the muse of poetry. McLaren was Glover's ideal, a master technician.[12] As an example of McLaren's filmmaking, Lipsett integrates *Blinkity Blank* (1955), in which a series of etched forms erupt intermittently on screen, in time with music. The film's impact had originally cohered around McLaren's use of colour and space: the eruptions are of various colours, many of them in subtle shades of red and blue against a black background. McLaren's film shares formal similarities with Breer's *A Man and His Dog*, similarities that are here underscored by Lipsett's presentation of *Blinkity Blank* in a black-and-white photonegative, such that McLaren's etchings appear as black-on-white forms, like Breer's black ink on clear leader.[13]

That Weinberg dismisses Breer as a purveyor of trash but regards McLaren as a poet of the first order supports Glover's point that the judgments of film critics are fickle, uninformed, even arbitrary, when it comes to experimental cinema. Glover's rebuke is a rare insight in a film that, despite its formal cleverness, is riddled with institutional compromise. Despite the drawback of its narrow focus on animation, *The Experimental Film* is unusual in its time for acknowledging this cinema at a time when the New York underground film was slowly seeping into culture, well before it burst into the popular imagination with reports of Andy Warhol's durational epics. The ignorant positions of Weinberg and Gilmour are of their time, and to Gilmour's credit, he would more actively cover experimental film in the *Telegram* in the mid- to late 1960s, when it became a harder phenomenon to ignore. Arthur Lipsett's treatment for *The Experimental Film* bears a more explicitly "personal vision" of the topic in his original choice of featured filmmakers. Stan VanDerBeek and Bruce Conner were the filmmakers with whom Lipsett shared the most common ground of anyone in the experimental film world. All three used found materials; all three were collagists who came to cinema from backgrounds in fine arts; and all three made films that offered tragicomic visions of life on Earth. All three men were contemporaries, and all became involved in filmmaking in the 1950s when any postwar idyll that North America had experienced had faded under the weight of consumer vacuity and the starved souls of artists, the same conditions that instigated the Beat poetry movement.

Of the three, Stan VanDerBeek, older by only a few years, had a history in television production, designing scenery for the cartoon *Winky Dink and You*, following an education at Cooper Union and the storied Black Mountain College. In making his own films, he took inspiration from Hannah Höch, whose disfigurative photomontages bore a sardonic humour, and Max Ernst, whose description of his own process may readily apply to VanDerBeek's: "the systematic exploitation of the accidentally or artificially provoked encounter of two or more foreign realities on a seemingly incongruous level."[14] Ernst's remark resembles an analytical summary of a statement central to Surrealist aesthetics found in the Comte de Lautréamont's *Les Chants de Maldoror*: "as beautiful as the chance encounter of a sewing machine and an umbrella on an operating table."[15] VanDerBeek's first films were collage animations in which still images were set to move through the interaction of paper cutouts—for example, the eyes within a pair of glasses would rotate independent of the face that wears them. The humour of his work is rooted in the influence of Surrealism, often engaging with a disjunction of scale, as evidenced in *A La Mode* (1959): the comedy of giant hammers striking tiny heads; bodies becoming landscapes over which vehicles ride; faces that are opened on hinges to reveal sitting rooms; and whole buildings that, when ripped open, reveal the piercing stare of a giant eye.[16] VanDerBeek's work would later morph as his interests in the geodesic dome, and the possibilities of intermedia and expanded cinema, consumed the bulk of his ambitions.[17]

That Lipsett and VanDerBeek were both working with found materials is a superficial connection in itself, but while their approaches were different, the way that they treated their objects shows common ground: grinning smiles in commercial images mix with historical photographs and paintings in surreal juxtapositions and with a joyous rhythm, a sign of a deeper bond between their work. VanDerBeek signalled the humour of his work by the use of rags and drum rolls on the soundtrack, as would Lipsett. Both filmmakers dealt with themes of hysterical consumerism, but the silliness of this hysteria is less ambiguous in VanDerBeek's films. VanDerBeek's overlapping collage constructs bear what Ernst had called the "spark of poetry" that joins disparate realities. Lipsett was dealing with discrete components, and so the spark of poetry is present not on the composition plane but in the rhythmic editing that joins his images in sequence.

There is no indication as to which of VanDerBeek's films Lipsett had intended to showcase in *The Experimental Film*, but at the time that the program was being prepared, a handful of them had gained considerable attention and might have provided great provocation to the roundtable. The aforementioned *A La Mode* was in wide circulation, and it features, more than any other, the influence of surrealism. In *Science Friction* (1959), humour arises from the consequences of actions (as when a hammer smashes a human face, which is replaced by the face of a dog) and a subversion of physics (a spacesuit with human faces bouncing up and down within its helmet, competing to peer out) to a conclusion of humanity departing from the Earth as its monuments float skyward. Nikita Khrushchev's "starring role" in VanDerBeek's *Achooooo Mr. Kerrooschev* (1960), as a kind of marionette that dances through many cultures and is continuously disassembled and reconstituted, is very similar to the Soviet leader's appearance in *Very Nice, Very Nice* the next year. Where Lipsett had Khrushchev leering from afar through binoculars at fabulous Western materialism, VanDerBeek places Khrushchev where the action is, trapped in a strange performance of imperialism. By the time that Lipsett and Millar made *The Experimental Film*, *A La Mode* and *Science Friction* were both in the collection of Guy L. Coté, making them accessible to Montreal's modest experimental film crowd.[18]

Bruce Conner had started out as a painter working in an anarchic, transgressive Neo-Dada vein, sensibilities that suited the scene of late 1950s American modernism. In San Francisco, he turned to other media, working in sculpture, assemblage, and filmmaking. Already toiling in refuse to assemble his mixed-media works, Conner turned to the idea of making films the same way, starting with what he would call a "poverty film," *A Movie* (1959), made from newsreels and clips from films he had purchased.[19] A patchwork of false endings and false starts signals the broadest definitions of cinematic action: in a startling reflection on the illusory spell of continuity in cinema, a wagon train becomes a stampede racing alongside an elephant and a military tank. *A Movie* plays on the indexical expectation of film editing, as a man looks through the periscope of a submarine and discovers a stag movie. A mushroom cloud blooms and is soon joined to images of surfing and boating in choppy waters. Throughout, these images achieve a sublime grace through the accompaniment of Ottorino Respighi's symphonic poem *Pines of Rome*. With *A Movie*, Conner anticipates the particular ridicule that Lipsett features in his own work, where images of banal, everyday life on Earth, of spectacle, of competition, of joy, are exposed for their silliness in the contrast created by Respighi's ominous music. The world is hazardous, and cinema itself is witness and death knell, but the humour of *A Movie* runs through each transition, the flume of a volcano giving way to the pope performing a mass. Even when Conner's focus is on tragic disasters, massacres, and death, their discontinuity, their compositional isolation, and the pomp of Respighi combine into a tragicomic farce.

In the year before *The Experimental Film* was produced, Conner finished his second film, *Cosmic Ray* (1961), cut to Ray Charles's "What'd I Say." Conner described *Cosmic Ray* as an anti-war film, an expansion on the form of *A Movie* in his rhythmic approach, the edits becoming denser, evidently propelled by the rhythms of the soundtrack. The film also departed dramatically from the parameters of *A Movie* in its integration of Conner's own photography of a dancer and light abstractions, elements that are superimposed as an erotic counterpoint to found images of war games and Mickey Mouse. Conner's integration of fragments, both made and found, mirrors Lipsett's prominent use of his own photography in *Very Nice, Very Nice*, an aspect of empirical witness that both men would soon make a prominent trait in their work.

Offered as exemplars of a movement, Conner, Lipsett, and VanDerBeek could no better demonstrate the diversity of forms in experimental film than the animators whom Lipsett and Millar ended up showcasing. In their common theme of consumer culture inertia, they were distinctive from the heterogeneity of experimental filmmaking, that cacophony of voices in which Jonas Mekas had glimpsed utopia. Lipsett's ambition to bring the three together in *The Experimental Film* suggests a great deal about his values and where he saw himself. The original subtitle of the program, *A Personal Vision*, has a double meaning: experimental filmmaking is work of personal vision, but further, this broadcast could be Lipsett's own personal vision of the field, one in which the influence of Max Ernst had survived to flourish in the communion of parts found amidst Conner's material apocalypse, Lipsett's driving rhythms, and VanDerBeek's surreal frottage. Lipsett would cast himself alongside his influences, but even more, alongside true peers, united in their own vision of cinema, not as a grand utopia, but as incendiary Neo-Dada folk art.

*The Experimental Film* was broadcast in late fall 1962. Michael Dancsok observes how innovative the style of the broadcast was for its time in eschewing narration and forgoing the presence of a moderator.[20] Lipsett, as the editor, becomes a silent moderator, arranging excerpts to guide the viewer into a questioning state. This is in sympathy with the NFB's push towards observational cinema, felt in the *Candid Eye* series and onward. Other techniques of Lipsett's declare his editorial interventions—in particular, his use of interruption, repetition, and laughter when Gilmour suggests the panel watch *Very Nice, Very Nice*, the style of the bull session suddenly mirroring the style of their subject. The unconventional approach that Lipsett used in making *The Experimental Film* did not go entirely unnoticed, nor was it welcomed in all quarters. Ottawa Citizen columnist Bob Gardiner wrote of *The Experimental Film* that "the editor of it needed to do a little homework on the old-fashioned variety…amoozin' but confoozin.'"[21] Gardiner's tacit suggestion that the piece lacked comprehensibility is a sign of how out of step Lipsett was from the staid expectations of NFB and CBC audiences. And yet, there was among concerned parties a warm feeling toward the project, that it had served an institutional purpose in bridging a gap and furthering the relationship between management at the CBC and the NFB and that, as such, Lipsett had done the Film Board a service. *The Experimental Film* was ahead of its time, not only in formal terms, but also in signalling interest in its subject. When experimental filmmaking became topical in the late 1960s, NFB staffer Terry Ryan would attempt unsuccessfully to get the film back into active distribution, insisting that the perspectives on display—both the methods and approaches of the artists, and the intolerance and ignorance of members of the roundtable—were still prevalent in the culture.[22]

It was after a film screening in August 1962 that Lipsett met Judith Sandiford, with whom he would pursue a relationship that would last for the next decade. At twenty, Sandiford was an undergraduate at McGill between her third and fourth years. Sandiford would later recall being taken with Lipsett: "he was tall, dark, elegant, handsome, charming, he dressed beautifully, he was funny."[23] Sandiford's recollections of Lipsett's charm and humour are a sharp contrast to the portrayal of him as antisocial, evidence that his shyness was taken by some as aloofness, a characteristic that, in combination with the perceived cynicism of his films, would gradually aggravate his relations at the NFB. Although Lipsett was a private person, there exist chronicles of his friendships in this period. He became particularly close to the actor Martin Lavut, who would later pursue an eclectic career as a filmmaker in his own right.[24] He enjoyed warm relations with his co-workers—among them, Neil Shakery, Kaj Pindal, Gerald Potterton, Derek Lamb, McLaren, and Millar—and his producers in Unit B became staunch advocates for him; in particular, Tom Daly, who had produced *Very Nice, Very Nice* alongside Colin Low, had initiated *The Experimental Film* and would go on to produce three more of Lipsett's films. Daly had a reputation for his supportive stewarding of projects and would be one of Lipsett's primary allies at the NFB.

That fall, Lipsett moved out of the Clifton Arms and into a larger unit in a four-storey walk-up at 4921 Coronet Street, where Sandiford would soon join him.[25] He hung a Union Jack in the window, a proclamation of his Anglophilia that doubled as a playful provocation to his neighbors, their home a strange, foreign embassy in French territory. As he had at the Clifton Arms, he would cover the walls with collages and clippings, a process that extended beyond his home and into his Volkswagen Beetle. Sandiford would describe this wallpapering as being "choc-a-bloc with images that Arthur found fascinating from every possible source."[26] The two would often spend Sundays together at Beaver Lake, a picturesque artificial basin on Mount Royal, and would bond over trips to second-hand stores and the Salvation Army. Lipsett's social life was evolving, taking train trips with Sandiford and Lavut to New York to buy jazz records and fashionable clothes. His collections of images, tchotchkes, and music were an extension of his ravenous interest in the topics that would occupy his filmmaking, from modern Western science to distant Eastern cultures. As Sandiford remembers, "he was always on the lookout for things that would feed his mind."[27] His next project at the NFB, offered under the working title *New Film*, was one that he would describe as a transitional film, a means of moving forward and away from the strategies that he had established in his earlier work. While *Anything Can Happen on Channel 6* and *Very Nice, Very Nice* had sported groundbreaking editing techniques, Lipsett would push his aesthetics into the increasingly personal and subjective territory of the underground film.

FOUR

# PROCESSIONAL

IN MAKING *VERY NICE, VERY NICE*, ARTHUR LIPSETT HAD engaged with themes that were distinctively eschatological. What resulted was a portrait of Western civilization teetering "on the side of a cliff." His sound collage was a minefield of stuttering, incomplete clichés, met on screen by the wretched superficiality of advertising, harrowing records of modern conflict, and long and longing faces starved for meaning. In the months following its acclaimed release, Lipsett had desired to transcend those surface realities, to pursue a more interior vision.[1] *The Experimental Film* had brought goodwill from his colleagues at the Film Board, but it was not a creative work in the sense that *Very Nice, Very Nice* had been. Lipsett's follow-up would balance his interest in candid street photography with found materials and sound collage of a more cosmic spiritual order, dispensing with the topical apocalypse of the bomb and instead confronting the eternal apocalypse of a godless universe.

After *Very Nice, Very Nice,* Lipsett became more invested in the tension of paired opposites, the bond of a work to antithetical concepts and representations, the possibility for a work to signal a cognitive dissonance or, short of that, to maintain a deep ambiguity.[2] The perceived ironies of *Very Nice, Very Nice* anticipate this: the absurdity of showing smiles amid horror, or preaching calm in the light of the bomb, or declaring the promise of springtime to the brumal frost of an expressionless crowd. Among the paired opposites Lipsett was drawn to, none were more all-encompassing than those of the material, visible world and the metaphysical, spiritual realm. He could relate this pairing to the theories of Siegfried Kracauer, who argued that the material world was redeemed through the poetic translation of the movie. Lipsett could also find, in the relation between the visible and the invisible, pathways towards a multiform religious awakening, a beatnik's tour of Buddhism, a tour of various faith definitions of the veil between the visible world and the kingdoms that lie beyond it. This pairing also speaks to emerging scientific knowledge, theories of cybernetics, relational networks between the material world, human constitution, and contrived, artificial intelligences.

As Lipsett assembled his next project, he began to think of it as a transitional work that would counter the deductive interpretations of *Very Nice, Very Nice* with more interior, elusive renderings of experience. It was thus a shift into a deeper subjectivity, a personal search for transcendence. To pursue so subjective an agenda, on March 14, 1962, Lipsett bought his own Bolex 16mm camera.[3] The Bolex was the iconic tool of the underground movie, a multitool that allowed for pixilation, various framerates, precise manipulations of the shutter, and other in-camera effects. According to Judith Sandiford, he didn't want to use the NFB's equipment.[4] This is in keeping with Lipsett's nocturnal occupation of the editing and sound studios: if his work was not actively consuming NFB resources, it could sidestep any petty complaints, proceeding with little oversight or interference. The skill he had developed in his 35mm still photography translated readily to the Bolex: his resulting footage maintains the candid, stealthy approach that made *Very Nice, Very Nice* so voyeuristic, but it also demonstrates his masterful control of shallow focus, exacting calculations of aperture, and a balance of ambulatory from-the-hip shooting and steady intent, often made steadier through slow motion. As a cinematographer, Lipsett embraced another inbuilt tension, between rapidly changing inscriptions of experience—a familiar allegory for days of tepid ritual—and images that linger, sustained, with his dynamic editing suspended, an engrossed stare at the human project.[5]

Lipsett began to make his new film with the working title *New Film* and the proposed title *Processional*. Lipsett's plans for *Processional* break the film down into six sequences. Like his chart for *Strangely Elated*, it begins in a state of dispossession and culminates in ecstasy. It describes a search for meaning ("looking for the existence of a creator") that ends in the joy and ecstasy of "hysterical laughter" in the dance halls of Boulevard Saint-Laurent, contrasted with Easter pilgrims on the steps of St. Joseph's cathedral. In between, there is a "concrete jungle" sequence, to suggest "utter depths of despair" in the drunken violence and aimlessness that Lipsett found in "St. Lawrence on a Saturday night," drawing on Boulevard Saint-Laurent's status as the city's red-light district. The titular processional sequence is not so much a literal funeral as "the feeling that everything is a funeral procession."[6] A sequence of escapist fantasy would follow, showing workers breaking through rush hour seeking distractions, a random listing of activities that includes shopping, antiques, opera, beauty rituals, parties, bar life, and the circus. Lipsett notes that this sequence includes "Belmont Park close-ups," suggesting that his catalogue was not altogether speculative at this stage, Belmont Park being an amusement park that operated on the banks of Riviere des Prairies in Cartierville in the north end of Montreal. The "escape phantasy" sequence is defined by Lipsett as "a profound dream of desperation—a kind of life or death search for something evolving into a cinematic mental break-down."[7] The penultimate sequence he planned as "Hieronymus Bosch or Kafka-like," angelic and demonic, a chaotic mix of the profound, the absurd, the insane, the grotesque, the mystical, "out of which comes the fear of the unpredictable and the suggestion of uncontrollable laughter."[8] The concluding sequence, of revellers and pilgrims, would end in "hysterical laughter on *very tight* faces from Belmont Park or Elsewhere."[9]

*Very Nice, Very Nice* had mixed found materials with Lipsett's travel photos to fashion an epic statement on the present moment in the Western world. His plans for *Processional* demonstrate Lipsett's desire to make films at a local level, as a witness, drawing on the conflict between the violent and hedonistic club culture of Montreal and the city's institutions, from the rhythms of the workday and the pleasures of the carnival to the stone basilica of Saint Joseph's Oratory, a pilgrimage site whose claim to miracles greets visitors at the door with a wall of cast-off canes. The canes are a relic of the basilica's association with early twentieth-century mystic Brother André, whose efforts in nursing the sick were claimed miraculous by some. Placing Saint Joseph's Oratory in contrast to the dance hall, the red light district, and the amusement park could be taken as a cynical gesture or as a recognition of the sympathetic flow that leads the dispossessed to one kind of confessor or another. A triumphant debasement of prayer, comparing houses of worship to the carnival, gives way to a greater and more compassionate absurdity: that revellers, johns, and worshipers are united not only in a quest to balm their wounds, but by the structures of their experiences, a continuity between dance, inebriation, sex, and prayer. As the film came together, Lipsett would find further parallels to reconcile piety and indulgence.

Working out of the metaphorical wastebasket of Unit B productions, Lipsett found inspiration in the outtakes from Roman Kroitor's interview with cybernetics philosopher Warren McCulloch, interviewed for the two-part documentary series *The Living Machine* (1961). *The Living Machine* was a survey of supercomputer programming in the contemporary world, as viewed within a framework of synthesized subjectivity, labour and machine learning, the limits of quantification, and the machine's future as threat or relic. It begins with simple automatons and the opaque operations of punch-card supercomputers ("the electronic brain"), and it concludes with museums and myths, with McCulloch and Margaret Mead addressing the question of whether machines can become sentient and what role they serve in the future of humanity. One sequence in particular caught Lipsett's attention, in which McCulloch describes the search for purpose and meaning: "Somebody walks up, and you say, 'Your number is *21-87*...isn't it?' Boy! Does that person really smile!" *Processional* was subsequently built around this statement as a theological reckoning with a chaotic world in which a palpable desire for recognition of one's humanity is lost in a sea of masks. When Lipsett's film was completed in late 1963, McCulloch's remarks had inspired its final release title: *21-87*.

Lipsett began to solicit outtakes in June 1962, and the editing process took him roughly a year, concluding in October 1963. For the most part, the film would be composed of Lipsett's own 16mm photography, drawing only a few materials from the Unit B wastebasket: a shot of

Alan Shepard aboard the *Freedom 7* preparing for launch, which had also been used by Kroitor in *The Living Machine*; shots taken from the museum sequence in *The Living Machine*, likely footage of automatons and of a mummified corpse being inspected by archeologists; shots from the outtakes of Kroitor and Wolf Koenig's *Lonely Boy* (1962), their portrait of crooner Paul Anka, likely scenes of youths dancing excitedly; footage of a paramilitary rally interrupted by a man who is subsequently beaten; and a shot of a figure collapsing in flames.[10] Lipsett's own cinematography ranged from candid shots taken in the streets and parks of Montreal, to staged scenes with friends, to event photography in the vein of cinéma vérité.

The visual character of Lipsett's work was evolving, and so too was his approach to sound. *Very Nice, Very Nice* had a percussive sound collage, its form built around truncation and eruption, and this was well suited to its mix of waffling speech and rehearsed narration, its assault on the cliché. The sound collage of *21-87* would assume, by contrast, an uncompromising focus. Percussive elements remained, truncation remained, but where *Very Nice, Very Nice* had embraced the emptiness of its speech content, *21-87* is stitched together from fragments both earnest and profound. When music interrupts, it isn't the comic "piano massacre" of Crazy Otto; it isn't mechanical in its rhythm. Antiphonal gospel and jug-band music that Lipsett selected meet the image rather than leading it.[11] The sound collage of *21-87* is a sign of another transition that Lipsett is making, in that it is slower and more deliberated in its sequence. The crisis of speech, declining into maudlin stupidity and aphorism, transitions into a crisis of spiritual expression, where words are not being used carelessly so much as they are insufficient to express great sorrow and urgent need. The voices of *Very Nice, Very Nice* were, for the most part, voices that obfuscate and frustrate, the voices of judgment. The voices of *21-87* are often wise, searching, and frustrated, rarely comic.

The relationship between humanity and machine is present at the outset of *21-87*, as mechanical bleats and clicks sound under a medical illustration of a skull. A trapeze artist, suspended high above the circus, hanging gracefully by one foot, arms outstretched, demonstrates exhilarating balance and muscle control before Lipsett cuts to a team of anthropologists, unseen but for their hands, sawing down the chest and poking at the eye sockets of a mummified corpse. This contrast, symbolic of the passage of life, is also a demonstration of the mechanics of the body and the intangibility of the soul, the body as a bone machine. From the eyeless face, Lipsett cuts to the aggressive stare of a mime performing a "mechanical man" illusion, a stuttering dance against the backdrop of a Dimplex heater display at a carnival or tradeshow. The "android" moves its hands and arms in violent, jarring movements, stopping with precision, and an actual automaton—a pair of mechanized pincers—pours liquid from a bottle into a vial, accurately but clumsily. Kroitor's *The Living Machine* had dealt with different kinds of programmed intelligence, from the entertainment spectacle of the automaton to the trained expertise of the supercomputer, but its survey, as a progressive evolutionary inquiry into the future of man, did not dwell on comic folly or the terror of the uncanny. For this reason, Kroitor showed toy automatons—a giant robot with flexible digits, a mechanical canine that could bark and sit—but did not cite the scatological example of Vaucanson's digesting duck, or the hoax of Wolfgang von Kempelen's Mechanical Turk.[12] Despite their certain relevance to the topic of automation and artificial intelligence, such examples represent heights of human absurdity. Lipsett's "automatons" are nearer to these examples and, held in contrast, form an ironic dyad, the hesitant, imprecise movements of the mechanical pincers in sharp contrast to the exacting turns of the mime's wrists. The first human voice to sound has the speechifying tone of a minister as he reads from Robert Dodsley's collection *The Œconomy of Human Life* (1749), a compilation of tracts, aphorisms and parables that claimed to be gathered from ancient Eastern wisdom. The excerpt welcomes the limitations of knowledge, declaring that knowledge of self, God, and the debt paid through worship is all that must be known.[13] In the context of Lipsett's montage, the statement is addressed not only to humankind but to its human-like creations, for whom humanity becomes godlike. The text is also a command, against inquiry, to accept only what is known. What follows is a persistent challenge to that command.

As the prologue ends, Lipsett's own cinematography starts to dominate the image: a man on a bench in Montreal's Dorchester Square, pigeons pecking at the ground, close-ups on a child's face, the sun cutting through branches, a miraculous dawn. An older man, flanked in a crowd of young and old figures, turns his face upward to gaze to screen right. His gaze is met with a hard cut to a monkey behind glass, looking out curiously, moving its head. Lipsett cuts to another older man with a wise but crooked smile. In his outline for *Processional*, Lipsett had planned for the film to begin with a sequence about the life cycle: "a slow awakening to the reality of now…looking for the existence of a creator."[14] This sequence is both highly contrived—the spectators, staring upwards, are not observing the monkey, which is at chest-level—and jocular, in the sense that, following on the Dodsley quote, Lipsett intimates that these faces are searching for the presence of God. That god is revealed as a monkey, and the next reaction shot, of the sly grin of an onlooker, implies that even the congregants are in on the joke. This tragicomic communion is reinforced on the soundtrack by the song "God is Alright" by Sons of the South, an ecstatic, early 1950s Excello R&B gospel single in which a forceful voice cuts through the bass bellow of a choir singing that every child of God has to cry sometimes.

An atmosphere of religiosity persists as a subway train, passing at night and lit by the reflections of street lamps, leads into a series of candid street shots, of a man walking through traffic talking to himself, of smoke pumping out of buildings, of well-dressed older women shopping, eating, and conversing. Inserted into this montage is another image of humanity's attempt at self-definition: a mannequin's head topped in a boater hat. The presence of the boater hat suggests another form of harmonized singing, the Barbershop quartet, a fading memory of twentieth-century fetishized dandyism, another example of absurd iconography. On the soundtrack, a woman talks about her devotion to the Book of Revelations, her faith in a punishing, world-ending salvation; her speech ends with an ambiguous tripping repetition in which she says, "I don't believe in mortality…immortality," another paired opposite mirroring the distinction between the visible and the invisible. People search the shelves of a shopping mall, grasping at strings of pearls, glaring at Lipsett's camera, all of them filmed in medium-to-tight close-ups that frequently suggest the density of a crowd. A man's voice declares that the world has no secrets, only facts, a sobering if condescending charge against mystery that sounds in accord with the burdened faces of consumers. A child covered in dirt breaks down weeping into the chest of an older child, while on the soundtrack, the staged, trained voices of actors speak in synthetic hysteria about being human and wanting to feel free, an incongruity of artifice and insuppressible, painful emotion. Returning to his street photography, Lipsett cuts to a slow-motion image of an elderly woman as, on the soundtrack, the voice of an elderly woman speaks about the social anxiety of feeling stared at in public, transitioning away from artifice and towards a coherent melding of image and sound. As Lipsett's montage continues to another paired opposite, the wide smile of an elderly woman passed on the street and the blank expression of a young woman feigning obliviousness to the camera, an interviewee is heard on the soundtrack, repeatedly asking their interviewer, "can I go back?" As if to pose an answer, a diving horse is seen plummeting into a pool of water at the end of a long and narrow platform with no option but to move forward off the edge.

In a scratchy intrusion of whimsy, the Memphis Jug Band plays "You Got to Have That Thing" as Lipsett's camera passes rapidly and from a low angle against a moving crowd. The penetrating stares of old women yield to the comically small lenses of a pair of pocket binoculars, held by a man who peers through them to return Lipsett's gaze. An eruption of violence at the podium of what appears to be a Nazi rally is punctuated with cutaways: a downward-facing shot of a man walking in the street; a transient eye-level shot of bodies passing against black; a dramatic upward tilt on a skyscraper; and a leftward pan following a man with a hearing aid, seen from behind. These directional subject movements and camera movements become entangled with the violence of the rally, in which a figure who has disrupted the scene is dragged and beaten by uniformed men. A pair of hands position another icon of commercial culture, a sculptural bust of a sailor in a Dixie cup hat, a cigarette in his mouth, posed in a shop window, framed by a rotating sunflower. The broad, toothy smile of the sailor beams in response to the beating. A staged drama unfolds in a rapid and compositionally abstract series of shots: a bearded man extends a revolver, and several figures, gathered around a boat on a shore, are seen feigning wounds and mock-firing pistols. The sequence ends with two men laying facedown on a grassy hill. In relation to Lipsett's plans for *Processional*, this has been his jungle sequence, "to utter depths of despair." His intimations of violence, brutality, and aimlessness are not filmed in the shadowy alleys of Saint-Laurent, but rather in the streets of the business district, in bus queues in broad daylight, in this mix of observed and imagined conflicts.

As Kroitor begins to speak on the soundtrack, slowly formulating a question, the aimless men of Dorchester Square feed birds and stare skyward. A flock of birds passes the Boer War Memorial and the Sun Life Building as Kroitor talks about the perception of God, the collective feeling that there is a force behind the mask of nature. With audible edits, McCulloch interrogates Kroitor to define whether what they're discussing is a matter of feeling or thought. An even more audible shift signals McCulloch delivering the title remarks: "Somebody walks up, and you say, 'Your number is 21-87...isn't it?' Boy! Does that person really smile!" A handbag is waved in front of a monkey through glass. Its eyes follow, and it sways in time with the motion as if being hypnotized. Various people, observed from a low angle, enter a shop, sunlight bleeding and refracting through the glass of the window, seemingly oblivious to Lipsett's camera. The low angle casts them as godlike, looming above, as, on the soundtrack, a man's voice calls out to a doctor for mercy, begging for relief from a terrible warmth, but his plea seems less for a crisis of the body than of the soul. In *The Living Machine*, science fiction historian Sam Moskowitz introduces Hugo Gernsback's visionary 1911 novel *Ralph 124C 41+*, a work that offers a precedent for McCulloch's remarks about 21-87. In Gernsback's novel, the population has taken on quantifiable codes in place of traditional names.[15] McCulloch's interview in *The Living Machine* speaks to Lipsett's sense of paired opposites, as he espouses a view that could be interpreted as both fatalistic and optimistic, suggesting that man is doomed to be swallowed by the sun but that man might survive in the machine relics that extend the presence of humanity in the universe. *The Living Machine* offers further clues to why Lipsett would be so attracted to McCulloch's exploration of cybernetics, as the mathematician speaks of how he reconciled early expectations placed on him to join the ministry with the seduction of mathematics. He describes his work as being driven by a theological question: "what is a number that a man may know it, and a man that he may know a number?" In this sense, his remarks about the "calling" of a human being's number, posed here out of context as a response to Kroitor's speculations on the animating force of life, are less about the dehumanization of humankind, the reduction of a human being to the status of a number, than they are about the human quest to recognize and to implicate themselves in a pattern, even by quantified or symbolic means.

FIGURE 4.1: *21-87* (Arthur Lipsett, National Film Board, 1964)

Lipsett had proposed that his new film contain "the feeling that everything is a funeral procession."[16] He realizes this with the film's most eulogistic passage: a fashion show, featuring models in fur coats and mask-like face paint, is intercut with scenes of the models preparing and of a man whose rubbery mugging plays in forward and reverse motion, casting into his features mechanical gestures akin to the mime seen in the film's opening. The fashion show is accompanied by whistles; the call-and-response of a Latin mass; and reverberating sound, some of it slowed to an inarticulate bass modulation. The liturgical elements are held in sharp relief to the decadence of the scene, but as the models pose on the catwalk in slow motion, their trained gestures assuming the uncanny, inhuman postures of automatons, the fashion show becomes a mirror ritual to the mass, a translation of body and blood into that greater force that animates the masks of the universe. The presence of cameramen standing in the spare, anonymous, backlit audience emphasizes the ghoulish, detached witness of those on the cusp of the scene. The winding mechanism on a 16mm camera spins as if it were an extension of a cameraman's head, conducting and reproducing the funereal atmosphere of the scene. A benediction is read as, in a rural setting, a figure collapses in flames, then stands and staggers forward, an image that would suggest the topical case of Thich Quang Duc, the Mahayana Buddhist monk who self-immolated on a busy road in Saigon in June 1963 as a protest against the persecution of Buddhists by Ngo Dinh Diem's South Vietnamese government. While Quang Duc was stoic in his act, this figure seems almost casual, staggering into the trees as if the flames weren't there. Images of modern conflict, which had played such a substantial role in *Very Nice, Very Nice*, are largely absent from *21-87*, with this exception, and its placement in this cavalcade, after the synthetic mass on the catwalk, is a reminder of the end of corporeal experience and the barbarism of the known world. As a segue towards the heavens, the image transitions to astronaut Alan Shepard, suspended in the cockpit of the *Freedom 7*.

The second episode of *The Living Machine* was largely built around this same image of Alan Shepard, trusting his fate to supercomputer calculations as he prepared for launch. As *21-87* begins its final descent, this same image appears, Shepard in the visible discomfort of the claustrophobic cockpit, as a staccato, interrupted benediction sounds. With the sound of a hymnal choir, Lipsett cuts from Shepard to scenes of people mugging at their own distorting reflections in the tilting funhouse mirrors of Belmont Park. Young people dance vigorously to an unheard big band, accompanied only by sounds of heavy panting, the gagging of suppressed vomit, the involuntary moans of a body in distress. A series of circus acts plays to the sound of a somber hymn, an elephant spinning a dancer in its jaws by her leg, a graceful gesture made all the more graceful by the austere religiosity of the music. Tired, haggard faces peer out from a crowd at a horse track, an evening at the circus having given way to an evening at the derby, where announcers rapidly call results, their voices overlapping in a complex collage, reverberating as if in an empty cathedral.

In a sequence of hard cuts, figures rise on an escalator, most of their faces oblivious, some guarded, one glaring, accompanied by a hymn that lends a spiritual dimension to their rides. As with many of the film's references to technology—automatons, binoculars, hearing aids, movie cameras, rockets—the escalator has become allegorical, a mechanical extension of human agency and of the progressive evolutionary project that is also an imperialist project: a shopping centre escalator is simultaneously an occasion for Lipsett's candid photography and a gateway to the last new world, a metaphor for final ascent. As the hymn fades, a low sound, like a slowed siren, accompanies a series of allegorically potent images—an elderly woman sitting on a bus staring out the window; a traffic jam; an elderly man digging in a garbage can; a statue of an angel in a cemetery; a cherubic baby; a tilt-a-whirl—all intercut with scenes of trapeze and highwire acts from the circus. The acrobats serve as an allegory for the risk of living in the modern world, while the scenes with which they are intercut suggest the poles of life—youth and old age—caught in an interminable waiting. In its parodic use of

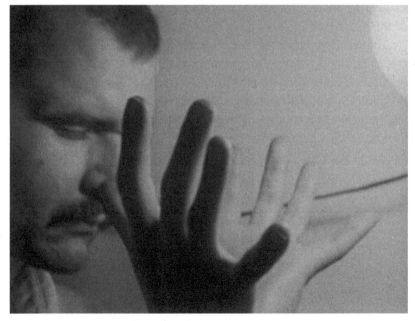

**FIGURE 4.2:** John Max offers a Buddhist prayer in *21-87* (Arthur Lipsett, National Film Board, 1964)

religious music, *21-87* becomes a mock epic, with activities as trivial as rising on an escalator or waiting in a traffic jam assuming the weight of a spiritual event.[17] The final sequence is filmed in the bathroom of Lipsett's apartment: his friend John Max stands to the left of Lipsett, his face close to an exposed light bulb above the bathroom mirror, his eyes closed in meditation. Max performs a Buddhist prayer with his hands raised in a gesture resembling the Uttarabodhi mudra.[18] The end credits are interspersed with images of the two men, Max holding his hands up to the light as if conducting its energy, Lipsett glimpsing his own brackish reflection. As the image collapses into darkness, McCulloch is once again heard on the soundtrack, repeating the exemplum of "21-87."

Even with its experimental collage form, *21-87* was suited to the contemporaneous output of Unit B, as a film that balanced observational cinematography with astringent humour. These were traits that it shared with *Lonely Boy*: an eagerness to look behind the mask of commercial culture at egotists, hysterical consumers, and their slithering conductors. Despite the rapid and disorienting collage of his soundtrack, and his clever juxtapositions formed by the application of religious music to secular spectacles, Lipsett had made a film that masterfully performed the technical maneuvers of his peers, subjective but not diaristic, experimental but not lacking in social relevance. Its social criticism was ambiguous but provocative. Even as it pilfers the materials of *The Living Machine* and places them in a satirical context, *21-87* maintains continuity with Kroitor's series, a necessary translation of the series's themes from a pedagogical mode into a poetic mode, opening onto greater territory for doubt and apprehension. For Lipsett's presence behind the camera, and his delight at candid shooting, *21-87* was as much a work of cinema vérité as it was a collage film. This suggests another striking oppositional pair: that *21-87* is a subjective exploration of spiritual forces, and yet it bears a formal approach that originates in the desire among filmmakers to exhaust visible information and to conceal subjectivity.

When Lipsett completed *21-87*, he provided the NFB with a statement, describing the film as a "shock-state which the spectator must grapple with, continuously counter-check and question" and an "extreme statement of anxiety by a young filmmaker who considers the film as 'transitional.'"[19] Lipsett characterizes *21-87* within the subjective context of personal anxiety, but in challenging the viewer to enter this shock-state, it becomes personal to them, a Litmus test of their capacities for religious fervour and terror at the alienation of contemporary life. The subjective nature of Lipsett's project opens rather than closes interpretation, for the curiosity, frailty and naked fear that his statement suggests is universal to the world as he represents it: "this film can also be viewed as an arrested moment in the work of an artist, caught in the act of departure from surface realities in the search for an expression on film of heightened inner states which could transcend experiences of the known world."[20] As editor, Lipsett subverts the observational power of his own cinematography, tangling strands of image and sound to provoke rumination. In a statement given to L.M. Kit Carson in order to contextualize the film for an undergraduate class, Lipsett later claimed that he had "started out with the idea of shooting trivialities, but as shooting progressed [he] began reading *The Tibetan Book of the Dead*."[21] For Lipsett, the two journeys intermingled, with the *Bardo Thodol* guiding him further away from material reality and towards the spiritual: "Each shot tends to have its own reality; by joining many obviously isolated shots each having their own reality, a multi-reality situation tends to emerge which has the ability to symbolically represent a larger multi-reality situation such as the collective consciousness (and unconsciousness) of a civilization."[22] For Lipsett, the indexical relations between shots open possibilities for summoning a network of commingling subjectivities, engaging the viewer in a subliminal, unrestrained dialectic.

Lipsett's acknowledgement of the *Bardo Thodol* also demonstrates his distance from the conventional Western experience of his colleagues. When Daly, Low, Kroitor, and other Unit B filmmakers set out to make films, they did so with attention to the spheres of Western historical and scientific progress. Their efforts were marked invariably with imperialist hegemony, casting the world, even at its most mysterious, as a puzzle to be solved. Lipsett would have read an edition of the Walter Evans-Wentz translation, published as *The Tibetan Book of the Dead* (1927), popular in the circles of the beats and other intellectual countercultures contending seriously with Eastern mysticism. Evans-Wentz's text synthesizes the *Bardo Thodol* with the author's Theosophical biases and his awareness of Hinduism, resulting in a syncretic text that patches together accounts of the state between life and death, a window on inner visions that struck a chord with Omnists and Western converts to Buddhism.[23] Lipsett's use of the term "transitional" as a qualifier for this project takes on a richer meaning in the context of the *Bardo Thodol*, an account of transitional states of being.

The full context of *21-87*, of Lipsett's working methods and his sound sources, is deepened by an undated, untitled six-page script that prefigures the film and seemingly prefigures his engagement with the *Bardo Thodol*. This script features sixty-nine bullet points consisting of either image and sound description or transcriptions of speech. It suggests a longer work, one with more overt humour and in which an emphasis is placed on consumerism ("in the supermarkets / soft lights and music and beautifully displayed food"), military-industrial technology ("screaming jets"), and the hypocritical platitudes of public life (in quotations of various politicians).[24] In this, the script marks a stronger continuity with *Very Nice, Very Nice*; its density of sentiments regarding spiritual crisis and its attention to political speech and ideas of the past would be revisited in Lipsett's future films. In the margins, he indicates the film's intended "shock states," which consist of a man speaking to his doctor about having haunting visions of the afterlife: it is the same voice that Lipsett samples, begging that the doctor "have mercy on [their] soul." The "shock state" is a summit of terror and desperation amidst all of these banalities. The intended processional of Lipsett's original title is also revealed, unambiguously, as the melodious gaiety of a New Orleans funeral march.[25]

As an inquiry into the natures of spirit, damnation, cognition, and mechanical intelligence, *21-87* continues Lipsett's tragicomic tour of the human condition, performing what Søren Kierkegaard called a "leap," that act of devoting oneself, by the sheer necessity of forward movement and by divine, irrational trust, to an impossible, invisible transcendence. Even Lipsett's leap is elastic, his own writings on transcendence less about concretizing an abstract experience of "heightened inner states" than it is preoccupied with the search itself.[26] In its openness, *21-87* is a work of negative capability, for it imagines cinema as a mysterious ecstasy, a vision, or a waking dream that gives, in place of answers, occasions for reverie.

FIVE

# THE GREEN FUSE

In Dylan Thomas's "THE FORCE THAT THROUGH THE GREEN fuse drives the flower," the poet signals "a natural process that links man with what surrounds him, inner with outer, above with below."[1] His image of an animating life force leads to a chorus of dumbstruck sublime. That this force bears both creation and destruction is met with a resignation that such a force defies description. Thomas's ability to cohere contradictory elements, making ambiguous reference to processes that are both metabolic and mythic, is a trait common to the strongest visionary art, a discomfiting overlap of body and spirit. Dylan Thomas employs, in his words, "the earthquakes of the body to describe the earthquakes of the heart."[2] Like many poets following in the tradition of visionary modernism, Thomas took after William Blake's concept of contraries, that the opposites embedded in the individual fulfill a complementary duty, a duty that the poet accepts as the translation of feeling into image. The force that courses through the green fuse is itself and its absence, life and death, water and fire, earth and air, flesh and spirit, a force that marks universal resonances among earthly things and moves the poet to disavow his own gift for articulation.[3]

Arthur Lipsett had a sense of that force that operates under the mask of nature, animating the human machine, and, like Thomas, his definition of what that force was remained willfully unfixed. As Roman Kroitor had said in *21-87*, some call it God. Lipsett had occupied a secular reality following the suicide of his mother and the consequent non-observance of his family. This secularism had fed his absurdist vision of the world, inasmuch as he was unhindered by any one devotion. In his work, he maintained a pantheistic openness to mystical ideas and spirituality, an Omnist sensibility evident in his esoteric library, the international scope of his image and sound sources, his citations to the rituals and traditions of many cultures. His poetics were guided by a tension between modern and ancient knowledge, between faith and empirical witness, between the invisible valleys of the soul and the stone and glass of Montreal. To reconcile this tension, to proffer solutions, was not the role of the artist, and all the better for the artist to recognize the boundaries of their voice, admitting themselves unable to tell "how time has ticked a heaven round the stars." Thomas's poem resonates with the surrender of meaning in Lipsett's films, how he navigates theme, his refusal of definitive statement, his denial of reductive conclusions in the face of the sublime. In his statements, Lipsett encouraged the impression that his films reflected a personal struggle through anxiety, through social and spiritual crisis, but the tumult between life and death was a universal circuit. As Lipsett was preparing to make his next film, Jean-Claude Pilon profiled him in *Objectif*, writing that Lipsett planned to adopt "a resolutely experimental form" for what would "obviously be his first major film."[4]

In the summer of 1963, Lipsett submitted his plans for his next film. It claimed inspiration from Dylan Thomas's conception of the energy force, and its title, *Free Fall*, suggested the apocalypse of a plummeting and ruined civilization; it provoked Milton's image of the fallen archangel in *Paradise Lost*, who, in falling to Hell, discovers a place where "here at least / we shall be free."[5] *Free Fall* would serve as a showcase for Lipsett's own cinematography, which had become highly kinetic and abstract. It followed a direct line from his previous film: while Lipsett was quick to note that the film was not an adaptation of Thomas's poem, and would not feature the poem in any explicit way, his inspiration to explore the invisible force of nature also had its roots in Kroitor's remarks to McCulloch in *The Living Machine*, that people "become aware of some kind of force...behind this apparent mask which we see in front of us." Lipsett's shooting style was evolving: with *21-87*, he departed from the animation of paper collages and photographic stills that had led to his ascent at Unit B, but he would continue to elaborate on the rhythmic tensions that had developed from his previous films. For passages of *Free Fall*, his cinematography would assume the form of vibrant pixilation, a technique in which the cinematographer uses the single-frame exposure function of the camera to expose lone frames which, when played back at twenty-four frames per second, are rapidly regurgitated.[6] Lipsett's use of pixilation would, nonetheless, be interrupted frequently by his trademark caesuras, maintaining the rhythmic tension between meditative and quick editing.

Lipsett wrote two proposals for *Free Fall*. The first, dated July 16, 1963, is notable for featuring a methodology section on "sleuthing and indeterminacy" in cinema. In this proposal, Lipsett does not declare a particular relationship with composer John Cage, but his use of Cage's term suggests a debt to Cage's philosophies of sound art and improvisation. In 1959, Cage had released *Indeterminacy*, recorded with his frequent collaborator, pianist David Tudor, a work in which Cage and Tudor, operating in separate rooms and out of earshot of one another, perform modular pieces that result in chance alignments. Cage reads ninety one-minute stories, his recitation fluctuating in speed in an effort to fit texts of various lengths to a predetermined duration. Elsewhere, Tudor performed selections from Cage's *Concert for Piano and Orchestra* and played fragments from Cage's *Fontana Mix*, a prerecorded tape featuring chance collisions of sound. Tudor's elements fuse in a spare dance of disruptions and silences. The disparate sides of this performance, merged in the recording process, testify to Cage's dedication to letting sounds be. Lipsett's approach to "sleuthing and indeterminacy" is not imbued with Cagean ideas; rather, he writes in terms of the perception of an audience engaged in disentangling a codified experience, a proposition with greater debts to Kracauer than to Cage. He argues that the presence of a hallucinatory element—effected through fragmentation—will give the film an intensity that can support an indeterminate structure. Where Lipsett departs from Cage most sharply is in his reticence to produce a clear definition of indeterminacy: he writes of immersion, materiality, and spectatorship, but his terms are willfully ambiguous.[7]

By the time that Lipsett had revised and resubmitted his proposal on September 6, 1963, it specified that the film was to be a full collaboration with Cage. He rationalized the unconventional aspects of his project by noting at the outset that "experimentation in film is considered to be a valid contribution to Film Board productions."[8] He provided a philosophical basis for his methods, but, like his earlier charts, this made what precisely he was proposing no clearer. Lipsett offered that *Free Fall* would examine "the transformation of physical phenomena into psychological ones," an adoption of hallucinatory vision in which "inner and outer events intermingle and fuse with each other" to create a "psychophysical" reality.[9] The relationship between the psychic and the physical was a relation of presentness (the body) to memory, psyche, and mediated perception (the mind). In his earlier proposal, he had argued that *Free Fall* would "create a new continuity of experience *through the fusion of recognized past correspondences and immediate sensory patterns*."[10] A post-production statement that Lipsett gave the NFB upon finishing *21-87* had described it as a search for states that "could transcend experiences of the known world."[11] This phrase reoccurs with his plans for *Free Fall*, with Lipsett offering that to "approach the known world in a hallucinatory state" will force "a new reality" to take hold, a new reality that he had come to see as an act of "psychophysical continuity."[12] For his colleagues at the NFB, the known world was the world as represented on globes and maps; it was a world of diplomacy aspiring toward total social and scientific comprehension. For Lipsett, the known world was the visible, material world, an environment defined largely as a counterpart to other unknown and unknowable inner states of being. Lipsett's second proposal ends with a block quote from Cage's 1957 lecture "Experimental Music," reprinted in *Silence*, that resonates with Lipsett's ontology, describing composition as a form of "purposeless play," in a statement that, presented in this context, defies the didactic and explanatory traits of Film Board productions: "this play...is an affirmation of life—not an attempt to bring order out of chaos nor to suggest improvements in creation, but simply a way of waking up to the very life we're living."[13] Lipsett emphasizes Cage's final dictum, to let this play "act of its own accord."

In their initial correspondence, Lipsett had told Cage that he desired to collaborate after hearing *Indeterminacy*. In proposing Cage's participation to the NFB, Lipsett noted that full creative collaboration with an outsider was not unprecedented, "in keeping with the policy established for Norman McLaren's film with Balanchine."[14] Although it would not be completed for several years, the film to which Lipsett refers is *Pas de deux* (1968), originally a collaboration with famed choreographer George Balanchine, an adaptation of Balanchine's celebrated *Tschaikovsky Pas de Deux* (1960).[15] As Lipsett was preparing to move forward, Cage wrote to conditionally decline participation. Cage's letter is courteous and supportive, but acknowledges the incompatibility of his aesthetics with the direction the film was moving in. "I am insistent upon letting things go together," writes Cage, acknowledging that Lipsett's attention to continuity and audience were philosophically distant from Cage's own beliefs.[16] Lipsett, embracing the controlled, cohesive needs of the Film Board, had proposed a much too constructed experience for Cage's comfort. Further, Lipsett had asked Cage to produce a temporary soundtrack that could be subject to Lipsett's manipulations, in the style of his sound collages, a suggestion that minimized the collaborative nature of their exchange, implying that Lipsett saw sound as both subordinate and complementary to image. It was this that most troubled Cage for his devotion to the natural arrangement of elements and his resistance to old ideas of authorial mastery and plotted, thematized signification: "If the visuals express something, there is no earthly need for the sounds to have the same expression...when we force things into our ideas of expression, we simply reduce the natural grandeur, robbing it of its potential total expression."[17] Lipsett's training had misled him; in attempting to coordinate the elements of the project and to situate it in a thematic structure, as he had been taught to do, he had alienated an artist closer to his own aspirations. Cage's gentle rebuke ended the possibility for collaboration and raises questions about the degree to which Lipsett's poetic and philosophical ambitions were being hindered by the expectations of government work.[18] At the Film Board, outsiders were not full collaborators: their contributions were licensed and acquired.

In his pursuit of a psychophysical continuity, Lipsett had all but abandoned his collage methods. The wastebasket was no longer relevant to his phenomenological quest, at least insofar as pictures were concerned: what few found images he used were rephotographed with his Bolex, often from book and magazine pages that show paper grain and reflect light, or from the natural décollage of fading and peeling street posters and signs. The astringent humour of his work remained, placed into dialogue with images of nature that were vital and euphoric, evident in the opening shots as Lipsett's camera follows an ant, twisting its body as it carries an undefined morsel of food equal to its own size. Moving rapidly and seen in close-up, the ant is continuously lost and recaptured, both compositionally (as it scrambles) and in a shifting focus (with the lens–subject distance changing as the insect is followed). The telephoto lens that Lipsett uses to shoot the ant's movements also magnifies his own search, casting a kinetic, ecstatic rhythm, as if lens and ant were dancing to Elder Charles D. Beck's Urban Holiness Service, singing "Drive Old Satan Away, Lord," which accompanies them on the film's soundtrack. In its original context, the gospel song is a hypnotic thirteen-minute spell in which the stomps and claps of revellers compete with the chorus of an organ, drums, and the strained wail of a trumpet. Lipsett's pursuit of the ant gives way to a stream of images of a massive crowd, their faces seen in rapid succession, changing with each second in short bursts of exposure. This single-frame pixilation allows the crowd to extend the frenzy of the ant, seeming to mirror the insect's scrambling, the natural flow of the crowd causing fluctuations of scale, from faces seen in passing close-ups to wide compositions of distant figures. The image briefly settles on a bubbling poster of a man in a tilting boater hat, his hand to his mouth as if to call out, an image that recalls the mannequin head topped in a boater that appears in a shop window in *21-87*. The presence of these figures summons images of carnival barkers and barbershop quartets, impresarios of the weird or icons of manufactured nostalgia. Lipsett shoots little pixilated bursts of the weather-beaten traces of posters, each time slowing to show the boater-hatted face a little more eroded, the mouth washed away to reveal wooden boards underneath. A leaf, its margins chewed away to reveal the netting of its veins, is seen in close-up, mirroring the digestion of the poster. When it appears, the leaf is a reference to the Thomas poem, the green fuse of its petiole feeding its venous skeleton; in this, it anticipates Lipsett's journey into a wilderness, yielding to his reverent pixilation of sunlight breaking through trees. These images of nature, seen through forceful, joyous movement, are punctured with sudden caesuras on still images of faces and eyes, the young and the old, a sleeping child, a monkey behind a wire enclosure.

Lipsett's pixilation recalls what Robert Breer had called his own search for new forms of continuity. If this is the psychophysical continuity that Lipsett describes in his proposal, its physicality is reinforced by the rapturous sound of the gospel choir, evidence of that "force that through the green fuse drives the flower." The rhythm of Lipsett's pixilation, although pitched at the metric constant of twenty-four frames per second, seems to mirror the drum patterns played at the Elder Beck service, such that when the image halts to linger on dumbstruck and sleeping eyes, it seems unnatural that the music should continue. Lipsett's use of frayed posters offers several potential interpretations: they signal the impermanence and erosion of human action; they are another casualty of the endless march of time; or, like the reconstituted eyes/ears/mouth of modern man in *Anything Can Happen on Channel 6*, they symbolize a fragmentation of the body, the disintegration of

FIGURE 5.1: Arthur Lipsett, self-portrait, in *Free Fall* (Arthur Lipsett, National Film Board, 1964)

call-and-response between humankind and the things humans make in their image. In the context of Elder Beck's mass, this final interpretation is compelling, and yet the presence of these posters is also reminiscent of the "tear-offs" of Neo-Dadaist Wolf Vostell, what Vostell called décollage, a design principle that embraced the incidental palimpsest of separating glue-soaked, weather-beaten posters from the surfaces on which they're fastened.[19] Their inclusion is a gesture that these repurposed things have a lifeline in history that gathers dust and weathers storms; Lipsett's own images are no more eternal than those he finds. They acknowledge the presence of an unfolding reality.

The upper windows of a house are destroyed with a wrecking ball, and the demolition is interwoven with superimposed images from early twentieth-century photography: a pair of bespectacled eyes staring through a gas mask, domes of institutional architecture, a faceless mouth shouting. In an art gallery, a man stands before Anne-Louis Girodet de Roussy-Trioson's *The Sleep of Endymion* (1791), his back to the camera.[20] Narrator Noel Stone speaks, his narration taken from the soundtrack to the NFB's *Angkor: The Lost City* (Morten Parker and Roger Blais, 1961): "Here was the crumbling skeleton of a lost civilization." In keeping with the apocalyptic generalizations of Lipsett's earlier sound collages, Stone's commentary engages in comic exaggeration as a melodramatic response to classical painting as seen in an art gallery; it implies the severity of the spectator's meditation on this painting. Further to that, coming at the end of scenes of the demolition of a modern building, the remark designates contemporary Western civilization as a hollowed-out museum culture, to be inspected with a clinical distance, like the Girodet painting or the ruins of the Khmer Empire.

As the image turns back from art and antiquity to the streets, a series of superimpositions and pixilations play out: a sidewalk artist chalks out a partially obscured plea in continuous dashes, the hyphen a primary act of continuity; a Black male singer is seen in close-up, mid-song; a vulture drags a morsel through dirt; and, as a monkey's clinging hands slip from the metal corner of a laboratory cabinet, a rapid series of cellular illustrations cuts to the illustrated, anthropomorphized face of a wise elephant decorated in regalia of the Hindu faith. Interspersed are shorter images, some lasting for only a few frames: a soft-focus image of a child's face; a man standing in the lights of a marquee; another in the gated outdoor stairwell of a sub-level apartment. As with *Very Nice, Very Nice* and *21-87*, Lipsett's portrayal of contemporary humanity is one of futility and alienation; the glassy eyes of the man in the street become indistinguishable from the synthetic warmth of the illustrated barker and the vacant stare of the commercial model. Such a gaze casts doubt on the earnest, consumed, searching stares that frequently appear in Lipsett's films.

In *21-87*, Lipsett had engaged the indexical nature of cinema to create a false impression of a reaction or shared space between two discrete shots, a gesture that resonated with the tensions of his provocative alignments of sound. In *Free Fall*, Lipsett engages in intercutting to establish a thematic network among shots: acrobats, suspended in mid-air, cut to a spider suspended in its web; scenes of nature culminate in the hands of monkeys and the tail of an elephant, punctuated by a brief movie still of Peter Lorre in a bald cap as Dr. Gogol in *Mad Love* (Karl Freund, 1935); dandelions give way to outtakes from Trevor Fletcher's *Four-Line Conics* (1962) that demonstrate a series of intersecting planes, circles rotating amidst a network of triangles, lines that, in the aftermath of the dandelion, bear a stylized resemblance to the flower.[21] Lipsett establishes thematic nests of image relations, but he likewise draws image and sound into a more porous relationship: where his earlier films had used harsh truncation to allow each fleeting image or fragmentary sound to maintain its own province, with *Free Fall* he employs superimposition and sound overdubbing to allow these elements a degree of co-penetration. This density makes the flow of Lipsett's vertical montage less reactive; the sound and image do not have independent operation, but their respective crowding deprives the film of the simple, sardonic exchanges that had so defined his work to this point.

This new density of sound and image is felt in the next sequence, as a barber finishes shaving a reclining man, and the soundtrack repopulates with fragmentary speech; in the sequence that follows, a stag movie, rephotographed in the hazy focus of a Moviola viewing screen, gives way to further images of décollage posters and the dense, malformed, fractured bark of tree trunks, a parallel between the destructive operations of civilization and of nature. Lipsett meets images of nature and civilization with the exceptional lone human presence: a woman offers a vacant stare off camera as she passes with unnatural stillness, as if on a moving walkway. Questions of dehumanization—or of what defines the human being—are held over from *21-87*. They maintain a subtle presence in *Free Fall*, as a circus performer raises her arms in a demonstration of aerobatic achievement, and a crash zoom introduces a large neon sign in the shape of eyeglasses, another frozen stare. Representations of eyes follow this, on a sculpture of an owl photographed through a shop window and a zoom on the illustration of the man in the boater. Natural phenomena commingle with images suggestive of the human eye, in scenes of a goose on brackish water; a sleeping child seen in all the intimacy of a 35mm candid snapshot; a glassy-eyed man lying on his back in the street, struggling to light a cigarette. The distance between the human and its representation is underscored at the climax: a life-sized doll of a little girl, undressed, sitting in a chair, has a small, elegantly dressed doll perched on its shoulder; this cuts to a close-up on a photograph of a woman's eyes, the thundering drama of Carl Orff's *Carmina Burana* sounding underneath from a dense collage of electronic and orchestrated music, the edit suggesting a Pygmalion transformation of giving life to stone—only in this case, Lipsett transforms a three-dimensional representation (the doll) into a two-dimensional representation (the photograph).

Lipsett's sampling of phenomena has been largely focused on contemporary life: in the next sequence, *Free Fall* shifts into historical considerations as it tips further into grotesquery. Scenes from carnivals and zoos mix with images of bees and other insects on flowers, punctuated with a photograph of a person in a "chin reducer," an early twentieth-century beautification device.[22] A sudden shift into the past finds a 1933 photograph of the trapeze artist Gaby Marces and a scene of Hideki Tojo and the Japanese imperial Command posing for photographs as they announce the Pacific War. Lipsett moves his hands over the stylized eyes and mouth of a totem pole, an image pitched between man and bird, a breaking of the fourth wall of the rostrum animation camera, a sacred space among his colleagues for their various attempts, from *Jolifou Inn* onward, to use the animation camera as a means to enter into an animated, cinematic space (*A is for Architecture*) or to enter scenes out of history (*City of Gold*).

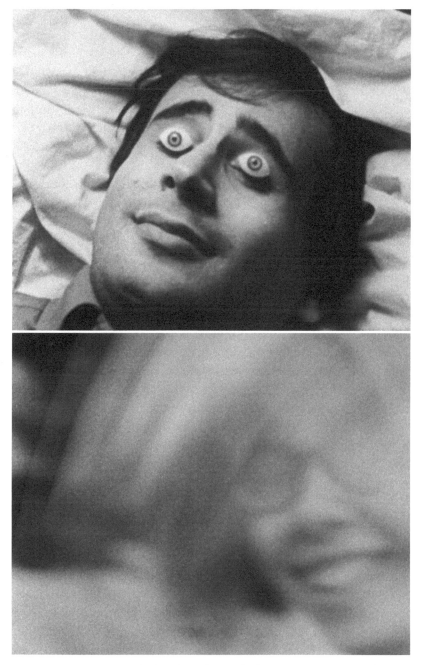

FIGURE 5.2: Martin Lavut (top) and Judith Sandiford (bottom) in *Free Fall* (Arthur Lipsett, National Film Board, 1964)

As Lipsett's hands flash across the totem pole, crossing as if to ward something away, the relationship among beasts and men takes on a newfound ugliness: a beetle eats a caterpillar, and a composite of a man's face is torn open to reveal a street scene.[23] A stern portrait of a woman dressed in nineteenth-century attire is interspersed, through a series of quick fades, with the decorative flourishes of the upper windows of an ornate building. A series of superimpositions combine statues, buildings, plants, and flowers, travelling shots along a skyline of sunlight breaking through trees. The stern portrait appears in a darkened room, under glass, and when Lipsett passes a light over himself, he captures his own reflection. Lipsett's friend, the actor and filmmaker Martin Lavut, lies, eyes shut, with plastic, stylized eyeballs resting over his eyelids; they fall as he winces and bursts out laughing, symbolic of an uncertain position between dream and reality.[24] A still image of Jean Marais's Beast from Jean Cocteau's *Beauty and the Beast* (1946) leads into a sequence of greater intensity, a crescendo in which close-ups of plants, flowers, and insects are intercut with scenes in a garden being toured by an elderly man in a white felt hat. Also present are images of Lipsett's partner, Judith Sandiford, faintly discernible in the intensity of pixilation. Scenes of beasts repeat: an elephant's tail, a bull's snout. The stamens and pistils of flowers and the spiked arms of cacti take on a menacing aura, fully realized with another bleat of *Carmina Burana*. As the film ends, a series of statements are made: a scientist's description of a semipermeable membrane; a staggering countdown; and, finally, a rambling statement on Khrushchev and Molotov that is interrupted by a yipping squeak, synchronized to the mouth of a frog, neck-deep in swamp water. The sound becomes denser with voices and music fragments overlapping, ending with Eldon Rathburn's score to *Police*, a callback to its appearance in *Very Nice, Very Nice*.

Throughout *Free Fall*, Lipsett develops his sound collage around the porous interpenetration of sounds—among them, music taken from Maurice Blackburn's score to the multi-authored NFB animated short *Christmas Cracker* (1963, co-directed by Lipsett's colleagues Norman McLaren, Gerald Potterton, Grant Munro, and Jeff Hale). Lipsett acquired the rights to use the 1956 Contrepoint field recording of Tibetan music of Sikkim, which he harvested for drones and percussion that are interspersed with other sounds.[25] Miscellaneous sounds play throughout, likely drawn from the Film Board's own holdings, but there is a consistent electronic synthesis through which sounds emerge, as in an animalistic howling that deflates into modulated noise. Orchestral swells, drones, and splinters of dramatic speech overlap. Lone instruments break through the cacophony, such as the distinctive plunk of an electric piano. Taken as a sound collage, *Free Fall* conjures up a transmission of coalescing radio waves, a group portrait of mid-century sound from the highly artificial—in dramatic and narrational excerpts and electronic tone generation and modulation—to the relative naturalism of gospel music and interviewed voices. Lipsett's spare use of human speech stands out in a film so aggressively focused around psychophysical experience. When coherent speech comes through, it is, in Lipsett's style, always lacking context and almost always truncated. At the midpoint, a speaker offers the non sequitur that whether "an electrical circuit, semipermeable membranes, a mathematical expression, or green cheese, it makes no difference," a statement that is in keeping with the cynical, unfocused rambling Lipsett drew from for comic effect in *Very Nice, Very Nice*. It is only in its final moments that *Free Fall* becomes fully self-conscious of Lipsett's prior exploration of the topical cliché, in the ramble that begins only to be shut up by the frog's comic squeak.[26]

The emphasis on pixilation in *Free Fall* reflects Lipsett's desire to extend the fast energy of his first experiments in a context that transcended the social critique inherent in using mass culture imagery. He is using mechanical means to make images of ecstatically human perception. *Anything Can Happen on Channel 6* and *Very Nice, Very Nice* found a perfect parallel in the piano massacres of Crazy Otto: rags that sounded uncannily like a player piano, the mechanization of the artist. Lipsett's pixilation and the guided force of his camera movements were, like the stomp and howl of the Urban Holiness Service, of plainly human origin, casting a confusion of perception familiar to the darting movements of the eyes. This is given in contrast to his earlier montages of perfectly suspended commercial and photojournalistic images. Gone was the pretence of clinical witness that placed *21-87* parallel to the observational forms practiced by Lipsett's colleagues, and gone with it was the comic leer, replaced with an intensity of feeling for earthly phenomena. Themes had survived the transition: still there was an apprehension of the relationship between humankind and its representations, mechanical mirrors, and aids; outrage remained, glimpsed in the crossing and glassy sightlines of human and animal subjects past and present, an impression of the world as abandoned, in free fall. Amidst all of this intense humanism, comedy remained, in his sound collage and in the contrasts of image and sound. The difficult form that Lipsett had engaged in, the negative capability produced by a melding of contrary parts, is at its most ecclesiastic in *Free Fall*, wherein an incomprehensible prayer is formed by the urgent religiosity of a darting, gospel vision; diaristic intrusions featuring himself, Lavut, and Sandiford; and grim citations of disarrays of the present moment and the recent past. His first three films reflect this transit: from the visible world, to purgatory, to an atmosphere of wild communion.[27]

Arthur Lipsett's collaborative relationships within Unit B had been fostered from his first years in the institution, when his co-workers had mentored him in the service work of animation. His sensibilities as an artist had been fostered from the weekend art classes of his childhood to his graduation from the School of Art and Design, but the community that Lipsett entered had given those sensibilities direction and purpose. Wolf Koenig had gone with him to purchase his first Leica camera from a pawnshop on Saint-Laurent; he lived in an apartment once rented by colleague Neil Shakery; he once went hunting with Derek Lamb, to the amusement of all involved; and candid photographs of Kaj Pindal's family figured prominently in his first film. The most valuable relationships that he had in Unit B, in terms of being able to continue his work with relative freedom, were with his producers Tom Daly and Colin Low, who understood that, while Lipsett's work did not perfectly fit the institutional model, it was inexpensive and promising, and it had an audience. Lipsett had been a beneficiary of the optimism of the institution and its players, the underlying sensibility that experimentation, even experimentation that those in power did not see an immediate value in, could produce valuable results; but he had also received opportunities, and been protected, out of affection and in recognition of his gifts.

The unit system came under distress in 1963, as members of other units began to resent the freedom and adulation that filmmakers in Unit B received. The films of Unit B were strongly associated with the organization's record of artistic achievements, and members of other units felt they were being denied opportunities to make art. A survey was undertaken that resulted in policy changes and led to the creation of a pool system, which would replace the unit system on February 28, 1964.[28] The pool system empowered filmmakers to bring projects directly to producers and a governing body, therefore creating a greater opportunity for the potential of an auteurist cinema. Norman McLaren had enjoyed a position of great distinction at the Film Board for his reputation as an artist, and with this transition, other members of the production staff could define themselves as filmmakers whose work dealt consistently with particular forms and themes. One consequence of this was the distancing of the labour of filmmaking from the tradition of service and sponsored films; another was the transformation of the process by which filmmakers got approval from an informal system of vetting proposals, or of assigning projects, into a nominating system whereby directors would pair with producers. This change would later be condemned by some critics as an era of the "dictatorship of the filmmaker."[29] Another outcome was that filmmakers whose relationship to the institution was already under strain, or whose opportunities were predicated on warm feelings towards them among their colleagues, would find themselves on the wrong side of a harsh popularity contest. When the pool system was introduced, Arthur Lipsett was in the midst of production on *Free Fall*. With this new process, Lipsett would have to rely, more than ever, on the aegis of his producers.

Between July and September of 1964, Arthur Lipsett filed three documents with the NFB that together comprised a proposal for a film with the working title *The Discovery Film*. This marks Lipsett's first attempt to make a film within the pool system. He noted his desire to make it into an entire series of *Discovery Films* that covered all aspects of education, but for the initial pitch, he focused on the formation of verbal and visual language in young children. It would be a twenty-minute film, mixing live-action and animation, dealing with child development with an emphasis on creative intelligence. The film would demonstrate the ways in which ideas are expressed through the assemblage of component parts of words and sounds, and it would relate this to pictorial systems. The proposal is riddled with optimism, and Lipsett characterized his working title as bearing "a sense of excitement and exploration."[30] He was carrying on the mission of his mentor Arthur Lismer and making an earnest attempt at directing the efforts of the NFB towards a form of social good that the Board could understand. His proposals drew inspiration from sources of varied and provocative origin—among them, art education expert Herbert Read, psychologist and theorist of child development Jean Piaget, art historian Henry Focillon, psychologist and theorist of dream interpretation Samuel Lowy, philosopher Martin Buber, architect and designer Karel Honzik, and writer and poet D.H. Lawrence. Lipsett's proposal gradually moves in the direction common to his other proposals, establishing a rhythmic arc in which an experience forms from a low ebb or nothing into an atmosphere of great intensity.

In his final document dealing with *The Discovery Film*, a formal approach appears that anticipates what would become his next film. He writes about "treasure-hunt continuity," giving a label to a common thread of the earlier research documents in which he had written about hints and clues that would be used to structure the film, in itself an admission that the film was developed from a pedagogical treatment that emphasized the puzzle, that the film could pose a mystery and offer glimpses of a solution.

# SIX

# TIME-CAPSULE

NOSTALGIA IS A TRANSFORMATIVE FORCE, AT ONCE INTImate and communal, a commonly held delusion that the brightest days of a civilization are in its past. Through the course of the nineteenth century, photography, and later cinema, challenged such sentimentality by representing, in exacting terms, life as it is, but they also produced their own forms of nostalgia, and in the perceived cultural and spiritual wasteland of the 1960s, Westerners could regard even recent images of the past—of a civilization climbing ever higher, of scientific discoveries, of the victories of war—with idealizing grandeur. The time capsule represents this effort on the part of a society to engineer its own wistful reminiscence, and the experience of cinema became, from its earliest actualities, an immaterial time capsule—that is, the time capsule in its apex form. There are records of pre-twentieth-century time capsules, but the ceremonial institutionalization of the phenomenon occurs in America in the twentieth century: where else but in a "new world" of recovered bones and arrowheads could the time capsule gain traction? Was it foresight or arrogance on the part of Thornwell Jacob when, at the sealing of the Crypt of Civilization in 1940, he declared his contemporaries as "the first generation equipped to perform archeological duty to the future"?[1] The time capsule is a memorial counterpart to the photograph, a window for the future onto the values of the present moment or a window from the present moment onto the values of the past. It is a modern culmination of archeological restlessness and navel gazing, for it recognizes in the average life a museum of oddities and wonders at future value and the possible obsolescence and meaninglessness of its contents. As a collage of curiosities readymade for burial, it is conceived to be found but designed to be lost.

Resonances between levels of experience—individual, group, and universal—were on Arthur Lipsett's mind throughout the summer of 1964, necessitated by his proposal for the *Discovery Film*, a project on youth development that would never move into production. His growing preoccupation with the writings of Martin Buber had led Lipsett to focus his concerns on the social perch of modern spiritual experience. Buber's conception of the philosophy of dialogue was fundamental in this, the notion of how subjectivity distinguishes self from object and other; Buber's thought was focused on mutuality and conflicts of will and perception among beings, themes relevant to Lipsett's conception of child development and to his fluid judgment of society as a whole.[2] The transitional phase reflected in *21-87* had led Lipsett to make *Free Fall* as an ecstatic expression of freedom, but the transformation of his workplace, and his growing alienation there, would inhibit these formal directions in his work. The adoption of the pool system meant that Lipsett would be going before a program committee, where there would be an even greater burden on him to explain the purposes of his films in plain language. Others at the NFB were adept at these tasks because the work that they were proposing was typically didactic, conceived for comprehensibility and to serve a discernible social good. As one of the institution's first filmmakers, Norman McLaren was protected from this explanatory process by virtue of the broad, international regard that his films invited; those who had made films at Unit B with a sociohistorical function, like Colin Low or Roman Kroitor, could continue to situate the virtues of their work within the new model. Lipsett's proposals had always been unconventional in part because to explain his intentions was already an onerous task for an artist inclined towards instinct and improvisation. His greatest merit was his capacity for abstract thought, which did not translate into the politically motivated, didactic expectations of the NFB. This incompatibility between Lipsett and his colleagues would lead him to encounter greater opposition and neglect than he had previously.

Donald Brittain had joined the NFB three years prior to Lipsett; he was recruited for his background as a reporter, and he learned his craft serving in various positions on sponsored films.[3] By the end of the 1950s, he was working as a writer and director of short subjects, primarily sponsored films—among them, *A Day in the Night of Jonathan Mole* (1959), a docudrama about racial discrimination in the workplace, and *Fields of Sacrifice* (1963), on Canadian war veterans. Brittain was teamed with Lipsett as the producer of Lipsett's next film. Having recently completed *Bethune* (1964), a portrait of Canadian doctor Norman Bethune, and in the midst of completing *Memorandum* (with John Spotton, 1965), a haunting record of the German concentration camps, Brittain seemed an ideal pairing with Lipsett for his own masterful integration of archival footage. Their collaboration is evidence that Lipsett was still regarded at the NFB as an artist working with found footage, despite minimizing the collage elements in his recent filmmaking. The partnership proved fruitful as Lipsett committed to making his first compilation film, one without the use of any original footage. Brittain would later recall, "I really respected his work and I knew his problems, and he could not deal with bureaucracy...I had to run interference for him. First I had to get him to the program committee to try and explain what he was gonna make a movie about. It was pretty baffling. Nobody could understand a word he said, and I would give some superficial interpretation and said that he has his audience, and should be allowed his voice."[4] That Brittain had been elected to survey filmmakers and make policy recommendations during the transition from the unit system to the pool system is, in itself, evidence of the political influence that he had among his colleagues and of his value as an advocate.[5]

By this time, Lipsett was securing his equipment with heavy iron chains when he left the facilities for the night, eccentric behaviour to some observers but done for practical reasons: to ensure that the equipment he was working with—his viewer, his synchronizer, his splicer—would be the same day to day.[6] In an effort to focus on his work, he also began to wear large earmuffs to block out distractions.

That his colleagues noted this behaviour as eccentric was a sign of the growing distance between him and the institution. Even the proposal for Lipsett's next film did not follow in the model established by his prior proposals; with the daunting task of facing a program committee, he had to provide Brittain with ammunition to get the project approved. This is the spirit with which his proposal, dated December 25, 1964, begins. With a proposed title of *Time-Capsule*, Lipsett offers Brittain a series of interrelated lists of phenomena, themes, and groups that guide him back, in conclusion, to a statement given by Martin Buber: "History is not the sequence of conquests of power, and actions of power, but the context of the responsibilities of power in time."[7] Further to Buber's statement, Lipsett poses the question, "what are the forces that have shaped, and are shaping, our new awarenesses, and what are our new responsibilities?"[8]

The proposal bears many statements that demonstrate a cumulative awareness forming through Lipsett's body of work, beginning with a conflict between a technologically determinant, behaviourally predictable "new type of man" and the human being as enigmatic and subversive, an agent of surprise.[9] Lipsett's explanation implicitly reflects on the role of intelligent machines in *21-87* and the spontaneous, improvisatory forms of *Free Fall*, as he argues that as science grows, faith diminishes; that machines have become tools of spirit and ritual; that the experiments of behavioural psychologists have invaded education and are reflected in everyday experience; and that, as a result of this collision of elements, the human being loses agency. Lipsett counters this determinist vision with a quote from Dostoyevsky's *Notes from the Underground*, on man's innate ability to defy prediction, that in this state, "he would still do something out of sheer perversity—he would create destruction and chaos—just to gain his point."[10] This new man still speculates on his nature, the finite and the infinite, the Nietzschean abyss; this new man is therefore all the more alienated and all the more aware of his alienation. Lipsett points to Buber, for whom salvation is found in communion with others, "the confrontation of existence and death together, in a mutuality, man to man."[11] The proposed film would explore these philosophies and conflicts through the avatars of altruistic spokespeople of various social groups, taken in combination with actions and reactions at universal, group, and individual scales. "In this film," Lipsett writes, "I am interested in exploring the connection between an individual's outwardly expressed inner reaction...and the influences that create this reaction."[12] Lipsett perceived chain reactions as occurring on an inward and outward scale among individuals, groups, and national or global forces. With *Very Nice, Very Nice*, he had started from a group awareness—felt by the awakened and the aware—of the tedium of the cliché on the verge of an apocalypse. The spiritual crises at the core of *21-87* and *Free Fall*, dealing with dehumanization and rapture, respectively, brought the individual experience—his camera as witness—into dialogue with grave universal concerns for the isolated provinces of science and faith. *Time-Capsule* is posed as an exploration of the reactions among these levels, the interdependence between scales of experience.[13]

As with his earlier proposals, Lipsett's final project, released under the title *A Trip Down Memory Lane*, would depart from these plans dramatically. The citation-cushioned philosophical inquiries that Lipsett had begun to integrate into his proposals were little more than a nicety for the program committee. While Lipsett's work was impacted by his readings, he was first led to his nocturnal experiments in the sound studio through fascination, not philosophy, and his process had always been guided primarily by instinct. The spontaneous camerawork that dominated *Free Fall* is evidence of his growing trust in instinct and chance. Despite anchoring his questions in the present, when *A Trip Down Memory Lane* was released in early 1966, it was Lipsett's most archival work to date, a comic collage of newsreels, an international tour of Western progress and its rippling impact on the rest of the world. From *21-87*, it inherited a fascination with technology and the curious and often spectacular adaptations of human beings to new knowledge. It bore a satirical optimism reminiscent of *Very Nice, Very Nice*, bringing a veneer of joy that was particular to the newsreel into contact with scenes of human failure, war, and scientific mastery, in a strange parade of the twentieth century.

*A Trip Down Memory Lane* had gone into production on the heels of Lipsett's proposal, evident from stock footage requests made by Brittain on Lipsett's behalf beginning on January 21, 1965. Production would last roughly a year. The film featured the subtitle "additional material for a time-capsule," and Lipsett had gathered these materials from many sources beyond the wastebasket of the NFB. As Brittain had done with Memorandum, Lipsett was no longer dependent upon the scraps of his colleagues, instead soliciting material primarily from news agencies.[14] This allowed the film to fulfill the promise of its proposal, assuming an international scope with imagery drawn from the archives of other institutions, representing imagery taken from all over the world. By confronting nostalgia, in the icon of the time capsule, Lipsett was also confronting the legacy of imperialism and the spectres of fascism and intolerance that had long haunted his films. To speak of dehumanization in the shadow of technology is to address only a recent history; in reflecting on a half century that featured the Great War, the Holocaust, and the Atom Bomb, Lipsett was returning to the theme of the crowd, driven, by mastery and hypocrisy, to acts of cruelty and destruction.

Time capsules are timed spectacles, their significance bound to the act of unveiling their contents. It was only appropriate that in making a cinematic time capsule, Lipsett would prioritize spectacles, some reflective of entrenched cultural rituals, others exceptional in their peculiarity. *A Trip Down Memory Lane* begins on the runway of the 1959 Miss World pageant, intercutting the rotation of contestants with the rapt attention of audience members and jurors. Among the jurors, the presence of actress Jill Ireland, one of two Miss Irelands in the room, is a promise of comic mirroring. After the winner is crowned, the beaming faces of her competitors are intercut with a mob of photographers, a declaration of the vantage point of the film, which will explore various episodes of a half-century captured on film. A fog of mystery and decadence surrounds the procession of a Rajput cavalry through the streets of Udaipur as they lead an elephant, atop which sits the Rajah with the Maharani. The camera's stationary focus on these exotic streets, crowds, and uniformed guards casts a distant, alien atmosphere onto this parade, far from Western experience and, yet, another pageant, a parallel to the runway walks of the Miss World contestants, a display of pomp and circumstance. The footage is narrated by a British commentator, his mannered, nasal voice stating that, "with a final superb touch of spectacle, the ruler arrives," as the figures seated on the elephant synchronously wave large feathers.

FIGURE 6.1: *A Trip Down Memory Lane* (Arthur Lipsett, National Film Board, 1965)

The next episode deals primarily with images of flight. In a sync interview recorded on an airfield, Eddie August Schneider, seated in the cockpit of his biplane, announces his intention to pursue the junior transcontinental record, a record Schneider would capture in 1930. As he shakes hands with his interviewers and his plane takes off, Bing Crosby and the Paul Whiteman Orchestra's 1928 recording of "Louisiana" starts on the soundtrack, a salute to the technology of its day (the train) offered in a spirit of nostalgia (a return to home and "happiness"). A child in a ceremonial gown waves to the camera from the top of a hot air balloon, which is then shown floating over a city, their distant figure balancing on top of it. In a sync shot, to shouts of encouragement from his customers, a waiter brings a plate of drinks and food to a construction crew at the top of a skyscraper in progress, which he delivers successfully despite the threat of a plummet. In another nod to the history of aviation, a test glider is set up on the edge of a cliffside road. A man sits in the glider as it plummets straight down at a ninety-degree angle. He is shown staggering from the wreckage and waving. A title card offers a nostalgic farewell to these oddities of early flight: "It was a nice job while it lasted." In *21-87* and *Free Fall*, acrobats served as ambiguous symbols of the human condition in the twentieth century, a century of technological accomplishment and wonder; the figure confidently suspended mid-leap, high above the circus, could embody both a leap of faith and an intimation of danger, the stupidity and brilliance of humankind in a startling spectacle. These newsreel glimpses of flights, heights, wonders, and failures extend this theme.

Lipsett's next antique music selection is *May Morning*, a theatrical march from a 1910 recording by Evan Williams and the Victor Orchestra, and, with it, the images are cast even further back. Digressing from the theme of aviation, Lipsett turns to footage of Kaiser Wilhelm posing for a photograph with an assembly of his generals who have near-identical moustaches, uniforms, and spiked helmets, reintroducing another of Lipsett's absurdist themes, the illusion of individualism, in the figure of the Kaiser, in a stifling atmosphere of conformity. Continuing this theme of the individualism of "great men," industrialist John D. Rockefeller's home movies reveal, as a title card announces, the "world's richest man at play": Rockefeller in his eighties is shown writing in his study, walking through a garden, playing golf, posing for a movie camera, and then running the movie camera himself. He accepts Christmas presents from a stocking-faced Santa Claus and then eats cake with his great-grandchildren. As he sits in a garden reading, the music cuts, replaced with an electrical hum; in a new setting, a strange car enters the frame, humming and bursting into flames. Its occupant is dragged from the flames. The domed edifice of the United States Congress in Washington, DC, rises in the background: this footage is of the Triphibian Car, demonstrated for the press in front of the Library of Congress in 1936. Intended to navigate air, land, and water, the Triphibian Car was a space-age dream of the interwar era, a concept that would find purchase in fantasy but that would prove impractical. The driver pulled from the car is inventor Constantinos Vlachos. However, to follow the logic of Lipsett's editing, the Triphibian car demonstration is integrated seamlessly with Rockefeller's home movies; the film imagines the thin Vlachos, pulled like a rag doll from the flaming wreckage, to be none other than the aged John D. Rockefeller himself. This is the first of several of Lipsett's comic manipulations of the indexical relationship between images in

*A Trip Down Memory Lane*, in which his lingering focus on scenes from the past, in contrast to the speed of cutting in his earlier films, allows for a finer overlapping of action.

Lipsett's film explores the procession across cultures, the foolhardy wonders of flight, and the pleasures of the idle rich, and it gives some suggestions of the conciliation between scientific marvels and the comic arrogance and vanity of humankind. A science teacher gives a demonstration of a heated piston driving a tinker toy; as the piston is heated, the tinker toy spins with the resulting airflow in a sudden burst punctuated by a comic pop, a modest success in the shadow of these epic failures.[15] Warren McCulloch speaks on the soundtrack, describing the formation of the nervous system and of complementary forms of communication. As he speaks, a behavioural researcher observes a monkey in an incubator, which reclines, fully restrained with its arms extended, a bar in its hands snapping up and down. This footage is of Sam the rhesus monkey, colloquially known as one of America's "space monkeys" and a subject of NASA's Project Mercury (1959), who had been placed in a "shock avoidance task and harness system" to aid him in triggering the emergency system of a rocket.[16] McCulloch's speech points to the disconnect between humans and animals—that there is a lacking desire for communication between beings whose communicative faculties have developed along different evolutionary lines. Now on camera, in an outtake from *The Living Machine*, McCulloch concludes this line by defining this network of communicative relations as "the give and take between an organism and its environment."

The lack of communication between human and monkey, an evolutionary schism, and the resulting clear conscience of animal testing, is archetypal of this give and take. As Lipsett has established in the film's opening sequences, technological progress is another form of evolution, speckled with strange and doomed experiments. He moves on to acts of technological mastery: the German Hindenburg airship and the battleships of Benito Mussolini's Regia Marina. The grace and scientific triumph of the Hindenburg dirigible is inextricable from the menace of the Nazi swastika on its tail, and Lipsett excludes better-known images of the airship collapsing in flames in favour of shots that correspond with his titular theme: three figures hanging from a rope suspended from the hull of the ship, falling, one by one, to their deaths. Subsequent images survey the Italian fleet, the majesty of its design and the menace of its cannons, ending in Mussolini's piercing, suspicious glare. The sequences are joined by a shot of an open-air religious mass, an implication of technological mastery in the continuity of faith and ritual, a theme further reinforced by the presence on the soundtrack of Gregorian chant, further imbuing these machines with a divine grace.

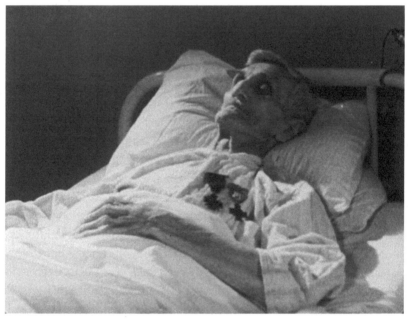

FIGURE 6.2: *A Trip Down Memory Lane* (Arthur Lipsett, National Film Board, 1965)

An elderly veteran reclines in hospice, a spare composition of a failing body bathed in sunlight, but for the presence of his medals prominently pinned to his hospital gown. As a newly freed concentration camp survivor is shown being deloused by an Allied doctor, the monastic chants give way to a hysterical Salvationist rant. The salvationist's voice is contrarian, as he speaks invitations of fellowship through extraordinary rage. The salvationist refuses his own Jewishness—declaring that "you don't have to be a Jew" to be one of "God's chosen people"—and shouts of his own conversion, "I, as a Jew, did accept [Jesus Christ] as my personal saviour; I'm glad I ever did!"

The Messianic frenzy of the salvationist bears out Lipsett's familiar strategy of paired opposites, preaching love with a mouthful of venom, but it also contains this pained admission that speaks to themes of dehumanization and spiritual degradation matched on screen by the scenes from the aftermath of the Holocaust. In another ironic turn, the optimistic homecoming of "Louisiana" is echoed in a confident title card, which reads, "We are doing our best and a bit more." Such is the spirit of optimism inherent in newsreels, and it is a spirit that has been glimpsed repeatedly throughout, as in Crosby's crooning about travelling back to happiness "and then some," and when a reporter tells Eddie August Schneider, with regards to his intended record-setting, "you try to do better than that." As the salvationist reaches a fever pitch, a series of politicians is shown, waiting, ending with Pope Pius XII who, in a series of awkward, casual shots, sits and gives blessings to a procession as a triumphant music cue sounds.

Dramatic music accompanies scenes that anticipate violence: a civilian is dragged by uniformed men through a gate, possibly en route to an interrogation; an airplane is destroyed in a planned explosion during a military demonstration, to the pleasure of the soldiers looking on; and, in a series of photographs from a 1930 celebration in the Weimer Republic, guests wear cheer and gaiety in sharp contrast to the rise of Nazism that, in a few short years, would erode their government. Lipsett's arrangement of these stills ends on an image of a bald man capped with a tiny novelty top hat, at once buffoonish and burlesque. A narrator describes a "milk run" by the air force on the Ruhr, "industrial heart of Germany." The stills from the Weimar Republic cede to a photograph of a woman's face, its surface punctured in a disfiguring pattern. The strange bedfellows of political theatre manifest in footage from the United Nations, of United States Ambassador Edward Stettinius Jr. and Russian Minister of Foreign Affairs Vyacheslav Molotov shaking hands as, on the soundtrack, a German commander shouts orders to an antiaircraft battery. This gives way to a series of still photographs: the injured face of a soldier and the intense stares of a Black man and an old woman.[17] In its early passages, *A Trip Down Memory Lane* is presented as a film about invention, aspirations to progress, and the exchange that exists between an organism and its environment. From the appearance of the Zeppelin, the film departs from the simple comedy of failure, instead offering a blank response that depicts aimlessness, ineptitude, futility, and suffering.

The film presents at length a stumbling 1939 speech from British aristocrat Lord Riverdale as he announces the Commonwealth Air Training Plan in Ottawa. Riverdale's recitation is stiff and pompous, but more telling is his sentimentalization of the Crusades, as his prepared remarks wonder at the technological marvel of being able to travel "three hundred miles in one hour." As he concludes, Riverdale hurriedly says "right?" off-camera, confirming with the director that his work is done. This abrupt breaking of the fourth wall transitions to another of Lipsett's antique songs. "Baby Won't You Please Come Home," as played by McKinny's Cotton Pickers, begins in comic punctuation of another of Lipsett's illusions: President Harry Truman exits an airplane, and a match cut to another plane maintains the illusion of continuity. From this second plane, a pilot exits and kisses the ground. As Truman is met outside a government building by the press, a couple waltzes in a dance studio by daylight. In the stillness of a laboratory, fluids are plunged from and remotely drawn up into tubes and irradiated chemicals are sealed with caution. A Japanese victim of the atom bomb sits for an on-camera examination, as a scientist points to the burns on his singed head with a pair of forceps, accompanied by the ratcheting sounds of a Geiger counter. Fluid is removed at a distance and placed in a barrel, marked "danger," initiating the film's final sequence.

Throughout *A Trip Down Memory Lane*, politicians of various nations and eras have been shown in suspicion, discomfort, and anticipation as they are observed by cameras. This flourishes into a central theme in the final sequence, as authority figures are shown waiting in prolonged silence. Atomic scientists are congratulated at a press conference as the montage begins: Vannevar Bush and Leslie Groves, representatives of the Manhattan Project, pose at a news conference in front of a world map, waiting to speak; elsewhere, a crowd of soldiers waits for something—several confer, and one checks his watch; at the White House, United States Defense Secretary Robert McNamara and Chairman of the Joint Chiefs of Staff Maxwell Taylor wait to speak on their findings regarding the war in Viet Nam; South Korean President Syngman Rhee and his American counterpart, Dwight Eisenhower, both seated at desks, wait to speak. German Chancellor

Konrad Adenauer sits alongside Japanese Emperor Hirohito, posing for pictures. The spell of suspense is broken by images of former Vice President Richard Nixon, first on a monitor, then on film speaking in front of his desk. Nixon had a lifelong struggle with television, a medium he had first used in 1952 for the self-righteous posturing of his Checkers speech and, later, in the first televised presidential debate, which would hold his impoverished charisma up against the magnetism of John F. Kennedy, all but winning Kennedy the 1960 election. The former candidate's presence in Lipsett's film has the added strangeness of coming at a time when Nixon's relevance was fading: he had lost not only the presidential election but a gubernatorial election in California, after which he threw a public tantrum over his dead political career, announcing that the press wouldn't "have Nixon to kick around anymore." Although he would, within the decade, come to represent an ultimate betrayal of oath, at the time of his inclusion in *A Trip Down Memory Lane*, he represented another stumbling block in the political consciousness of the West. Lipsett enters on Nixon midspeech, but the only sound is stock orchestral music.

As the film ends, a sword swallower at a carnival performs for an audience. His act is filmed in slow motion, a meditation on the horror of the spectacle, a rite that profanely commands the focus of the crowd. Circus music plays on the soundtrack, modulated so as to distort the sounds of carnival barkers and canned pre-recorded music. In two final stills, Lipsett declares the discontinuity between spectacle and wisdom. The first is an image of a man in oversized novelty glasses sporting a political slogan: "the eyes have it, vote for George McLain."[18] The second is Philippe Halsman's 1947 photograph of Albert Einstein. Einstein's face is the final statement of the film, and his sober expression, his penetrating, pooling eyes recall the words of Puck in *A Midsummer's Night's Dream*: "Shall we their fond pageant see? / Lord, what fools these mortals be!" That Einstein was a pacifist and a fierce critic of the bomb, whose efforts to warn the world about Nazi atomic research provoked the United States to start the Manhattan Project, gives added weight to this, the film's last judgment.

The clichés of speech that had crowded Lipsett's first films are not present in *A Trip Down Memory Lane*, which instead turns its criticality on the relationship between humanity and the camera, where each wave of the hand becomes an inadvertent wave to the future. This provides an overarching context for Lipsett's exploration of various scales of experience, but to acknowledge these scenes as the product of a half-century of cinematic witness makes the pattern they weave no less mysterious. Most remarkable is Lipsett's culling of the recent historical record for images that suggest myth: from the exotic Udaipur to grand instruments of war to Lord Riverdale waxing poetic over the Knights of Old, *A Trip Down Memory Lane* becomes less a survey of mere failure than a survey of eternal ideals. When Dusty Vineberg reviewed the film for the *Montreal Star*, she commented that Lipsett's source materials were oracular: "they seem to prophesy—if you could only read them correctly."[19] In its last sequence, the film poses an explicit search for reassurance, among all these uncertain, waiting faces. Now absent is that facile voice, that rushed show business clap, that affected, almost hissed, "very nice, very nice."

As a phenomenal catalogue of then-recent history, *A Trip Down Memory Lane* shares less in common with the average compilation film than it does with *Mondo Cane* (Paolo Cavara, Gualtiero Jacopetti, and Franco E. Prosperi, 1962), the lodestar of exploitation pseudo-documentaries that birthed the "mondo" genre.[20] An international travelogue of strange and violent customs presented in an ethnocentric framework, *Mondo Cane* revels in giving a shock to Western propriety, emphasizing man's cruelty towards animals but also featuring sequences that deal with modern art, the exploitation of women, and the impact modern Western technology has on Indigenous Peoples. As a cynical leer into hypocrisy and barbarism, its makers have little in common with Lipsett from an ethical and moral standpoint, but as a work of weird anthropology, *A Trip Down Memory Lane* fits the mondo style, a copious inventory of curious visions. The mondo style was, at its core, carnivalesque, the freakshow of modern life; Lipsett's film is an Expo unto itself of oddities and aspirations. The compilation film had, until the 1960s, generally taken as its focus a defined historical epoch or a narrow topic or was, more commonly, taken as a technique of integration for work that mixed found and original footage, like the films Stuart Legg had made for the NFB in the 1940s.[21] *Mondo Cane* and *A Trip Down Memory Lane* stand apart from the compilation films, despite their episodic structuring, and are united in the broadness of their inquiries, taking on massive, ill-defined topics and populating them with strange evidence towards an uncertain conclusion.

Taken as a time capsule, *A Trip Down Memory Lane* anticipates NASA's Golden Records of the late 1970s, literal twelve-inch records of the history of human achievement sent out into the universe aboard the Voyager, a rocket-fuelled carte de visite or, as Carl Sagan described it, a message in a bottle in the cosmic ocean. Lipsett's film is an absurd mirror of such ambitions, long present in civilization, and it revealed, as *Mondo Cane* had, a ridiculous Earth where failure leads the blind steps of success. Grand ambitions and great inventions make good on their promise to inevitably fail, as does the Zeppelin, as does the Triphibian car. The trip of the title is a fall: not a fall from Paradise as in *Free Fall*, but the clumsy trip of humankind on their own shoelaces, hoist with their own petard. The death defiance of the sword swallower is a conditioning of the body to do what the body should not, much like the robot mime in *21-87*. The theme of consumerism that had been most dominant in *Very Nice, Very Nice* never fully departed from Lipsett's work: he had simply turned away from everyday consumerism, which is defined by plenitude and aimlessness, and looked to the consumption of spectacle. A sea of faces, those of scientists and leaders, waits to speak. Not pictured is Enrico Fermi, but on July 16, 1945, he was taking bets on whether the atmosphere would ignite in the minutes before the Trinity test. Do they await disaster, or do they wait in anticipation of being consumed?

Under the pool system, Lipsett continued to receive occasional assignments that were relevant to his passions: Guy L. Coté, who had been a catalyst in Lipsett's exposure to the world of underground filmmaking, would make a two-part documentary series, *Regards sur l'occultisme* (1965). Coté would co-edit with Lipsett, marking the first instance of Lipsett collaborating with his French colleagues since his years of service work. The two episodes, each an hour in length, focused on magic and miracles, and science and spirits, respectively, and the second episode draws from Coté's interest in underground cinema, as a discussion of Aleister Crowley and Thelema culminates in a long excerpt from Kenneth Anger's *Inauguration of the Pleasure Dome* (1954). Lipsett's style is evident in the editing of still images within the film. Stills are integrated throughout, among them symbols of occult significance (hexagrams, patipembas, sigils) and paintings cropped so as to generate a narrative progression through details.

Even without easy pathways to approve Lipsett's own projects, his former Unit B colleagues attempted to assign him projects that he would find interesting. Joseph Koenig, brother of Wolf Koenig, arranged for Lipsett to serve as director of a series of filmed lectures commissioned by members of the psychology faculty at McGill University, coordinated by prestigious neuropsychologist D.O. Hebb, a leading figure in behavioural psychology.[22] The resulting films were simple affairs: each lecture was performed in a single uninterrupted take, in front of a blackboard, with some speakers employing simple props for visual interest. Neither Koenig nor Lipsett was acknowledged in the credits. Koenig would later remember that Lipsett was eager to take the job on because he found the subject matter interesting, a mix of human–animal relational psychology, explorations of the genetic and social means by which humans respond to fear and pain.[23] Taken in the abstract, with titles like *The Puzzle of Pain* and *Animal Altruism*, the material resonates with the morbid side of Lipsett's own filmmaking; in practice, service work had changed from the meticulous skill of the graphic arts to the dull routine of pointing and running a camera.

The next year, Joseph Koenig would go on to make another film with the McGill Department of Psychology, again with the participation of D.O. Hebb. *Restricted Dogs* (1966) is an illustrated explanation of the department's sensory deprivation experiments conducted on dogs. The film itself was, like Lipsett's films with Koenig and Hebb, a sponsored project; the director, Henry Zemel, would not stay with the NFB for long, getting fired after only three months. By his own account, Zemel was ill-suited to the agency: "I was a total goofball. I didn't fit in. I alienated everyone for no reason. I was high, man. I didn't understand that you're not supposed to say anything."[24] Zemel was a member of Leonard Cohen's circle of friends, along with fellow NFB filmmaker Derek May. He would befriend Lipsett, and, as Lipsett began to formulate plans for new films, he would draw on his friendship with Zemel, the two men forming a kind of partnership. Although Zemel was no longer on staff at the Film Board, Lipsett, having the freedom to choose his on-camera subjects, would bring Zemel into his circle of creative collaborators.

In the limbo between films, Lipsett continued to navigate the bureaucracy of the pool system. Guy Glover arranged for Lipsett to co-edit *The Continuing Past* (1966) with the film's director, Stephen Ford. Made for the Geological Survey of Canada's Department of Energy, Mines and Resources, *The Continuing Past* was a straightforward film charting the efforts of the country's surveyors, and its form was a utilitarian mix of long takes on geologists and poetic sequences in which the phosphorescent qualities of ores, seen under microscopes, express a resonating beauty from out of the past. Lipsett would play a more substantial and solitary role as editor and animator on Patricia Watson's *The Invention of the Adolescent* (1967), again produced by Guy Glover alongside Cecily Burwash, a square portrait of youth rebellion that, despite its alarmist narration, gave Lipsett opportunities to work with observational footage of children and the elderly, common subjects in his own work. The animation involved historical paintings and illustrations treated in the style established at the board by Colin Low, moving the images beneath a rostrum camera. Lipsett developed parallels between the contemporary footage and his historical sources: a mother holding her young son's hand at a crosswalk yields to an image of a child hand in hand with an adult in a Renaissance illustration. The focus on childhood and social development resonates with Lipsett's interests, albeit within a framework of historical division, between the modern world and pre-eighteenth-century sharing of experience between children and adults. Lipsett's interest in the topic of childhood was both constructive and philosophical, focused primarily on the development of communication and cognitive systems; Watson's film, by contrast, adopted a sociological framework.

For some at the Film Board, the manipulation of found still images had become a trademark technique of Lipsett's, though he'd seldom employed such materials in his own work after *Very Nice, Very Nice*. The lone exceptions that exist in *21-87* and *Free Fall* stand out as exceptions in the flow of the works, and where he used still images in *A Trip Down Memory Lane*, they became declarations, acts of response and weighted judgments. At Joseph Koenig's urging, thanks to Lipsett's Anglophile fascinations, he was assigned as editor to Josef Reeve's *Imperial Sunset* (1967). Reeve had benefited from the pool system, which allowed him to make his first film as director, *Judoka* (1965), an accomplished but conventional portrait of Canadian judo champion Doug Rogers. By 1967, Reeve had made a film that bore the obvious influence of Lipsett: *Poen* features, on its soundtrack, outtakes of Leonard Cohen reading excerpts from his novel *Beautiful Losers*, readings that are frequently stunted by mispronunciations or merely by Cohen's desire to start over. Cohen's readings are accompanied on-screen by still images that suggest war, torture, and imprisonment. When Cohen's reading ends, a laughing crowd is heard, edited in like the canned laughter of a sitcom. *Poen* is one of several examples of Lipsett's sideways influence at the board, his influence being felt on aspiring rivals and even his enemies: Julian Biggs, who had been openly dismissive of Lipsett, made his own humorless film about the bomb, *23 Skidoo* (1964), a docudrama of an empty city, tailor-made to compete with *Very Nice, Very Nice* as a definitive NFB statement on the atomic bomb.[25] *Poen* follows in the same line, a result of cynical misunderstanding of Lipsett's style and wit, straining out the resilience.

*Imperial Sunset* was billed as a satirical documentary, and the NFB would promote it as a comedy. It engages in maudlin treatments of the collapse of Commonwealth colonialism; Lipsett's participation was in keeping with his use of archival imagery in *A Trip Down Memory Lane*, *The Invention of the Adolescent*, and *Regards sur l'occultisme*, and the material he drew from was at times striking. However, the film is largely conventional in its structure, an affair governed by a narrator. There is an editorial complexity to the presentation of viewpoints only inasmuch as lordly delusions of colonial righteousness are maintained against evidence of the suffering of the colonies. In the NFB's words, "many of the film excerpts and photographs were chosen by Arthur (*Very Nice, Very Nice*) Lipsett whose apt riposte of picture with word previously pricked other illusions and almost won an Academy Award."[26] While the film illustrates hypocrisies and ironies, claims that Reeve's film is a "wry and amusing" satire demonstrate the organization's failure to understand what had made Lipsett's films funny: their rhythm, their vision, and, to a degree, the potential for loose collisions of sound and image. Despite a tacky eagerness to exploit Lipsett's participation in the film, the final third is devoted to talking heads and panel discussions about racism, colonialism, and the present state of the Commonwealth, topics that the film treats with heavy-handed earnestness. Many of Lipsett's own notes on the film suggest he had planned for a tension of fast and slow edits, but none of this came to pass; instead, those sequences that were made with Lipsett's input are a languid march through scenes from the slow processes of independence.[27]

At the end of 1966, as Lipsett was beginning production on his next film, he purchased three items from the Rand McNally & Company's in-house map store: John B. Sparks's *Histomap of World History* (1931), *Histomap of Evolution* (1931), and *Histomap of Religion* (1947).[28] Sparks, a chemical engineer and polymath with a lifelong interest in history, was following in a long cartographic tradition of flowchart visualizations of time when he made his Histomaps, widely adopted as essential learning tools in twentieth-century education. For Lipsett, the Sparks Histomaps would serve as a new inspiration for the shapes and rhythms of his work, which was steadily accommodating less and less, with sources glimpsed and flowing over, a copious inventory of incomplete gestures.

# SEVEN

# PRINT-OUT

ARTHUR LIPSETT'S MATURATION AT THE NFB HAD STARTED with a television advertisement. In 1960, *Anything Can Happen on Channel 6*, which Lipsett referred to as the "feet clip," promoting cultural programming on the CBC, was one of the NFB's sponsored films destined for broadcast. Despite the distance of the two government agencies, they formed a national media cluster, and Lipsett's interests in consumer inertia inevitably turned back on a growing consciousness of the overall media habitat. By the mid-to-late 1960s, his intrepid collecting of curiosities had turned to the television as a resource. Instead of the wastebasket of trims, Lipsett began gathering material for his sound collages by recording to quarter-inch tape directly from television broadcasts: game shows, sitcoms, advertisements, late night movies. The television was useful for Lipsett for one of the central ways in which it differed from cinema: where cinema was linear, television was non-linear. Broadcasts could be changed with the turn of a dial, a set could be tuned to another station, and, in this, it was closer to the radio. His sound collages, in their switching of elements, had followed the precedent of the radio dial tuner, as did television. From these tapes, he made charts, lists of elements that he had captured: dialogue from movies, interviews, jingles, and stories from the news.[1] It was a chaotic, intuitive approach; some sources he could later identify, others he could not. Like the chance invitation of the radio dial, the television was a tool for immediate modulation, which brings with it a kind of amnesia.[2]

Arthur Lipsett first proposed *Fluxes* on November 12, 1965, even as *A Trip Down Memory Lane* was moving into production. It was later given the working title *Print-Out*.[3] In advance of it reaching the programming committee, Guy Glover signed on as Lipsett's producer. Glover, along with his partner Norman McLaren, had been protective of Lipsett since his early years at the NFB, and, like Brittain, Daly, and Low before him, Glover would serve as an advocate and interpreter for the filmmaker despite the reluctance of the top brass. Lipsett's proposal begins with playwright Henrik Ibsen's observation that man is an onion, which he interprets as "layer upon layer of coverings...pain suppressors of past mistakes."[4] Lipsett aimed to film traces and tracks left behind by passing organisms, combining imagery of track- and trace-worn subjects with footage of "this process-in-action."[5] The examples that he gives are both broad and ancient, cultural and religious, universal, resonating through history: the building of an empire; the fossils of prehistory; cave drawings and Mayan stone calendars. *Fluxes* would be an investigation into an underlying theme of continuous, renewing processes. The mistakes of humankind's past form feedback that guides collective experience towards survival, a concept he reconciles with Darwinian evolution, an inherited wisdom. He concludes, "we too are evolving, leaving tracks."[6]

As Lipsett had originally conceived it, *Fluxes* would be in continuity with his prior films, ten minutes in length, a mixture of live action and animation. It differed only in his desire to make a colour film, but the final work would be in black and white.[7] The title of the film, close to the Latin word *fluxus*, suggests the postmodern art movement and magazine *Fluxus* that emerged from New York's downtown scene through the labours of George Maciunas. *Fluxus* was dedicated to a kind of anti-art. In Latin, *fluxus* means "flowing," as in English, "flux" means "a flowing out," and Maciunas imagined their art as a purging, a "revolutionary flood."[8] Without unifying styles or media, the Fluxus artists ranged from filmmakers and performance artists to musicians, painters, and sculptors.[9] Much like Lipsett's engagement with John

Cage's concept of indeterminacy, his conception of fluxes overlapped but did not replicate Maciunas's ideas. For Lipsett, flowlines were the course of an overarching structure, like the arcs of energy he had tracked in his charts and proposals, a malleable and elemental link between image, sound, and subject. By the mid-1960s, the flowlines of Lipsett's films were becoming more opaque. His first three films had been highly regimented in their sequencing. Like advertisements, these sequences tend to come and go within a minute, always advancing in their densities and energy patterns towards plateaus—those "leaps of greatest intensity" that often served as caesuras, destinations of energy that becomes suspended in an instant of sublime recognition.[10] In his proposal, Lipsett recognizes such flowlines as an omnipresent pattern of the past. In the forced plurality of *Fluxes*, Lipsett signals many acts of flowing out, be it in terms of circulation or exsanguination.

Lipsett's use of the term fluxes is only tangentially related to the Neo-Dada movement. For him, the concept of fluxes came from a familiar source: Warren McCulloch. On December 9, 1965, Lipsett put together a six-page transcript of Warren McCulloch speaking about genetic knowledge, the possibilities of the supercomputer in the wake of MIT's TX-0, and the anastomotic model of information indexing, by which various branches of information become mixed and the resulting output is fed data by all parts of the input.[11] McCulloch's preferred term, anastomotic, referred to the forking paths of rivers, and his metaphor is that a final output—be it an ocean or a print-out—draws from all of its component parts. Lipsett set upon applying McCulloch's metaphor to the forms of flow that he recognized in culture: tributaries conforming to an anastomotic course. But where McCulloch spoke in the abstract about the computation of information, Lipsett saw a medley of faith and science, modern and ancient experience commingling, intermixing, and becoming interwoven. This is the source of Lipsett's proposed title: in Lipsett's poetics, the twentieth century becomes the *print-out* of all the traces and tracks that came before it.

*A Trip Down Memory Lane* had represented something of a farewell to the West for Arthur Lipsett. The major themes of modern Western civilization that he had explored in his first films, which had been gradually met by his spiritual interests and his fascination with Eastern mysticism, had been more central than ever in his survey of the newsreel consciousness of white Westerners. *Fluxes* represented a major departure from this, but it would be a gradual departure. Like *21-87* before it, *Fluxes* would serve as a transitional film, a tour of cultures in flux. His passion for cybernetics remains, most evident in his exploration of two subjects: the space monkey and the space-age monk. Lipsett's interest in automation spanned from the prayer wheel to the supercomputer, but it was at its most focused when dealing with images that suggest an impacted humanity. An old theme takes on new urgency: the depths of barbarism and torture had maintained a persistent presence in Lipsett's films. In *Fluxes*, the wild and predatory violence of the twentieth century and the dual nature of humankind as builder and destroyer are explored through allusions to the myth of the werewolf. The werewolf becomes an anastomotic figure, a trinity of man, beast, and blend. Against these themes of cybernetics and lycanthropy, Lipsett is working on his own collage-based model of evolution, a palimpsest that runs from the drawings and diagrams of early encyclopedias to the metaphoric scrapheap figures of Giorgio de Chirico paintings.[12] Lipsett's notes on *Fluxes* have an archeological thrust to them, demonstrating his desire to throw the ancient and modern worlds into relief. When he inscribes at the top of a list of possible sources "the writings on the wall," Lipsett is engaging the duality of the expression, changed by an apostrophe. That "the writing's on the wall" is as an eschatological declaration of the last calendars of humankind, while "the writings on the wall" signals a long history from cave painting to the commemorative placard.[13]

*Fluxes* was completed September 11, 1968.[14] It faced further bureaucratic obstacles prior to its release, raising alarms in the NFB's legal division over the untraceable sources of much of Lipsett's sound collage. The ensuing discussion suggests the mutual difficulty faced by both Lipsett and the Film Board, a consequence of an artist working in a regulated institution. Staff copyright specialist Gérard Bertrand was tasked with addressing the film's complicated authorship, concluding that "Lipsett is unable at this date to identify much of this material which, as mentioned above, was recorded over several years and in various places (including his own home)."[15] On November 26, Bertrand circulated a memorandum as a show of the NFB's good faith, a means of indemnifying the board against any future claims. In coded language, Bertrand promises that he will ensure that such a measure is never taken again and insists that it is only being done in this case because of the strength of Lipsett's work, the message being that even Lipsett would not be allowed to pursue such loose processes in the future. NFB Director of Production Frank Spiller added, in an address dated November 29, that in future, planning for the potential copyright claims against collaged materials would prevent delays in release.[16] Lipsett was later encouraged by Tom Daly to note these objections in order to avoid conflict in the future.[17]

*Fluxes*, more than Lipsett's prior films, uses motifs as a structuring element. Throughout the film, monkeys are shown tapping at panels of blinking squares, as if their operations are setting in motion the strange pageant of Lipsett's montage. What might have originated as a behaviourist experiment has become an ironic parody of NASA's ground control. Adolf Eichmann is shown standing trial in 1961 at the Supreme Court of Israel in Jerusalem, an event that inspired Hannah Arendt's theory of the banality of evil.[18] The "Wacky Wizard of Waukesha," Russell E. Oakes, demonstrates his gadgets, odd inventions he had made in his own basement workshop. Control panels and measuring gauges are shown frequently, at times in a context that clarifies their use (with measured phenomena declared: "milliseconds," "degrees centigrade"). At other times, their purpose remains mysterious, as if these dials and knobs, like the monkeys at ground control, are the cause of the events that Lipsett absorbs into his montage. Interspersed are various experiments, diagrams, and religious rituals. Oddities are afforded their own prolonged sequences or serve as focal points.

In his notes, Lipsett writes of a fluxes machine that is a "world-machine," an imaginary machine that quantifies the logic of the world.[19] Lipsett's fascination with imaginary machines became a fixture in his project notes for the remainder of the 1960s and might explain his interest in the Wacky Wizard of Waukesha, an entertainer-inventor of needlessly complicated gadgets. Russell Oakes recorded films as a series for *Popular Science*, demonstrating his eccentric inventions; for the most part, he did so under the moniker "the Wily Wizard of Waukesha." With all the futile chain reactions of a Rube Goldberg machine, Oakes's best-remembered inventions suit Lipsett's absurdist sense of humour: a dripless mechanical doughnut dunker, a snore-activated light system for people afraid to go to sleep in the dark, and a hydraulic cigarette lighter powered by a lab rat.[20] In *Fluxes*, Oakes demonstrates a large pair of novelty headphones that have the appearance of loudspeakers, suggesting the amplification of thoughts; a pull-apart bowling ball with modular finger holes and large, protruding dowels; and a sandwich holder that also brushes the beard of its user. Oakes serves as a counter to serious, mysterious scientific experiments: an orb plummets through a series of tripwires; a rifle fires a bullet with its trajectory graphed; a man sits with wires covering his body. Later, this conflict between appearance and function continues, with a machine for stocking fabrication, on which fabric is pierced by artificial legs to give a perfect fit, and a scene featuring a hair salon's perm press, an elaborate machine that suggests an Orwellian torture device.

The Wacky Wizard's mugging is echoed by Henry Zemel, who appears on screen in a series of stills, his face distorted by being wrapped in a transparent sheet. These portraits are intercut with an animated demonstration of a physics experiment. Elsewhere, Zemel appears with an icosahedron suspended in front of his face, meditating in the lotus position. At this point in their friendship, Lipsett and Zemel had begun a process of active collaboration. In Lipsett's notes, he had planned for sequences featuring both Zemel and Lavut; only Zemel appears in the final cut. By the end of production, Lipsett would begin to identify with Zemel as a stand-in for himself in his work; Zemel's appearances in *Fluxes* even suggest this, echoing Lipsett's own appearances in his earlier work: when Zemel's mugging face is crushed under plastic, it is reminiscent of Lipsett's contorted grimace glimpsed in *Very Nice, Very Nice*. Zemel's intrusions are the only sequences of the film that are not made from found footage, and *Fluxes* is otherwise a compilation film, albeit of a violently heterodox arrangement. That heterodox construction was reaching a fever pitch in Lipsett's montage. Lipsett had evolved his amusement at artificial forms of speech into new forms of material self-awareness, with a debt to Bruce Conner's discontinuous countdown: he even interrupts his first sequence with a temporary, numeric title.[21]

The opening sequence establishes the themes of *Fluxes*: the monkeys at their "control panel"; rotating, anonymous mechanisms; the Wacky Wizard; Adolf Eichmann in his glass booth. A still image features a pair of hands, extending towards an evidence card that reads

"6." The evidence card is one sign that Lipsett's phenomenal catalogue is clinically apocalyptic, a backward-facing record of life on Earth. Counters and dials are shown to be linked to experiments—an orb dropping through a series of tripwires, a rifle firing—that relate to units of time, using cameras that register in extreme slow motion, and are augmented by on-camera graphics in the form of plotted white lines. A soldier turns to demonstrate the woolly camouflage he's wearing, a mane of fur that he models for the camera. He shows his rifle clips, five bullets in each, one in each hand, like a pair of claws. The first sound heard in *Fluxes* is dialogue from Stuart Walker's *Werewolf of London* (1935): "The werewolf instinctively seeks to kill the thing it loves best." This becomes an overarching ethos through the film, a warning of the hypocrisy of mastery, amid all these acts of invention, so many of them with an inbuilt goal of destruction. The werewolf serves as an avatar of this unreconciled duality between creation and destruction. That the soldier-werewolf's bullets double as claws is made further ironic by the mythic claim that a werewolf can only be killed by a silver bullet.

Aerial bombs drop from a plane, their descent filmed from a topographic perspective. A figure lies on the ground, immersed in flames—the same figure and the same shot that had appeared in *21-87*.[22] When Lipsett used the image in *21-87*, the figure merely collapsed in flames; this begins where that shot left off, with the figure standing, in slow motion, and walking, still in flames, into the jungle. The eerie calm of this action gives the sequence a dreamlike artificiality; there are no tears, no hysteria, no urgency. In a museum, a woman measures a sculpted head; when she rotates it, the head has been sheared cleanly, the stone lopped and smoothed into a perfect flat surface. The recurring images of graphs and instruments allow the woman's measurements to suggest the pseudoscience of phrenology, Franz Joseph Gall's process of determining mental traits by measuring bumps on the skull, long since discredited; the transformed head of the sculpture, meanwhile, suggests trepanation, the act of boring a hole into the skull in order to release evil spirits, gain new wisdom, or otherwise relieve pressure from the brain or treat illnesses of the mind, a crude and brutal precursor to neurosurgery. A samurai is seen, first in close-up, then in a medium shot holding his sword, the bulk of which is out of frame. The operations of a stocking machine, which combines the comedy of an elastic stretching of fabric with the serious machining of artificial legs, leads to the titillating image of a woman demonstrating their success by raising her stockings above her knees. Lipsett is engaging in paired opposites: the war machine and the weird machine, the modern soldier and the feudal samurai. The samurai represents conflict as a calling, while the soldier, like the werewolf, represents the Jekyll-and-Hyde hypocrisy of modern warfare, where the wholesome civilian identity is psychically amputated from the gruesome, violent hunger of the hunt. The disembodied legs of the stocking machine reinforce this theme of fragmentation and amputation.

Back at ground control, the monkeys continue to press at the lighted panels. In many of these experiments, human presence has been erased. The monkeys are exposed, like Eichmann, as exhibits under glass. In a scientific demonstration, from a top-down angle, a figure walks from set points on a wooden floor, in straight lines and then in curves, their origin point marked with a star, their paths forming constellations and triangles that are charted in animated white lines. Without context, these experiments form mysterious rituals. This figure is intercut with Zemel, an icosahedron suspended over his face, cross-legged in a lotus position, further amplifying the ritualization of the scientific demonstration. That his face is obscured by an icosahedron, a twenty-faced geometric form and a symbol for water in Plato's cosmology and thus a parallel to the themes of flows and flowlines, reinforces the icosahedral complexity of the human being.[23] Its symbolism suggests the theme that human activity mirrors the natural coursing of the elements, that human history is elemental theatre.[24] It is Lipsett's variation on a Giorgio de Chirico figure, the scrapheap of symbolism that reimagines the head as a smoothed balloon.

A Japanese man lowers an 8mm movie camera from his eye to return the gaze of the camera that films him. An implied reverse shot shows a still image of the head of a vulture as Leonie Rysanek sings "Una macchia è qui tuttora" from Verdi's *Macbeth*, the musical setting of Lady Macbeth's "out, damned spot" soliloquy. A man is seated at the control panel of an electrical generator. As Adolf Eichmann testifies, the soundtrack oscillates through a series of comic speeches, exclamations, and fragments of advertisements, as if queued up by the operator. The indexical relation between these component shots suggests an overarching action, repeated throughout, where control panels serve to animate the world; like the monkeys at ground control, the man seated at the generator is tuning the floodgate of Eichmann's testimony. That Eichmann and Lady Macbeth both represent attempts at denying obvious guilt—and at that, guilt by proxy—parallels a line of Dylan Thomas's that appears in Lipsett's notebooks but that he never used: "The hand that signed the paper felled a city." The copious inventory of *Fluxes* obscures, at times, the degree to which this theme is insinuated throughout, of the ghastly consequences of giving and following orders. In one of his flowcharts, Lipsett draws from another quote, likewise about distance and living with horrific deeds: "The man who drops the bombs cannot see his victims."[25]

Lipsett integrates sequences from Kaj Pindal's *What on Earth!* (1966), a film Pindal and Les Drew made for the NFB that is typical of the organization's animated fare, a simple entertainment in which a conga line of odd machines manufactures a line of automobiles. Each car evolves through this process to become an anthropomorphic apex predator (in the source film, these cars are called "the earthlings"). Pindal's animation is intercut with Eichmann, whose grimacing testimony is met on the soundtrack with the calling of a lottery and dialogue from police dramas. Pindal's strange mechanisms typify Lipsett's imaginary machines. They also hold all of the rapturous curiosity of a Rube Goldberg machine, the Mod animator's reimagining of the assembly line as a site of bulbous curves, toothed gears, crushing tools, all of it machining a human-like automobile with a grill for teeth, a windshield for eyes, and a steel body for a head. In Pindal and Drew's original, humans are introduced in the final moments as parasitic creatures, there to be destroyed by the "earthlings." Pindal and Drew made a film using the conventional premise of what-ifs: the result is a simple joke with a disquieting but undemanding conclusion. Lipsett's approach differed so dramatically from that of his colleagues, with its blank questions and negative capability, that his inclusion of Pindal and Drew's film in *Fluxes* transforms Pindal's assembly line into a bizarre, violent carnival, shielding its menace from the corny humour of its original context.

Peasant-farmers trek through tall grass. The footage is taken from a documentary on the displacement of the people of Xuzhou. From this tragic rural scene, Lipsett revisits ground control, where the monkeys tap at panels to trigger another revolution. This begins what Lipsett referred to as a "psychological landscape sequence."[26] A mass of men in skullcaps march in synchronized unison, arms raised to their chests with each step, an abundance of figures stretching out in the distance. Maps of animated landforms are piled up in a three-dimensional graph, with an eye peering down through these translucent layers. The animation is borrowed from David Millar's *Data for Decision* (1968), on which Lipsett served as editor. Millar's films served as some of Lipsett's primary sources on *Fluxes*: much of the footage of religious ritual is taken from the four-part series on world religions that Millar made in collaboration with William Greaves, James Beveridge, historian Arnold Toynbee, and philosopher George Grant. In its original context, this illustration demonstrates the ways in which the Department of Forestry and Rural Development's Canada Land Inventory system operated, a computer to index and compare landforms in order to manage and develop Canadian land. Relocated into *Fluxes*, the penetrating line of the eye is coursing through not mere data but the tracks and traces of history. Human action that has played out on the Earth, from farming to the displacement of farmers, from the synchronized marches of soldiers in training to the locked formations of men at arms, has left deep-rooted traces, both visible and invisible. A monk collects an offering of food from a villager, and, without making eye contact, he exits. A projectile hurtles through space, and animation shows the Sputnik satellite and its inner workings, a translation of Lipsett's world-machines to the cosmos. Hands tie an espadrille around their ankle. A ship's captain looks out a deck window with binoculars, and an implied reverse shot sees a monk climbing the steps to Angkor Wat.

Lipsett's "psychological landscape sequence" is, in part, an act of communion between modern and pre-modern values: the Land computer, like the modern ship voyage, represents an act of mastery over information and distance. Lipsett holds these inventions in contrast to cultures where ancient values and monastic virtues have survived into the present, typified in the humble construction of the espadrille, or in the silent dignity of monk and villager. As a deep, growling chant begins to sound, the dance of the modern and ancient turns futurist and populist: a man stands beside an airplane dressed, mysteriously, as an umpire; a Chinese orchestra plays traditional instruments, the fury of their movements at odds with the low, slow dirge of the soundtrack; men wait in pensive silence until a globe is unveiled as the centrepiece at a dining table, and a dining hall erupts in a standing ovation; a holy man, clad in a black robe, leads a crowd in prayer; a Japanese soldier at the front receives good news over the phone, and, in an act of wild rebellion, a crowd of dignitaries struggle over a microphone at a press conference. The sheer chaotic diversity of Lipsett's tour of the East makes attempts at identification increasingly hazardous; where *A Trip Down Memory Lane* had suggested something of the strange competitions that arose in the theatres of war during the 1940s, *Fluxes* is a work of chaos where wonder and horror overlap, and where cultural distinction is trumped by a force-feeding of sheer spectacle. The copious inventories of *Very Nice, Very Nice* and *A Trip Down Memory Lane* were overflowing, but thematically constrained; in assuming the flowlines of a half-century of religious and political culture, *Fluxes* draws from the tracks and traces of international news culture where, alienated from their root meaning, images form new and tenuous contexts. A rocket takes off, and its ascent is recorded in a series of uncanny, ghostly images, hurtling up into the atmosphere and circling the Earth. A group of people examine an unseen compound through microscopes, en plein air, on a bridge with classical European architecture rising in the background, a muddling of the minutiae of the petri dish with the epiphanic vastness of the cosmos. The overlapping of East and West forms a furious dialectic. The sounding of a singing bowl invites a Movietone headline about the Dalai Lama: "Fugitive God-King Says Peiping Lies," dated to his 1959 exile to Dharamshala. An elderly white politician begins to speak but is interrupted by footage of a Buddhist religious ritual. A Buddhist teacher leads his disciples in prayer. When he speaks, he appears to say, in an inexplicable North American accent, "if you examine it closely you will note the simplicity of construction."[27] Lipsett's editing of sound and image is full of such episodes, small, thematically potent acts of alignment that provoke discomfiting laughter. The teacher's statement is met with the humorless, skeptical expression of a devout Buddhist woman. Her presence here is a silent, self-directed scold for the filmmaker's subversive comedy.

A party of Japanese and European military officers and scientists descends the steps of a government building, posing for the camera.

In its popular consumption, Arendt's argument about the banality of evil was simplified to the perception that ordinary, unexceptional people were capable of horrific acts, and in Lipsett's films, the public-facing warmth of military officers, scientists, and politicians only faintly conceals "the hand that signed the paper." A ritual dance is performed before an altar, while, on the soundtrack, dialogue from a movie intrudes: "Perfect physical structure, perfect," a new effusive declaration to take the place of "very nice, very nice"—and just as superficial. Lipsett's use of dramatic dialogue builds parallels between the mannered choreography of the priest and the spasms of the screwball comedy. A topographical map of military targets cuts to a bombardier, observing through the viewing window in the floor of his airplane. In another play on the indexical bridges of montage, the image cuts to a procession of men in India pushing a giant transport, three storeys high with huge stone wheels, something akin to a construct from another ancient civilization, the Trojan Horse. Two operators prepare a hair perm press around a client, wires dangling around her head as she smiles at the camera. This is humorously synthesized into another

FIGURE 7.1: *Fluxes* (Arthur Lipsett, National Film Board, 1968)

of Lipsett's imaginary machines, in his use of the menacing dialogue of *Dr. Cyclops* (1940), as the doctor declares his own Frankenstein complex, as if the perm machine represented technological mastery over life: "Now I can control life absolutely."

The inventory of *Fluxes* includes many forms of ceremony, be it Tibetan priests performing sacred hand dances, or Eleanor Roosevelt cutting a ribbon at the opening of Macy's Latin American Fair in 1942. Smoke billows from an oil field, a glimpse of ecological strain. Admiral Andrew Cunningham of the Royal Navy smiles at the camera, and plotted lines animate the Tyrrhenian Sea with military targets; on the soundtrack, a dramatic voice recites, "I've always been very careful," whispered, inadequate words to accompany the schematics for wartime military raids. In a ballroom, decadent partygoers drink, as the soundtrack declares, "Now here's what you do." By this, the partiers' merriment becomes an exemplum of pleasure. Lipsett surveys a series of figures: a man intently staring at the camera; one man measuring another's head, another allusion to phrenology; and the umpire-pilot, strapping on his helmet. An elderly politician signs a paper, and bombs drop from an airplane, their plummet observed from a topographical angle. Lester B. Pearson poses with the Liberal cabinet for broadcasters and photographers. The ceremonies continue as a man is given a necklace of ornamental grapes to wear like a lei. This pomp and circumstance, a confusion of honorific ceremonies, cocktail parties, and implied declarations of war, ends with the performance of a robot music trio—drummer, saxophonist, accordionist—their mannequin heads capped with helmets that resemble the Pickelhaubes of the Prussian Army. These expressionless heads, without eye sockets or nostrils, extend from coiled tubing into broad metal bodies. The saxophonist, the only one with a mouth, seems to be in the process of standing or dancing, the plates of his body shifting to support this illusion. At the Eichmann trial, witnesses and prosecutors turn as if to hear the band. In Germany, a giant papier-mâché effigy of a man in glasses and suit—resembling Eichmann—is toppled.

The effigy is given context in a later shot that shows a pageant of large papier-mâché figures atop floral parade floats, waiting stationary on a lot: a man walks through the grounds wearing a grotesque East Asian papier-mâché mask, which is playfully clubbed apart by his co-workers. Chinese street theatre performers on stilts loom over a bustling crowd. Hands count a massive pile of bills and jewelry as the sound is dominated by dramatic music and increasingly hysterical and urgent voices. This breaks as a theatrical voice declares that "it was hand lotion…*hand lotion*! It was an emollient." A soldier is wrapped in bandages, and a man in a top hat tips it to the camera; the dramatic intensity of this actor as he speaks of hand lotion is in contrast to the dire silence of the soldier, and the showy decadence of the gentleman serves as another of Lipsett's trademark collisions between the pedestrian and the terrifying. The street performers walk on stilts through a market in rapid strides, their leg span making them more gods than men. Another title card interrupts, this one reading "temporary title." Such title cards are another sign of an unhinging of the copious inventory, that the container is under such duress that conventions of arrangement have been abandoned. It is a further evolution of the rapturous denouements that featured in Lipsett's films from *21-87* onward, where end titles signal false endings, interrupted by prolonged cadenzas. The bombs drop again. Students gathered on a campus green throw their arms up in a "boola boola" wave, a symbol of entrenched competition. The Statue of Liberty towers over Manhattan in parallel to the Chinese street performers.

A woman on the steps of a government building and a man in a tuxedo seated in the pilot's seat of a biplane both give perplexed expressions as a narrator says, "perhaps someday wherever they were it could happen there too"—but where is wherever, and where is there? This ambiguity is surrendered to the judgment of the viewer. There is an implication, in the puzzled, apprehensive expressions of these decadent Westerners, that what happened in Hiroshima and Nagasaki could happen in America. The carnivalesque continues with a Chinese acrobat, balancing six spinning plates on sticks while performing bodily contortions. Cartoonist George McManus, creator of *Bringing Up Father*, draws on a blackboard, a puzzle of lines and curves that come together in the winking, cigar-chomping, clown-like face of cartoon icon Jiggs. A Catholic priest begins to speak, but his speech, like that of the Buddhist teacher, is substituted, this time with the corny menace of a hammy actor playing a ransomer. As the details of the ransom are expounded, animations show a stylized globe with rotating parts and the patterns by which the Telstar satellite sends and receives information. A monk looks blankly into the camera as it interrupts his meditations, his own invisible acts of sending and receiving.

As the monkeys press their lighted panels, *Fluxes* returns to uncanny, twisting images taken from an object in orbit moving up through the atmosphere. At a Buddhist ceremony, figures move in a pathway around an altar, performing hand dances in a procession as an American science-fiction program sounds, a stiff dramatic voice declaring that "we have made everything on our planet invisible." As *Fluxes* has reckoned with war, competition, and rocket flight, an unspoken theme of overpopulation emerges from its sheer density. The speaker has made everything on their planet invisible by an imaginary subterfuge, while earthlings have made their planet invisible by chaotic plenitude. An image of the Earth appears, clouded by its atmosphere, oceans and continents invisible, as, on the soundtrack, actor Adam West as Batman offers one of the hero's characteristic pseudoscientific speculations: "perhaps if I activated the accelerated concentration switch." As he speaks, the globe slowly comes into focus. Buddhist ceremonies continue as this dichotomy of cosmic and East Asian imagery and American popular culture provides a thesis, in the form of an invading alien's mission statement: "we come from a hungry planet... as a matter of survival, we raid other planets...our only morality is survival." In its original context, this mission was a faintly masked metaphor for colonialism; in *Fluxes*, it is placed in direct relation to imagery of religious, national, and racial competition, where it becomes riotous for the actor's histrionic delivery, but equally haunting for its global resonance, an unvarnished admission of a ravenous, werewolf cabal.

As a Tibetan priest performs a hand dance, rotating in circles and alternately enclosing and releasing his fingers, the credits play. In a rapturous flow, an image of a child monk cuts to lights shifting along the curves of a series of bulbous dials. Monks are intercut with a rocket launch, as a voice intones that "power transfer will begin immediately." As the monks, gathered in meditation, become another ironic mirror of NASA's ground control, the film assumes the eschatological themes of Arthur C. Clarke's *The Nine Billion Names of God* (1953), in which Tibetan monks exhaust the names of God with the help of a modern computer and Western technicians, provoking the whimper of

FIGURE 7.2: *Fluxes* (Arthur Lipsett, National Film Board, 1968)

a dimming universe. Modern computation becomes an extension of the prayer wheel, an apogee of media as the extensions of humankind, where spirit and technology meld in a moment of *satori*, but where *satori* is merely a bated breath before ignition. A monkey seen through murky glass, his head twitching and turning rapidly in pixilation, stares up into an unseen, sublime eternity. A final dialogue from *Werewolf of London* returns the film to themes of lycanthropy and predation, as two characters discuss the Tibetan "phosphorescent moon flower" that "blooms only under the rays of the moon." As one admits to the other that he cannot get his flower to bloom by moonlight or any other light, a voice interrupts with a concluding declaration of futility, and a final threat: "whether you get it or not will not matter much…tonight."

Lipsett imagined *Fluxes* as a "mechanism with human fleas," an allusion to the flea circuses of the nineteenth century that gradually abandoned their tamed insect stars for pure mechanical illusions, another simulation of the force that through the green fuse drives the flower, a visible manmade world host to invisible labour.[28] His notes suggest an interest in timekeeping, that the film should bear imagery of various ways of keeping time: the metronome, the chronometer, even the Land computer's graphs; these are interwoven with what Lipsett refers to as "mechanical tick-tocks," EEG charts in progress, needle gauges moving, sometimes paired with their units of measurement.[29] The clinical distance of the Histomap, conceived to demonstrate at once causality and simultaneity in human progress, was the long view of time. Here it is supplemented by Lipsett's "tick-tocks," measurement tools and gauges, to develop a total vision of time, from ancient customs to a contemporary futurism, a "pushbutton culture."[30] Lipsett's friend Mark Slade, working in the distribution division at the NFB, wrote an article for the *Montreal Gazette* praising *Fluxes* when it was released: "it's no secret that Lipsett distrusts switches...once an electric current is introduced into the grammar of man's ritual languages, fuses are needed... Arthur Lipsett still hopes to discover adequate circuit breakers."[31] These switches and gauges function in an arena of pure symbol, signs of the contemporary world that, prey to a behaviourist society, predict the coming of the "new man," as imagined by the filmmaker in 1964.[32]

When Lipsett worked in the unit system, he could count on being able to pursue a given project because his work was so inexpensive, employing virtually no production personnel save for the sound re-recordist. He used his own equipment, and that spared him additional scrutiny. Now facing the program committee, Lipsett's projects began to overlap, a sign of his uncertainty that his pitches would be approved. While making *Fluxes*, Lipsett had proposed another project—a television series titled *The Search*, with the additional working title *Prayers*. It was an extension of themes found in Coté's *Regards sur l'occultisme*; Lipsett was exploring the rise of an esoteric spirituality, a result of the same curiosity that had made Coté's series fashionable. In his proposal, Lipsett writes of behavioural patterns operating in New Age philosophies that mirror the early stages of civilization and reflect an ancient, magical perception of the world: "Are some of the veneers of civilization peeling away to reveal inner man once again?"[33] This image—of peeling away layers—mirrors Lipsett's use of Ibsen's onion metaphor, and the tracks and traces of the past here become "veneers of civilization."[34] The series would explore emerging forms of prayer that operate as defensive magic—for instance, the rise of the mantra in Western experience as a form of affirmation. Lipsett's long-held curiosity about the causes for spiritual atrophy derives from Alan Watts's *The Wisdom of Insecurity*, on the disparity between faith and science in the modern age. Watts gives this re-emergence of magic a vivid description, writing of the necessity of new myths, a violent political religion that "betrays the anxiety beneath them—for they are but men huddling together and shouting to give themselves courage in the dark."[35]

While working on *Fluxes*, Lipsett took on other tasks at the NFB. He served as editor and assistant director on *Data for Decision* (1968), directed by his former neighbour David Millar and produced for the Canadian Department of Forestry and Rural Development, a film about computation and its role in solving human problems, the automation of storing and analyzing data. Millar's film followed on themes established by Roman Kroitor's *The Living Machine*; like it, *Data for Decision* deals with the interface between computers and human beings. Where *The Living Machine* was a work of poetic inquiry, Millar's film is fundamentally educational, its scenes illustrating processes described by a stentorian narrator. Brief glimpses of Lipsett's editorial imagination show through the film's utilitarian form, as he inserts still images into gliding shots through the hallways of map cabinets in a map library, in timed punctuation with the voice of the narrator. The bulk of his work obeys the conventions of continuity editing for which the material has been shot.

In the midst of his making *Fluxes*, Arthur Lipsett's work was acknowledged and commemorated through the efforts of a small group of his colleagues at the NFB in the form of a special program, initially developed for television and the educational market. *Two Films by Lipsett* features *Free Fall* and *A Trip Down Memory Lane*, contextualized by a debate among uncommonly articulate and insightful secondary school students over the style, merit, and perceived cynicism of his work. They meet the work with a mix of prejudices and projections, drawing opposite conclusions from the film, reinforcing the notion that Lipsett's films were like a Rorschach test—in other words, that the films reflected the individual viewer. These interstitial sequences are presented in an observational style, directed by Donald Rennick, but the project itself was instigated by some of Lipsett's most stalwart supporters at the NFB: Mark Slade, Robert Verrall, and Joseph Koenig. That this presentation was thought necessary is a sign of both the esteem Lipsett had inspired in those close to him, who wanted to acknowledge and celebrate him, and the widespread sense that his films were puzzles, mysterious, possibly unknowable. The students reach the disquieting conclusion that their generation is entering into a hell of meaninglessness exhaustion and pain, recalling Slade's remark that "there is a generation of young people whose own survival is linked with the survival of Arthur Lipsett."[36]

Despite such celebratory treatments of his work, Lipsett found himself the subject of malicious rumours. In January 1968, he addressed them head on in a memorandum to twenty members of the production and distribution staff. "I understand that there are wild rumours which seem to be emanating from the Distribution Division concerning sales figures for my films," Lipsett writes, "One rumour has it that only seven prints have been sold in the past eight years."[37] Lipsett refutes these claims by providing up-to-date sales figures totalling an impressive 334 print sales out of the 593 made. Further to that, he notes that in the three months prior, bookings for loans of prints totalled 77.[38] The baffling rumours are indicative of an increasingly hostile workplace. Lipsett's films had not been the sole cause for the shift away from the unit system, but they were emblematic of the freedom that had infuriated his colleagues outside of Unit B. They denigrated his work out of jealousy and bitterness, and only partly because they could not understand its success. Audiences wanted to see Lipsett's films. Students would rather have a dialogue with *Free Fall* than be lectured by the sanctimonious *Imperial Sunset* or be asked to reflect on *23 Skidoo* and its superficial illustration of a post-nuclear silent world.

The NFB did not know what to do with Arthur Lipsett. While a minority felt either that his work was essential to the artistic integrity of the organization or that it had a proven audience and he deserved his voice, rumours were spreading that would make Lipsett's transition to the pitch-based pool system even more difficult. The didactic bias of the National Film Board had little room for modern artists, and none at all for artists whose work was not conceived for quick comprehension. His role as an outsider was what had given Lipsett's work its power—but without the shelter of Unit B, his eccentricities and unconventional sense of humour would become liabilities.

# EIGHT

# LANDSCAPES

The "n-zone" is a hypothetical plane of philosophical speculation: n is nirvana, n is nihil and none, n is nadir. As in algebra, n has a specific but concealed meaning that is revealed by inquiry, by the working out of an equation. By the poetic properties of the phoneme, n can suggest infinity. By those same properties, it is the end zone, the scoring plane at either end of a football field, the goal. For Arthur Lipsett, who had spent a decade making films about consumer society, the dense plenitude of worldly content, and Western civilization's hunger and pitilessness, the n-zone represented something ultimate and final. The n-zone first manifested when Henry Zemel came to Lipsett's Coronet Street apartment one day to find that Lipsett had cut out a series of letters from black and white paper. One man took a black surface, the other a white one, and they arranged and rearranged the contrasting letters until the expression appeared. Even as they settled on it, they played with the orientation of N, the n-zone becoming the z-zone and the z-none and back again, z as zero and as the end of point of the Latin alphabet. Between nowhere and eternity, the zone became host to a legion of potential meanings.

As the unit system gave way to the pool system, Lipsett's standing at the Film Board came under strain. The institution's growing intolerance for his absurdist underground sensibilities combined with taxing disruptions to the social order of the workplace: his contributions were undervalued, and his support system was scattered. Outside of the Film Board, Lipsett was held in high esteem: his films had been highly influential, encountered by Americans and Europeans thanks to the higher standing afforded them after his Oscar nomination, and by an emerging generation of Canadian filmmakers through campus screenings and television broadcasts. A new scene of independent experimental filmmakers was taking shape in the country's civic centres, bolstered by the creation of distribution networks and the emergence of cinema and media studies courses at universities. Lipsett would never connect with this new underground cinema, nor had he connected with his peers in the American underground at the time of his own emergence. With few exceptions, the limits of Lipsett's peer network were in the hallways of the National Film Board.

Henry Zemel had come to Montreal from New York City in the mid-1960s with the hope of making films with the NFB. His one film with the organization, *Restricted Dogs*, on sensory deprivation experiments conducted on dogs by the behaviourists at McGill University, ended in acrimony because of conflicts with his co-workers.[1] Zemel was a charismatic, fiercely intelligent outsider. He had a social ease that juxtaposed with Lipsett's shy demeanour. This provoked envy and affection from Lipsett. His invitation to Zemel to participate in the creative groundwork for a new film was a novel process for Lipsett, whose films had been solitary affairs. Lipsett's only formal collaborators had been his sound re-recordists and his producers, whose contributions were primarily technical and political.[2] The friendship between Lipsett and Zemel had a utility to it for each man: Zemel wished to be involved in filmmaking and had gained the support of an important film artist, and for Lipsett, it might have fed a desire to share the burden of his voluminous work, and to use Zemel as a conduit, to draw some secret knowledge out of the universe. Their collaboration also grew out of a newly formed social ritual, hosting parties where they took drugs and played spontaneous music on Lipsett's collection of Asian flutes and Indian percussion instruments.

In September 1968, Lipsett delivered a proposal for his next film to the program committee. With a requested budget of less than $15,000, it was a more modest outing than his recent films, a sign that the enmity he had encountered from the NFB had led him to set low expectations for support. The methodology was different from his prior films as well, stipulating non-sync "documentary-type shooting...no candid material."[3] This would prove a departure from his earlier camerawork, which had developed around candid shooting: the faces in the crowd of *Very Nice, Very Nice*; the shoppers and dancers of *21-87*; and the figures seen through cover in *Free Fall*.[4] He described the new film as a document of "landscapes of our time," a study of the interconnections of various "reality levels" as they were unfolding in 1968. By that fall, 1968 had been host to an exceptional series of turning points in Western consciousness: the civil unrest in Paris that resonated with workers and students internationally; the assassinations of Martin Luther King Jr. and Robert F. Kennedy and continued progress in the American Civil Rights movement; growing condemnation on the part of the American public of the war in Viet Nam; and the riots at the 1968 Democratic National Convention in Chicago. There was unrest in Canada as well: in the aftermath of the nation's 1967 centennial, Pierre Trudeau's landslide win in the federal election coincided with separatist riots in Montreal, giving proof that the country was facing its own interesting times. Lipsett's preparatory notes focus on the format of his presentation, explaining his use of loose-leaf papers, what he refers to as "idea notebooks."[5] The film's working title was *Landscapes*, but when it was finished and released two years later, it was called *N-Zone*. Lipsett would be reunited with Tom Daly, who would return as his producer for the first time since the unit system had given way. Daly, alongside Colin Low and Robert Verrall, had made Lipsett's first films possible, and their support had allowed Lipsett to take the NFB in the strange new directions of an emerging underground cinema. While such work failed to gain serious traction among his colleagues, it brought him admiration that had allowed him a degree of agency and solitude. Lipsett was also joined by Henry Zemel, who would be credited on the film as a co-writer and as one of four cinematographers, alongside Lipsett, Wolf Koenig, and Paul Leach.[6]

In one of his idea notebooks of the period, Lipsett offers a fragment that gives further indication of his intentions in making *Landscapes*: "And the landscape never looks so enchantingly lovely as in the hour when a man thinks he may be viewing it for the last time."[7] The eschatological promise of this statement comprehensively applies to all of Lipsett's films, which had dealt with apocalypses of varying scales—the bomb as messenger in *Very Nice, Very Nice*; the confusion of man and machine in *21-87*; the ecstatic collapse of *Free Fall*; the hubristic optimism of *A Trip Down Memory Lane*. When Lipsett seized upon the idea of anastomotic pathways in the mid-1960s, he engineered the flow of mythic, scientific, and spiritual tributaries into an apocalyptic output in *Fluxes*. *Fluxes* declared the inevitability of a quiet massacre on a rocket-bound journey to a full moon: this is the way the world ends—not with a bang, but with a werewolf. Lipsett recurrently fixates on a Tibetan Buddhist expression he drew from Walter Evans-Wentz's *Tibetan Yoga and Secret Doctrines* (1935): "And may all karmic debts be paid and cleared. Phat!"[8] The loose-leaf papers that Lipsett presented for the program committee's consideration were more definite in their imagery: a man dying of thirst crawls into view in a desert; a herd of elephants pass by in a savannah; pans of Russian leaders on a balcony "looking like deadly foreign spies."[9] This attempt to concretize his abstract thoughts on the spirit of 1968 was noted by the program committee when they approved the project; unmentioned is the fact that Lipsett's 1968, in keeping with his recent compilation films, appears to again be assembled from the distant memories of newsreels.[10]

Lipsett began to conceive of his diagrams and flowcharts as "secret museums," a phrase he borrowed from one of his many collage sources, *The Secret Museum of Mankind*, a five-volume exploitation book published in 1935 with no author, credits, copyright, date, page numbers, or index. *The Secret Museum of Mankind* was sold through mail-order services, advertising "1,000 revealing photos" of "various secret societies, civilized love vs. savage, exotic rites and cults, strange crimes and criminals, omens, totems & taboos, mysterious customs, dress & undress round the world."[11] It was a window on the unscientific, leering fascinations that underscore anthropology. For Lipsett, calling his art a "secret museum" was a strange joke, not only for the pornographic nature of his source, but as a kind of oxymoron. His secret museums followed John Cage's advice to let things go together. Lipsett was not so much a curator or architect of these secret museums as he was a conduit himself, his film the output of an anastomotic force. It was a concept that extended from his earliest wallpaper scrapbooking: the secret museums were paperboard collage flowcharts, but they were also the spaces in which he lived, and images of his Coronet Street apartment show walls covered in clippings, another secret museum. In advance of starting production on *N-Zone*, Lipsett made a flowchart that alternates between technical plans for an unrealized film and observations of Buddhist dualities. *The Mundane (Sangsāra) vs. Nirvana: A Farewell to the Material World* is thus filled with descriptions of precise images and lists comparing states of existence. He writes of "the moving force of the sangsāra" in contrast to "nirvanic non-moving," a relation of his Buddhist readings to that force that through the green fuse drives the flower.[12] The chart takes the form of a numbered list of forty-three items—sequences, images, philosophical observations. The text shows an evolving poetics, pantheistic with a heavy helping of Tibetan Buddhism, focused on bodily experience of the visible world as a contrast to the psychic experience of an invisible world. Quotidian experience—the trivialities of the life cycle as embedded in the concept of Sangsāra—keeps company with a search for enlightenment, at its most practical in the form of instructions ("one must free oneself from all hope and fear," "the 'doors of action' [the body, the senses, the mind] must be closed").[13] *The Mundane vs. Nirvana* follows from other posterboard collages that Lipsett had prepared for his projects beginning with *A Trip Down Memory Lane: Man's Psychic Evolution*; a series serving his *Discovery Film* proposal (among them, *Dreams of Empire*); and untitled series dealing with graphic concepts, political science, and newsreels.

Lipsett's diagram for *N-Zone* is a series of intersecting shapes forming a cone, marked along its trajectory by motifs (noted in the legend as "woozy dog," "x-ray man," and appearances by performers—among them, Lipsett's friend John Max, Henry Zemel's parents, and Lipsett himself).[14] Evolution and history overlap in a "wandering ghost area" of mystical portents, and the trajectory travels from one triangle ("thesis") to another ("sleep area"), joined by a "karmic deeds record."[15] Iconography mixes with these general labels, marking appearances by Hindu goddess Kali, master of death, time, and change; Charon, mythological ferryman of the Greek afterworld; and John Diefenbaker, "Dief the Chief," Canada's former Prime Minister whose whistle-stop train tours of the 1960s are noted in Lipsett's diagram. Lipsett writes

FIGURE 8.1: Arthur Lipsett poses with his Secret Museum in *N-Zone* (Arthur Lipsett, National Film Board, 1970)

"switters," likely a reference to Kurt Schwitters, the Dada artist whose philosophical conception of Merz was defined as a form of psychological collage, with his "Merz Pictures" combining commonplace objects, non-traditional and traditional materials, to the end of forming multidimensional, abstract assemblages. For Schwitters, the Merz Pictures were a natural consequence of the Great War; as he said, "everything had broken down...and new things had to be made out of the fragments."[16] Much as Lipsett would, Schwitters had developed a quotidian poetics that recognized in the transient nature of rubbish the potential for new expressions, in itself an act of resilience. Turned to a vertical orientation, the *N-Zone* diagram forms a face with a third eye. The overlapping forms of squares, triangles, circles, cones, and parallelograms become the features of this face, tracking an evolution from primal needs to a rapturous climax, described only as "garden events etc."[17]

Lipsett's charts became less functional and more an extension of his thought process as time went on. By the end of the 1960s, he began to think of his films and his collages as a reconciled continuity, as when he described *N-Zone* as a "fold-out mural."[18] Lipsett already regarded film as being guided by the energy flows of modern art, a perspective that is evident with his kinetic, ambulatory shooting in *Free Fall*. By 1968, in public addresses, Lipsett was speaking of his films as being guided by flow and flowlines, his language modelled on the ideas of Alan Watts and Warren McCulloch.[19] The notion that a film could be a component part of a multiform work that enfolds its process is particular to the optimism and porous processes of art-making in the 1960s. The growth of happenings and the relative ephemerality of moving-image art presented a freer range of expression, opening new possibilities for art's embattled containers.[20] In Lipsett's case, the paperboard collages, or secret museums, were more than roadmaps for his films: they were paracinematic art objects, another container for the copious inventory, an overflowing of information, their content ranging from editorials, to scientific breakthroughs, to news imagery and stills from movies. These secret museums marked a transit back from the scathing tours of common history in *A Trip Down Memory Lane* and *Fluxes* towards the quotidian banalities glimpsed in his early films.

On July 25, 1969, six months after his memorandum to production staff regarding the rumours of his films' purported unprofitability, Lipsett wrote to NFB Director of Production Frank Spiller. He resigned his contract, effective October of that year. "I will be finishing my present film by that date," Lipsett wrote, "and will not want to begin any new projects at the National Film Board for the immediate future."[21] Lipsett's plans for a hasty departure did not come to fruition: by the end of the year, it became clear that *N-Zone* was going to be longer than he had expected and would take more time to complete. Once the film was approved for a longer runtime, Tom Daly ensured that his contract was extended.[22] Lipsett's unhappiness with the NFB hinged partly on his mistreatment (typified by the damaging rumours from the distribution division) and partly on his growing frustration with filmmaking, a craft that, for him, had become inextricable from the NFB and its bounded definitions of what constituted "art." It must have been a source of some dissatisfaction for Arthur Lipsett that he was so strongly associated with the process of recycling elements from the films of his colleagues. Their wastebasket had provided some early inspiration, but for the most part, his collage materials were chosen with careful intention from a myriad of sources. With *Fluxes*, his use of television as a tool for sound collage mirrored aspects of his creative process, a tuning among channels; and, like the subjective and interior experience that forms when caught in that abstract zone between channels, Lipsett's sources became more diffuse, more intimate, and all the more open in their meaning.

The pre-credit sequence of *N-Zone* is typical of this ambiguity. Lipsett establishes the film's party atmosphere, with the sounds of Henry Zemel and their friend Israel Charney commenting on Lipsett's newsreel imagery. As a nod to the guessing-game experience of watching a Lipsett collage film, they ask among themselves, "Do you have any idea what this is?" There is a rehearsed, performative quality to their voices, a self-consciousness of the recording that only becomes more prominent when they begin prolonged vocalizations, recalling the ahs and uhs and Oms of *Very Nice, Very Nice*. They describe the action on screen, as well as shots that aren't on screen—"a ping pong ball is bouncing." A number of sequences repeat as motifs: a man crawling in the desert, a procession of elephants, a promotional film about the Ride-a-Roo-Kangaroo bouncing rubber ball, and footage of fishermen on a pebbled shoreline. Before it is over, *N-Zone* extends Lipsett's persistent themes of the conflict between real and artificial organisms: facile, ridiculous, and occasionally charming gimmickry of toys and inventions; and the mysteries of civilization that form across valleys of time and culture. That the entrance to this zone is initiated by a struggling, crawling figure gathers it all under the sign of a declining, fated humanity, ensuring a continuity that links it back to his earliest films.

Lipsett structured *N-Zone* in six reels, woven together by recurrent sequences: the Zemels—Henry Zemel, his wife Carol, his mother and father, and his extended family—have a family gathering with the serving of tea as a focal point, a surrogate for an East Asian tea ceremony; another party at which Zemel, Charney, and others talk, sometimes pointedly but often mindlessly; and a scene focused around a floral-print armchair that is occupied variously by Lipsett and Zemel as they perform strange rituals for the camera. As with Lipsett's earlier films, *N-Zone* would end in a rapturous crescendo, but the length of the film, almost twice that of *Fluxes*, allowed him to embrace the idle chatter of his sync footage of conversations. Lipsett's early filmmaking had been strongly associated with anxious dancing rhythms; the piano rag and the piano roll were ideal models for the rapid changes and sensory deluge of his early CBC advertisement, *Anything Can Happen on Channel 6*. However, Lipsett had reached a new point in his aesthetic evolution, setting aside the density and metric precision he had come through to pursue a newly durational and meditative form. In spite of this change of rhythm, *N-Zone* was never so still or silent as to stand in for a state of *satori*; Lipsett's intercutting of historical footage, performative mugging, and parties both young (bohemian) and old (familial) are no less an articulation of universal anxieties. He has merely transformed his mode of representation from lilt to lamentation.

As the credits end, fishermen along a pebbled shoreline catch catfish, stroking them and keeping them wet. A montage of 35mm stills begins with a photonegative image of a statue with a line drawn through it, crossing out its face, the monument made futile. This montage proceeds through stills of wall-mounted artificial fish, their bulging eyes a point of focus in the compositions. The image of the real catfish impinges on the novelty of a wall-mounted plastic fish; it suggests something like the statue, a cold stone surrogate as a memory aid. A recurrent image, taken from Zemel's *Restricted Dogs*, shows a woozy dog struggling to its feet. As a voice talks about a hypothetical movie title—"the return of fossil man, fossil man lives"—Lipsett is shown reclining in bed, a neutral countenance, illustrations and clippings decorating the wall behind him. A close-up on his face, looking away from the camera, yields to an image of two mice running in rapid circles in a tiny dish in a behaviourist experiment, a ready exemplar of futility that suggests, by its proximity to the shot of Lipsett, the artist's own idle disposition. A frog skeleton, a dinosaur skull, a turtle skull, and stuffed birds: all are signs of the past, but they assume an apocalyptic finality when placed in relation to another image, of wide, smiling eyes seen through a gas mask, a staged and literal illustration of laughing into oblivion. The bohemian party begins as Zemel, offscreen, draws Israel Charney into a discussion of Roco Cola, the two men tripping as they rehearse the words, as if preparing to shoot a commercial. Lipsett's work had always been about the long project of human history. The dog and the man in the desert are metaphoric avatars for the viewer and for Lipsett, navigating an n-zone in which fossils, like statues, never mark a true return from death and where newly shorn skulls may one day join those of the dinosaurs in outnumbering the species to which they belong.

The dog is shown variously struggling to its feet and limping, or lying in the sun, breathing with difficulty. A series of individuals perform for the camera: Lipsett opens a Fluxus anthology, a small photographic book with fold-out pages, and clumsily thumbs it; he sits in his apartment, playing a flute; Rick Raxlen, then an animator at the NFB, is seated with dark sunglasses, pressing an object to his mouth; Zemel plays with his lips, forming a duckbill. These scenes are markedly solitary in contrast to the party atmosphere, scenes of individual communion between Lipsett and art, Lipsett and music, Lipsett and individual friends in silent portrait sittings. The same mugging is present as when the camera lingers on Charney, but the performances are stranger, disentangled from a lively social atmosphere. When the film returns to the party, Ben and Marie, a couple, sit and have a casual discussion about White Plains, New York, as traffic noise and a child at play are heard offscreen. The moment is meandering, a paragon of the mundane. John Max and Zemel are shown in profile facing one another as two Chinese speakers have an animated discussion on the soundtrack; by way of this vertical montage, the white men are implied as surrogates for the Chinese speakers. Zemel's father sits at a dining room table and proudly unfolds rolled-up class photos, cueing the nostalgic reminiscence of a family gathering. Back at the bohemian party, Israel Charney declares that he can't write on the wall, then begins to draw on the wall behind him, as the child offscreen objects to the sound of Charney's squeaking marker. This is intercut with figures gathering in the Zemel family's dining room, to the sound of Lipsett repeating ad nauseam "I am the love drug, the love drug." Surrogacy is at its most explicit in the editing of Max and Zemel to the Chinese recording, but surrogacy is an inescapable theme in *N-Zone*, wherein Lipsett's documentation of his friends and of Zemel's family suggests that Lipsett is making a portrait of the informal kinfolk who were coming to populate his life.[23]

As reel two begins, Lipsett is shown more animated, bobbing his head along as he continues to intone "I am the love drug." Scenes from the bohemian party are interwoven with newsreel footage of prohibition agents smashing bottles with pickaxes, an ironic nod to the history of contraband and a scene that any hip audience would read as an act of square hypocrisy. Ben and Marie tease each other, and crosstalk culminates with her taking a rhino-shaped squirt gun and spraying it across the room into Charney's open mouth. Truncated speech and radio dial tuning dominate the soundtrack as the film tours various images of mouths and hands: the grotesque mouth of a cartoon mask hung in a store window, Martin Lavut's grinning mouth as he bites down on the tail of a rubber mouse, and, later, as he chews on a rubber cricket, a vivid, comic demonstration of the evolutionary axiom to eat or be eaten. An illustration of a disembodied, gloved hand becomes a motif amidst still photography of rubber masks, paper skeletons, and novelty gags. The faces, both illustrated and cast in rubber, recall the mannequin heads of earlier Lipsett films, only these toys are defined by performative, stereotypical exaggerations of the human face, not unlike the mugging faces of his friends. Scenes from the bohemian party are interrupted by the newsreel memory of the archive: two women walk to and enter a car; an older businessman sits at a desk, looking up and down from what he is writing, as if in contemplation; the soundtrack features a scribbling pen, and a woman's voice that gives a sound effect description that become an unsynchronized caption—"potato being peeled"—her professional, clinical voice used to misalign word and image, mirroring what Charney and Zemel were doing in the film's opening minutes. These machined misidentifications form comical riffs on the look-and-respond structure of the Rorschach test, demonstrative of Lipsett's amusement at the search for meaning in his use of stock shots. Lipsett is again shown thumbing through his Fluxus anthology, as a means to transition into an explanation of these mysterious events.[24]

That explanation comes as Lipsett sits in his bedroom, backed by the clippings on his wall. He explains his secret museums with a list of increasingly comical non-sequiturs: "you could look at all the separate little boxes, each box containing a soul, an object, or something. Some have a man scratching his head, some have a door or an x or a samurai falling, or a word that says word," Lipsett narrates, "Or a twenty five cent photo strip. Or a man with a piece of paper crinkled in his eye. Or a man with a little black thing exploding in his head. Or disembodied hands that connect to a painting by a mad Englishman who likes red rooms."[25] The secret museums become a storehouse of extraordinary refuse, a phenomenal catalogue, at once semiotically potent and signalling nothing. His explanation of the secret museum, offered without specific reference to the wall beyond its appearance on screen, is also a suitable commentary on the structure of the film itself, a stream of images, each in sequential boxes (of the frame and of the film strip), placed into dialogue by their arrangement. Kurt Schwitters had conceived of the Merz Pictures as the output of such arrangements; to respect the discretion of the object and the dialogue of their assembly brings Lipsett's psychological collage closer to that of Joseph Cornell and John Cage: the secret museum marries the dollhouse logic of Cornell's boxed assemblages to Cage's philosophy of indeterminacy. Lipsett's description rationalizes the form of *N-Zone*, but it also mirrors the undertakings of other collectors, real and hypothetical: the unseen consumer for whom these novelty gags exist; the devout who house idols of their gods; even Zemel's father, as he passes around a photo album, is sharing a secret museum.

As Lipsett's narration continues, Henry Zemel, with a patterned cloth covering his forehead, rubs a deer's foot on his face. Marie moves her foot around in the air while the partygoers tease each other, forming a parallel between Marie's extended leg and the hoof of the deer. As the sound of the bohemian party intrudes on the family's party, the scenes are intercut. The bohemians discuss Rabbi David Hartman, a prominent spiritual leader and influential teacher in Montreal known for his progressive, universalistic approach to modern Judaism. The unseen child continues their protest, insisting that they want to go home, barking "I'm serious, you know!" The reel ends with a still image of two men carrying a large mirror through the streets. In a separate act of reflection, *N-Zone* has brought together themes of difficult, even impossible homecomings: Hartman, who believed in the possibility of Israel as a progressive humanist utopia, was then in the process of moving to Israel himself, a gesture that would prove a strange homecoming for many members of the Jewish diaspora—while the unseen, frustrated child desperately insists on leaving the party, on going home, their pleas falling on deaf ears. Like the parallel between the hoof and Marie's foot, this arrangement thematizes but does not invite a conclusion. These events are neighbouring boxes, crossing in the flow.

In his third reel, Lipsett begins to integrate still images of East Asian idols. They become a structuring element. His approach involves showing an idol and then something else (John Max's balding head, Henry Zemel assembling a bauble from a plate of strings and beads, masks in the gag store, a security mirror) before cutting back to the idol. This A-B-A structure repeats subtly throughout the sequence, as various East Asian statues become witnesses, their patient, placid features peering into Western anxieties and junk-throngs. This exchange of East and West—an extension of the transpacific themes of *Fluxes*—is also present in a scene of a Japanese surrender ceremony circa the Second World War, with Japanese and nondescriptly Western military officers present, culminating in one Japanese officer relinquishing his *guntō* (a sheathed sabre). When the security mirror is shown, first in a wide shot and then cropped in as a detail, it displays a dense horde of totems, gag gifts resembling trophies, lamps, and idols. It hangs in a corner next to a stereotypical Fu Manchu mask that is suspended from the ceiling. *N-Zone*, like *Fluxes* before it, deliberately confuses earnest and grotesque depictions of Asians, orientalist visions of an eternal other. Lipsett's archive of representations lingers on Buddhism, felt in the ceremonial soundtrack, in which an infrequent cymbal and distant

FIGURE 8.2: *N-Zone* (Arthur Lipsett, National Film Board, 1970)

chanting signal the monasteries of Tibet.[26] The faces of the soldiers betray no emotion, their stern discipline a strange distance from the racist grins of figures and masks. The copious inventory can host irreconcilable ideals: the carnivalesque of the illustrated, plastic, or papier-mâché face; the eternal tranquility of the stone idol; and the flat, neutral expressions of monks and soldiers.

The sustained chants and call-and-response of a Buddhist congregation accompany mice as they scurry in a dish. John Max, mirroring the movement of the mice, paces before the camera. The number of mice fluctuate between shots—two, then one, then two again—but the scurrying is always furious. Carol Zemel's father smokes a cigar. Lipsett sits in bed turning a hand-held light on and off. The Zemel family continues to review photo albums. Lipsett, still in bed, plays a miniature xylophone. These contrasts between the Zemel family and Lipsett's solitude resonate with the scurrying mice, Lipsett's arch-metaphor for futility. Among the most terrifying images in *N-Zone* is that of the lone mouse darting in place in dizzying circles. That this sequence represents limbo is evident in Lipsett's notes on the sequence. He had described it as a "Karmic Judgment Aftermath Bardo Plane Limbo," which he represents through a variety of interspersed images: bubbling, pale, opaque mud; a still image of a man getting a shoeshine; and a scientist peering into a microscope, an image so open that anything joined to it would be taken as the contents of a petri dish.[27]

The karmic themes of the sequence remain mysterious, but that it is a limbo explains the presence not only of the statues, as witnesses and judges, but of the very image of death. Judith Sandiford appears with a cut-out paper skeleton affixed to her head, arms, and chest, her hands behind her ears, her face obscured by the Halloween-decor grin of the skeleton, against a backdrop of other, smaller skeletons. She begins to move her hands, and the image cuts to details of a foot in a Japanese illustration—what Lipsett refers to in his charts as "Buddha foot on lotus flower," a symbol of the placidity and serenity of the Buddha, whose foot spares by its grace the force that through the green fuse drives the flower.[28] Sandiford's skeleton dance is interspersed with various images: a blank notice board; an inflated lifeboat stood upright in front of a shop; a perfectly formed water droplet as it courses across a clear surface.

At the Zemel home, an elderly woman enters the parlour with a tray of tea. Her arrival is interrupted by a portrait photograph of Mao Zedong, which slowly pulls out to show the Chinese chairman with his hand raised in a wave. Tea is poured. It becomes a strange joke, this aging Jewish family whose teatime has become crowded with suggestions of East Asian rituals and images of Chinese secular leadership. Lipsett's gallows humour is made all the more potent by Mao's position as the central persecutor of Tibetan Buddhists. John Max paces, chanting and spinning his fingers in mid-air. Lipsett, in bed, turns his portable light on and off against a grid cabinet, a literal illustration of his secret museum of "separate little boxes." The third reel, more than anywhere else in the film, serves as an exploration of this aspect of Lipsett's collecting, one that is less concerned with symbolic interrelations than it is with sheer abundance. Further to this are his attempts at staging ritual scenes, which at once appear an earnest investment in the aesthetics of prayer—its contemplation and repetitions—and acts of witty substitution. The dollar-store skeleton decoration is enhanced as it becomes a strange costume, returning this Western consumer-culture symbol to the station of a corporeal absolute. The East Asian statues, too, find a Western correlative in the figure of John Max, whose pacing and hand gestures are acts of communion with the fragmented reality of Lipsett's montage and with the sounds of distant, foreign worship. He becomes the Buddha.

The fourth reel focuses this ritual energy on the floral armchair. Zemel is seated in it, a black pendant strapped around his head. He begins to place objects underneath it, using himself as the living base of an assemblage: first a carrot, then a pine branch. He holds a folding rack in front of his face and places a black feathered brush in his mouth, laughing and taking a drag on his cigarette as he does so. His performance is made comic not only by the ridiculous gesture of building a collage atop a laughing face, but by the resulting balancing act, the careful positioning of these elements, held in place by the tenuous grip of the pendant's strap. A ball of foil, seen in close-up, rotates. It becomes a cosmic object, suggesting the rotations of planets even as it draws and shapes the light that strikes it. The tea ceremony continues, as does the skeletal dance. A photograph of a paper skeleton in a shop window faces out at storm clouds, and the reverse shot is of a dark liquid in a pot with shimmering, granular particles on its surface, a witch's brew; in a subsequent shot, vapours rise from it. This dissolves to a close-up of the mask of the skeleton costume. Lipsett sits in the chair with a crystal held to his head, his eyes wide with intensity. In an illustration, a silhouette stands under a chrome band, an image that suggests the teleportation of science fiction. Throughout, still images of empty rooms with bare walls recall the futility of the blank notice board. From his armchair, Lipsett lights a candle on a cutting board, then raises it onto his head. Zemel stares out from the same chair, equipped with his black pendant, at a supernova as it forms; the supernova is intercut with the pendant, as if it is being summoned. Zemel puts his cigarette out in the black pendant, thumbing his nose at eternity. Lipsett holds a toy propeller to his forehead, staring out with a deadpan expression. A series of death masks lined up in a row appears under glass in a museum. In contrast to the neutrality of Lipsett's deadpan countenance, the death masks are contorted in agony. The performances of Lipsett and Zemel explore two ways of getting "out of your head": Zemel becomes the defiant conductor of universal energies, while Lipsett's props—the crystal, the candle, the propeller—suggest an inward journey through the skull, new and futile means of trepanation.[29]

As a sustained chant sounds, Martin Lavut is shown with a paper bag on his head, a hole torn in it for his face. He is reflected in a mirror, holding a drawing of a rhinoceros. The rhinoceros imagery in the film, between this illustration and Marie's squirt-gun, is symbolically potent and particular to the time: the Parti Rhinocéros was a satirical political party started in Canada by Quebecois surrealist and physician Jacques Ferron in 1963.[30] Their credo was "a promise to keep none of our promises." They had been inspired by the election of a rhinoceros to the city council of São Paulo in 1958. Lavut even holds the same Albrecht Dürer woodcut that the party had chosen as its symbol. Any search for political affiliation in Lipsett's films is likely to align him with the liberal humanism of the Film Board, but this citation to the Parti Rhinocéros might be taken as a truer reflection of his values, prizing, as they did, the surreal and the absurd as ethical signposts. For the Parti Rhinocéros, wordplay and ironies were a potent defence against the reduction, factionalism, and moralizing of mainstream politics. At the same time, Lavut's madcap costume, the general sarcasm of *N-Zone*,

Lipsett's embrace of ambiguities, and the Parti Rhinocéros's own eager, inbuilt frivolity complicate the earnestness of this endorsement.[31]

Lavut's paper-bag candidate is interspersed along with images of x-ray cinematography. The surrogate skeleton—Sandiford in a paper costume—has given way to an actual moving skeleton, seen in fragments, its wrist bending, its jaw opening, closing, and, later, chewing a candy bar. In his diagram, Lipsett indicates that the x-ray represents a "ferryman to the spiritual shore," but while this suggestion implies a degree of sober and severe thematizing, the presence of the candy bar subverts this.[32] The skeleton is no longer an image of death, the Western Halloween decoration weighing judgment on the Bardo Plane; it is a living and present thing, as ridiculous in its corporeality as any viewer. As it devours the candy bar, it recalls an earlier image, of Lavut chewing on his plastic cricket, the curious appetites of 1969. Lipsett, in his bedroom, runs his portable light over a photograph of monks and a tchotchke of a preserved lizard; John Max, against a black backdrop, drinks tea and holds his free hand up, in the same pose as Chairman Mao, which is also, ironically, the Buddha's gesture of peace.

The image of an ornamental throne under glass is the first of a series of still images that suggest stations and figures of judgment: grotesque masks, scenes from a botanical garden, and discarded viewing chairs in the Oka National Park culminate in a newsreel scene of a line of camels being led through a desert. In his assembly chart, Lipsett describes this shot as a representation of "reaching the other shore," situating his montage in the narrative of a journey through the afterlife, a passage across the Bardo. The camels are intercut with scenes of the Zemels drinking tea, of the lone man crawling in the desert, and of a rotating striped pole, an image that Lipsett describes as "generating all yin yang energy."[33] The reel ends in the Zemel home, lingering on an empty teacup. Lipsett's use of the striped pole is, like his line of camels, an allusion to the energy force that had become explicit in his aesthetic philosophy from *21-87* onward; in his notes, these energies assume a distinctively Taoist dichotomy. When Henry Zemel balanced objects under his black pendant, the balancing act itself became a source of humour; the striped pole is a reminder that the balance of energies that lies at the core of Lipsett's film—of yin and yang, light and dark, positive and negative—is also a source of humour. Where yin and yang represent natural dualities, Lipsett draws in scenes from a world of plenitude, overstuffed with meaning.

Two scientists pass through a gate that bears a sign warning of radiation. Charney and Zemel prepare to play a game of Wei-chi (Go)—another image of yin and yang. Their discussion of the rules of the game synchronizes to the images of the two scientists as they carry on an unheard discussion of plant life in this forbidden zone. Zemel's explanation of the rules of Wei-chi gives way to another of the film's orientalist declarations: a recording of *The Red Lantern* with piano accompaniment, itself an important work in the reconciliation between Chinese and Western aesthetics. For this recording, premiered in July 1968, a major work of the Peking Opera is performed with a Western piano, an object long held by the leaders of the cultural revolution to be a symbol of Western decadence. The pianist, Yin Cheng-Tsung, explained his use of the piano as a kind of tank storming the fortress of Peking Opera on behalf of workers, peasants, and soldiers.[34] The result is a rapturous assimilation of East and West at a time when diplomacy between China and Western nations remained closed, anticipating the cooling period of the early 1970s. As the recording plays, a series of still images is shown: a Chinese photographer; a close-up on the tread of tires; Mao Zedong; a group of Chinese and Russian officials sitting around a table with teacups. A close-up on Mao's face dissolves to an advertisement for an armchair, a play on Mao Zedong's title of Chairman. The triumphant melody of the recording accompanies scenes of a zebra being led through a pasture, an echo of the striped pole, of yin and yang. The ruins of a massive row of ancient Egyptian statues, three of them missing their heads, gives way to an image of Lipsett playing his flute. As the music crescendos, the line of camels appears again.

The sequence restarts, this time with sync sound as the scientists open the gate. As they crouch to investigate, the image cuts to Israel Charney being interrogated by Lipsett about what word he's thinking of. Lipsett gives him the word "eggs," and the sequence is intercut with an egg held in place and eggs shattering on a black surface. The sounds of farm animals run under images of Charney thinking. He is too high to play word-association games with ease, and as he squirms, laughs, and jokes with Lipsett and Zemel, he offers spontaneous aphorisms and validations in response; despite his protests, he is playing the game anyway. Lipsett asks, "Do dreams come true?" Charney grins and responds "never," erupting into fits of laughter.

Zemel rearranges the cut-out letters, changing "z-none" to "n-zone." This is intercut with images of Zemel's family—his father on a lawn with a wheelbarrow full of bricks, his father-in-law and other relations gathered around the dining table looking through photo albums. Throughout, the sound of a fly is heard. Lipsett and another man, identified in his notes as Bob Merz, walk in the woods. Merz catches a fly, which is shown moving along his thumb in close-up. Lipsett is seen in various angles, a cover of leaves high above him, his hands forming mudras as he laughs. Like the moveable type that Zemel rearranges, Lipsett poses for a camera that is alternately upright and turned on its side at a ninety-degree angle, caught in the transition between N and Z. Zemel demonstrates what Lipsett refers to in his notes as "the three stages of pointing": a declarative upward-and-forward aim, an accusatory forward aim, and directly up, next to the face, as if in sudden realization. The phenomenal catalogue of Arthur Lipsett's earlier films, from the exhausted faces of *Very Nice, Very Nice* to the historical oddities of *A Trip Down Memory Lane*, are met here with a gestural catalogue, an account of variations, of mudras and finger-pointing, joined to subjects that command attention: the communion between a man and a fly, the social bond of the family photo album.

A bearded Black man with a trace of a Caribbean accent, identified in Lipsett's notes as Mcloud, sits cross-legged on the floor opposite Lipsett, the two preparing for meditation. Mcloud tells Lipsett, "you must concentrate on what you are doing to get the full benefit of the exercises," direct instruction that obliquely comments on Lipsett's own editorial disruptions. As Mcloud speaks, Lipsett turns away, distracted, to address someone else in the room, another comic subversion. A cut finds Lipsett back in the armchair, miming concentration, attempting to get the "full benefit" of the exercise. At the trigger of a percussive sound, he holds a portable electric fan to his head. The determination in Lipsett's deadpan expression amplifies the absurdity of this exercise, as do the severe images that follow it, of monkey skulls and grotesque Tibetan masks; ice crystals forming against a granular black base that suggests a universe of starlight; and a still image of a sculpture of a priest, laid out horizontally as if for a wake, almost certainly a recumbent effigy. In his notes, Lipsett describes this effigy—the sculpted priest, his arms folded in death, his eyes open without pupils—as the film's entrance to the netherworld. The netherworld suggests states of transition: a triangular bacterium, growing in size; a skull with a crack in its forehead, evidence of trepanation; and a human embryo mounted on a display stand. A television set is tuned "between channels," and its distorted images feature a man and a ghostly figure; a baseball game; and scenes of dancers and musicians, evoking *American Bandstand*. The common encounters of dial flipping are abstracted by this un-tuning, but the legible details suggest transformation, myth, and competition.

These distorted broadcasts are intercut with a catfish and medical diagrams of skulls, peeled open from above and from behind, held apart with forceps, another variation on the trepanned skull. A centipede courses along the earth and a close-up of the sculpture's face emphasizes its blank eyes. In a parallel to the centipede, elephants are assembled in a procession, a consonance between the great and the small that recalls Lipsett's interest in relations between scales of being, or, "reality levels." This parallels Lipsett's exploration of the microcosm of experience represented by his immediate social circle, as well as its resonance with the macrocosm of a turbulent world. The netherworld is drowned in Tibetan chanting, a deep, guttural undulation, a sound that represents a final transit to a new plane, an interplay of voices and bells so spare and, to some Western ears, menacing, that it could readily signal the presence and ultimate transcendence of death.

The climactic reel introduces a new couple, identified in Lipsett's notes as "Zav and wife." They lay in bed, Zav smoking a pipe, his wife waving a hand fan. They speak to the cameraman, asking about mutual friends, another mundane conversation that alludes to a dispersed network of urban Jewish bohemians. In the Arctic, a group of men prepares weather balloons, while on the soundtrack, a recording from a CBC TV travelogue series, *How Do You Say Hello*, finds the host in an African village listening to melodious reed music played by villagers on—the host observes in amazement—tiny pieces of hollow bamboo.[35] Lipsett, offscreen, points to medical imagery among his wall collages, creating parallels between the breast-like appearance of the weather balloons and the breast-like appearance of a diagram of a contact lens, an illustration Lipsett refers to in his own notes as a "breast diagram."

The men from the Ride-a-Roo-Kangaroo silently confer about the toy, another exaggerated stand-in for a sex organ, like a breast or a swollen testicle. The Zemels continue their gathering, showing their photo albums to the camera. Back at the bohemian party, wind-up toy sharks move in circles in the shallow waters of a bathtub, as Charney and friends try and fail to push Zemel in. As the conversation with Zav continues, an offscreen speaker, Lipsett or Zemel, cheerfully offers that "everybody's innocent till they're caught."

This will prove to be the final synchronous dialogue in the film, as the soundtrack turns back to *The Red Lantern with Piano Accompaniment*, a particularly rapturous section of it, as voice and piano hit notes in unison. The film mirrors this rapture, in a montage that speaks to the relation between collective and solitary action: Zemel's father peels an apple and eats it from the tip of a knife; Zemel plays with a necklace, a tin heart spinning on its end; Zav's wife whispers to him while he fans her; and, finally, Lipsett himself appears at the Zemel family gathering, drinking from a glass of water as Zemel's father smiles up at him and the camera. Zemel's father resumes stabbing into the chopped pieces of apple and bringing them to his mouth, a gesture that is repeated as the faces around him smile and laugh joyously. A still of Lavut, in his paper-bag hat, smiles to the camera; in his notes, Lipsett describes this outfit as "Chagal Jew," a possible reference to Marc Chagall's 1937 painting *The Praying Jew (Rabbi of Vitebsk)*, in which a hooded figure sits in contemplation, a posture of piety to make an ironic contrast out of Lavut's wide grin. In a final image of Zemel's father, the camera seems to wrap around him, turning at a ninety-degree angle, mirroring the free orientation of N and Z throughout. In his notes, Lipsett describes this shooting style as "no more gravity, no up, no down."[36]

Throughout the evolution of Arthur Lipsett's filmmaking, he consistently attended to flexible, progressive ideas of continuity. Kracauer's theory surrounding the revelatory function of continuity, those acts that expose the "blind spots of the mind," remains embedded in Lipsett's work, both in a utilitarian sense (the centipede, the scientific photography) and in a mystical sense (the resonance of flow among images). Lipsett's "flow" trounced the potential for metaphor to editorialize and close meaning; his punctuating images—of totems, striking expressions, and comical oddities—often embody both ready and complex metaphors. In his earlier films, this had made it possible for an audience to walk away with a false sense of comprehension. For them, *Very Nice, Very Nice* was about consumerism and *21-87* was about faith under fire. These are not untrue, but they are reductive conclusions about what Lipsett achieved, for his formal approach, paired with his sense of the ridiculous and his playful humour, unwound the predetermined theses that the NFB expected of their films and gave his work a wild absurdity. By the time he had made *N-Zone*, Lipsett had an internalized concept of continuity, one that would allow him to draw from long, sync takes, knowing that those scenes of stoned laughter and humdrum chatter, like the dancing piano rags of Crazy Otto, had their own rhythms and gave further definition to the stiffness of the straight world. *N-Zone* is proof of Lipsett's interest in the open attitude towards cinematic continuity that was articulated by Robert Breer in *The Experimental Film*, as a search for new kinds of continuity. That search, undertaken by makers of underground movies, was defiant to the logic-focused approach that, proven effective, had left convention-bound cinema in a state of arrested development, doomed to patronize and underestimate its audience. Lipsett's philosophy of continuity was offered on tape, in the form of an endlessly encircling deadpan double-talk monologue. Before devolving into comic, 'pataphysical nonsense and repetition, Lipsett offers this glimpse of the wellspring of a new continuity: "Endless, endless, endless. Endless numbers of streams, continuities everywhere. Streams number continuities and continuities are everywhere. Are these continuities straight lines, or are they circular?"[37]

The process of making *N-Zone* found Lipsett exploring the greatest comic heights of his absurdity, and his loose-leaf notebooks attest to this. In his notebooks, treasured Chinese wisdom of Laozi ("great perfection should be like a cracked vase which lets all of its contents escape") kept company with its stereotypical, punchy Hollywood shadow, Charlie Chan ("mind, like parachute, function best when open"), sentiments that come together in the mordant comedy of a trepanned skull.[38] Text for potential stentorian narration and title cards suggest an overtly comic tone that mirrors the language of advertising and instructional media: "now here it is in slow motion," "need help getting up?", "how to tie up a brown paper parcel," "what to do with a piece of paper," "how to blow over a brick," "many uses for concrete," "more uses for concrete," and "how to use chopsticks."[39] Other notes are pitched between mysticism and the mundane: "100 uses for the elastic band" and "100 miles of strange continuous footprints."[40] Quotations from Zemel are littered throughout—for example, "without reading the instructions you're in trouble."[41] Lipsett's process pivoted between rhetorical questions and a fortune-cookie consciousness, with non sequitur asides throughout: "his interest in life would seem to be elbows."[42] A ponderous, open note ("the movement of things") is met by mundane instruction ("turn on 2-way radios at this point"), which, next to educational how-to titles and facile, self-fulfilling questions, declares a grinning dedication to futility. The final film does not contain any of these statements.

Despite the party atmosphere, *N-Zone* marks a shift for Lipsett, less joyous and raucous than his earlier films. Largely absent are the winking ironies of *Fluxes*, and in their place are strange rituals from an artist with an unyielding poker face, the last straight man in a gallery of stoned mugging and vocalizing. Lipsett himself described the bohemians, without judgment, as drifting into "mindlessness" in his reel assembly chart, a mindless freedom in which he himself could become a love drug.[43] When Colin Low saw rushes from these sequences, he reprimanded Lipsett, telling him it was "just dumb stuff" and that the Film Board ought to fire him. "I think it wounded him badly," a remorseful Low later admitted.[44] After all, it was Low who had hired Lipsett, topping his judgment with the added ammunition of lost confidence and regret. Low's remarks might be interpreted as a sign of how square the NFB was, but they also demonstrate the superficial engagement of Lipsett's colleagues. That Lipsett was pursuing something thematically complex in these scenes did not matter to Low, who understood images within a system of clarity of statement, self-assured rhetoric and simple metaphor: it is these qualities that made Low's film *Corral* (1954) so aesthetically and ideologically successful. When Low saw Lipsett's footage, he took it as mere endorsement of a lifestyle he found objectionable. For Low, this was also a sign that the esteem in which Lipsett was held by some had protected him from critique and that being sheltered from critique had inflated his work. It may have appeared that way to Low, himself among the most cherished sons of the institution, but Lipsett's conflicts with his colleagues tell a different story, suggesting he was patronized and tolerated until their contempt for abstract thought became stifling.

Lipsett's intention to leave the NFB was no secret within the institution. Terry Ryan announced Arthur Lipsett's resignation in an article for *Artscanada*, noting that "on a short-term extension of his contract he is finishing his last film."[45] Both trepidation and optimism followed, a suspicion that life outside of the safety of the institution would be hard, but that it might also represent a necessary freedom for a man who had been constricted by the nature of government work. Lipsett's greatest challenge at the Film Board had been in being made answerable for his natural instincts, in having to write statements that encumbered his films with planned utility and social significance. His films had flourished not because of this structure, but despite it. His struggle with these aspects of the work, and even more so under the pool system, was a strain even without the burden of uninvited professional rivalries and having his accomplishments run down by malicious rumours. While Terry Ryan was not skeptical about Lipsett's future, he admitted in his article, "when [Lipsett] leaves the Film Board, it will be either for a radically different environment or for a radically different way of interacting with the environment."[46]

In anticipation of the film's release, Henry Zemel put together a short article for *Artscanada*, titled "N-Zone Continued." It wouldn't appear until the following summer. Zemel's text is discontinuous, but the bulk of it is formed around Lipsett's conception of the grid, presenting that template, so dominant in the secret museum, as a formal rationale for his editing style. The article also assumed the form of a collage in itself, weaving imagery from the film with behind-the-scenes production stills and diagrams, interspersed with pithy, sexist jokes offered as non-sequiturs (from a "campaign to market paper lingerie— RIP IT OFF" to an unnamed speaker declaring that "a woman has a prerogative to die if she wants to").[47] That these remarks are eerily similar to the casual misogyny found in the writings of Zemel's friend Leonard Cohen is no coincidence; Zemel's text was not a contextualization but an attempt to break from the meditative, tragicomic, apocalyptic aura of Lipsett's film. To his credit, Zemel made other efforts to support Lipsett's work, putting together a retrospective of Lipsett's films at the National Gallery of Canada in Ottawa, entitled "Zebras and Crosswalks: The Films of Arthur Lipsett." The event served as a premiere for *N-Zone*, at which Zemel attempted to present a serious critical framework for interpreting Lipsett's films.[48] The NFB had made no such efforts to mark the passing of Lipsett's tenure. Regardless, Zemel's article is offered less in praise of Lipsett than it is an assertion of Zemel's authorial voice, sprinkled with counterculture affectations, captioning the image of a preserved embryo "SPACE FASCISTS" and closing with his cherished expression "THE TRIANGLE IS UPON US."[49] The exchange between the men is a story of two hysterias: the humanistic urgency of Lipsett and the aphoristic declarations of Zemel. "*N-Zone* Continued" illustrates the divide between Lipsett's cool beatnik and Zemel's controversial hippie.

The social aspect of *N-Zone* did not pass without acknowledgement. On its release, the NFB announced *N-Zone* as "a surrealist sampler of the human condition."[50] Acknowledging it as a self-portrait, the announcement continues, "In *N-Zone* the film-maker himself also emerges for the first time. He is seen with his friends and contemporaries and with his elders. But, like the *objets trouvés* of his films, Lipsett's people also form their own metaphors. They too are in the *N-Zone*, awaiting the final move."[51] While the Film Board's publicity had consistently suggested that Lipsett's films were sardonic treatments of a despairing human condition, regarded at a distance, here they note the agency of "Lipsett's people," whose presence, statements, conflicts, and play support an anastomotic structure, their tributaries flowing together with newsreel memories, decontextualized Chinese propaganda, religious idols, and other discreetly observed details of ritual, both quotidian and rapturous, in crossing the n-zone.

As Lipsett was working on *N-Zone*, he was assigned to collaborate with Josef Reeve again, this time on *North* (1969), a sponsored film made for the Canadian Department of Indian Affairs and Northern Development, to demonstrate the vastness and diversity of northern Canada. The film mixes observational material of northern villages with imagery that takes advantage of the NFB's then-recent fixation on aerial photography, following on Eugene Boyko's epic, celebratory *Helicopter Canada* (1966), a tour of the Canadian landscape from above. As Boyko had done, Reeve attempts to characterize the diversity of Canadian society through the gliding triumphalism of aerial photography, exploiting the natural beauty of the landscape. The result is a tribute to the Griersonian model of the poetic documentary, machined for impact. Like many films that followed late in that ossifying model, its only morality is optimism, and, like *Imperial Sunset*, it asked little of Lipsett's creative discipline. According to Mark Slade, Lipsett's work was thankless and uncreative, meticulously cutting flies out of the footage at the request of Northern Development. "They didn't want bugs to appear in the film, they knew people weren't attracted to black flies," Slade recalled. "For months Arthur literally had to edit out the flies that appeared in the image."[52]

To be set to such tasks while plagued in the dust of rumours and facing persistent obstacles to his own filmmaking would prove to be the last straw for him. Even before he gave notice to Frank Spiller of his intended departure from the Film Board, Arthur Lipsett and Judith Sandiford were planning for a different future.

# NINE

# MESSAGES FROM SPACE

I N 1969, AS ARTHUR LIPSETT WAS IN THE MIDST OF EDITING *N-Zone*, he began to experience a period of unprecedented anxiety. Judith Sandiford, with whom he had been living on and off for years, had moved out of their Coronet Street apartment in order to be closer to the school where she was teaching. Lipsett came to the boarding house where Sandiford was renting a room and told her that he had to leave Montreal. He disclosed to her then that he was beginning to feel emotionally and mentally unwell, an admission of illness that foreshadowed the struggles he would face for the remainder of his life. The two of them devised a plan to take a trip to England, a move that they hoped might be permanent. Before that was possible, he had to finish *N-Zone*. Lipsett ended his lease on Coronet, packing up the contents of his apartment into trunks and placing them in a storage facility in Montreal. He moved into a room in Sandiford's building, at 37–39 Chesterfield Avenue in Lower Westmount. With her support and the structure that she provided to his days, he was able to find the strength to complete the film. Lipsett maintained his preferred nocturnal schedule: he would go to the NFB overnight to edit and would return every morning, sharing Sandiford's breakfast as his dinner. *N-Zone* was submitted to Tom Daly, but Lipsett did not wait to see a release print. His fatigue and anxiety were too urgent. The couple travelled to England on July 12, 1970, cashing in Lipsett's pension and packing a year's worth of clothes, intending on a long, and ideally permanent, trip.[1]

Lipsett would remain in contact with Tom Daly as the film was in its final stages. Daly wrote to inform him that the opticals were held because of warbling "as if seen through heat-vapour on a hot day."[2] The titles were also suffering from minor technical issues. The titles and opticals were reshot in Lipsett's absence, but Daly's letter assures that the work was done only to maintain his intentions. The fate of *N-Zone* didn't trouble Lipsett, but he was troubled by a growing awareness that his illness was worsening. As they toured the picturesque villages of Great Britain, he maintained his funny, charming exterior, and Sandiford was not able to recognize the degree to which he was struggling. He began to have bouts of quiet distress and grief. One morning in September, she returned to their lodgings and found him in their room crying uncontrollably. She took him to a doctor, who prescribed him Librium to cope with his anxiety. It did not help. What Lipsett was experiencing, they would only later come to learn, was the emergence of schizophrenia. They made the decision that he was not well enough for them to rebuild their life in a new country.

Lipsett and Sandiford returned home to Canada on October 14. Lipsett's breakdown had coincided with political unrest in the country: Prime Minister Pierre Trudeau had invoked the War Measures Act in response to the kidnapping and eventual murder of Deputy Premier Pierre Laporte by the separatist group the Front de libération du Québec (FLQ). The October Crisis, as it would come to be known, was an unprecedented moment in Canadian history, a suspension of civil liberties that empowered police, bolstering their numbers with support from the military and allowing them to arrest and detain suspects at their discretion.[3] Over the course of eleven days prior to Trudeau's invocation of the War Measures Act on October 16, tensions were high; after, it made Quebec a place of extraordinary danger for vulnerable people. When Arthur Lipsett and Robert Verrall had been detained by the FBI on their road trip to Connecticut in the early 1960s, Lipsett's instinctive response was hysterical and comic, gleefully shouting to strangers that they were being arrested by government agents. In that moment, he had been tolerated; during the October Crisis, Lipsett's sense of humour could land a person in his condition into an unpredictable, hazardous situation. Lipsett and Sandiford could not return home and instead temporarily moved in with Martin Lavut and his partner Suki Falkner, who were living at 1384A Bathurst Street in Toronto's Wychwood neighbourhood. By mid-October, Lipsett had recovered enough to write to Daly with the news that they had returned to Canada and to request that a test print of *N-Zone* be sent to the NFB office in Toronto for him to review.[4] The couple settled in an apartment at 25 Slade Street, a small unit close to Lavut and Falkner's, behind the Christie streetcar barns. They would remain there until the spring of 1972.

In February 1971, Lipsett again wrote to Tom Daly, this time to ask whether there was a possibility of televising *Fluxes* and *N-Zone*. The request was motivated in part by his desire to see *Fluxes* exhibited in this format—he considered it a televisual work because of how he had sourced the sound—but it also demonstrates that he was hopeful that his films might be given a greater audience and circulation, as when the NFB packaged *Free Fall* and *A Trip Down Memory Lane* together in *Two Films by Lipsett*. The letter also offers a glimpse of how he spent his time in the aftermath of the crisis in England: "I've spent much of the last 3 months in Toronto reading books on ancient Egypt, Greece, Rome, etc, discovered a Sumerian king called Lipit-Ishtar, and also getting heavily into 20s-50s printed material. All these activities are directed at eventually doing some murals, probably in the countryside."[5] The NFB would decline to package or televise the films, but Lipsett's account of his activities suggest that, even as he was planning for a tranquil future, he was maintaining his curiosity and his sense of humour.

Lipsett's growing research collection, of paper materials and books, was a sign that he was regaining his strength, and in February 1972, he was able to make a trip to England and Wales on his own, to visit shops that specialized in books of arcana and esoteric knowledge. He would later describe the years following his departure from the NFB as a "period of research," but it also appears to have been a time of transition, as Lipsett contemplated what direction his art could move in, should he no longer make films.[6] The contents of the Coronet apartment, which he had packed away in trunks, needed to be unpacked for him to continue his work, and so the couple decided to rent a two-storey house at 38 Belsize, in North Toronto.[7] Sandiford had found work at the Toronto French School, a short drive from their new home, and the house was large enough to contain Lipsett's voluminous materials and collections. Judith Sandiford remembers, "There were rose gardens all around the house. There was a big living/dining room on the main floor. Upstairs were two bedrooms, and a sun porch. The sun porch was my space. The rest of the house was Arthur's."[8] By late spring 1972, they were settled there, with Lipsett converting the upstairs bedrooms into studios for his collages and research—but where he had sought tranquility, and where Sandiford hoped to provide it, the degree to which he was again deteriorating became undeniable.

Sandiford's earlier departures from their apartment on Coronet Street had been motivated by a variety of factors, but a persistent one had been the lack of space for her amidst Lipsett's stuff. Now that they had space to accommodate his materials, his needs became more complicated. Sandiford witnessed Lipsett's eccentricity, which until then had been harmless, as it assumed a new, destructive form. The moment that Sandiford points to as a turning point in their relationship was when Lipsett, for unknown reasons, destroyed a chair that had been important to him. When he had been living in austerity at the Clifton Arms, as his career was taking off, he had bought a valuable antique oak chair. He had been so proud of the purchase that it spurred him to upgrade his living conditions to the unit on Coronet. One morning in June 1973, Lipsett woke early and began sawing the chair into little pieces and making a package out of the pieces. This erratic and destructive energy led Sandiford to realize that their situation was becoming dangerous.[9]

Martin Lavut, now alerted to Lipsett's deteriorating mental health, consulted with doctors at the Clarke Institute of Psychiatry, later known as the Centre for Addiction and Mental Health (CAMH), a hospital for those experiencing and living with mental illness in Toronto's Little Italy. Their advice to him was, "you cannot force, but you can inform," and they gave Lavut a contact that Lipsett could reach out to if he was feeling unwell. In July, of his own volition, Lipsett took a cab to the Clarke Institute and had what would be the first of many hospitalizations. When he was released, he phoned Judith, claiming that the doctors said he had "made a miraculous recovery" and that they had wondered "why my wife had not come to visit."[10] Sandiford knew the unlikelihood of a miraculous recovery. Even the exaggerative connotations of "a miraculous recovery" show that Lipsett's absurd spirit could surface in even heartbreaking circumstances like the distance they now found themselves facing. With Lavut's help, Sandiford found an apartment of her own on College Street. She moved to Ottawa the following spring, where she would work on a community newspaper and continue to teach.

Without Sandiford, Lipsett found himself alone in the Belsize house. His behaviour was becoming more erratic. By one account, friends would visit to discover him mid-conversation with household appliances.[11] The line between Lipsett's absurdist sense of humour and his emerging madness was fraying. As an artist who had assembled experiences out of fragments, engaged in a continuous process of breaking and rebuilding, the nature of Lipsett's condition was doubly tragic: his humour, his intelligence, and his skills were all intact, but his puckish sense of misdirection was becoming indistinguishable from his delusions.

In the midst of all of this upheaval, Lipsett had been trying to change his art practice. He had regained a degree of the freedom he had surrendered when he first joined the National Film Board, the freedom he had had in his days at the School of Art and Design that had led him to sample a variety of forms, including sculpture and collage. From the time he was hired in 1959 to his departure in 1970, Lipsett had to shift his focus entirely to filmmaking. His newfound autonomy allowed him to entertain other ideas—chiefly, the making of large collages, which Lipsett referred to as murals and which seemed at times to follow the lineage of photomontage, while at other times to serve as an extension of the flowcharts he had called his secret museum. In April 1969, prior to his resignation from the NFB, Lipsett began to inquire about the possibility of assistance through the Canada Council for the Arts.[12] The advice he was met with was not what he had hoped for: because his history of exhibition was in cinema, the Canada Council encouraged him to continue to apply for grants to support his filmmaking. Lipsett's first arts council grant was as a filmmaker, a short-term grant in support of his research and costs of living, awarded in 1970–71.[13] For the next round of awards, in 1971–72, he would serve on their cinema and photography juries for both awards and bursaries and would receive another short-term grant, this time for visual arts.[14] In this period, he was seeking advice from John Max and others in the visual arts about the types of paper and glue he should be using in his collages, a sign that he was making serious efforts to move away from filmmaking.[15]

The clearest sense of what he intended is given in an undated document, circa the early 1970s, titled "Composition Notes," in which Lipsett describes "chakra-murals," murals with a mandala or chakra in their centre and "equally radiating lines of activity," conceived as two-dimensional constructs of paper collage on plywood.[16] Both the mandala—a geometric, graphic, symbolic space—and the chakra—physical focal points in the body or, alternately, visions in meditation—are concepts inherited from Hinduism and Buddhism, an extension of his Eastern fascinations. These notes are not only a record of Lipsett's ambitions as an artist, but a record of the degree to which New Age and occult fascinations—Omnist preoccupations with "Eastern wisdom"—had persisted in his thought after the pantheistic tour of *Fluxes* and the Bardo journey of *N-Zone*. Lipsett's notes anticipate the direction his New Age interests would take—that is, that his chakra-murals should be "elevating and curative" and that the form should be principally instructive.[17] His interest in chakras show a growing concern with managing the circulation of energies within the body, a further internalization of the flowlines and arcs that had shaped his films. The document describes his murals in relation to borders, clippings, and graphic forms (squares, step pyramids, rings formed from blocks), all of which readily suggest two-dimensional, static composition; however, the language in the document bears a filmmaker's shorthand, marked with contractions for "medium-long-shot" ("MLS") and "close-up" ("CU").[18] This is, like his exchanges with John Cage, a sign that the influence of his time at the NFB might hinder his more general ambitions as an artist. It is also a declaration of the dominance of cinematic thinking in his work such that, even when he attempted to reposition himself into new territory with these collages, Lipsett's conceptualization remained essentially cinematic.

As his plans for these collages stalled, Lipsett began to maintain a notebook of ideas for a new film, one that would not use found footage at all but would instead take the form of a strange performance. The new film would have among its working titles *The Occult Wars*, under which title Lipsett described it as "a film like a big coo-coo [sic] clock with many doors," and, as it developed, another prominent title would emerge: *Strange Codes from Space (or, Messages from the Future)*.[19] *Strange Codes*, as it would come to be called, marked the culmination of a number of ideas that had come to interest Lipsett from literature and theatre during his sabbatical from filmmaking. Lipsett's inspirations speak to his own self-definition as a thinker following in a bevy of footsteps: he cites Heinrich Schliemann, the visionary but amateur archeologist whose discovery of the ancient city of Troy was accomplished only by penetrating and destroying many layers of the city; he cites Raymond Roussel's *Impressions of Africa* (1910), the armchair fantasy of a mad poet; he cites Arthur Rimbaud, having long since adopted the title of *A Season in Hell* (1873) as a cheerful adage, here inspired by Rimbaud's claim, "I became a fabulous opera: I saw that everyone in the world was doomed to happiness."[20] Lipsett, too, was becoming a fabulous opera. Of novels, Lipsett cites Laurence Sterne's *Tristram Shandy* (1759), Terry Southern's *The Magic Christian* (1959), and Hermann Hesse's *Steppenwolf* (1927); in short, his notebooks make reference to some of the great comic absurdities in Western culture from the eighteenth century to the twentieth.[21] Of all of his sources, one that he dwells upon is *Steppenwolf*. Lipsett was preoccupied with Hesse's Magic Theatre, a site of phantasmal projection for those in search of epiphany, a metaphor for the life cycle, for the masks that the individual wears in society, and for the human condition.

*Steppenwolf* is self-reflexive, presented as a manuscript within a manuscript and featuring therein further digressions. Its protagonist, Harry Haller, is one of twentieth-century literature's great outsiders, a middle-aged man who has borne witness to the absurdities of bourgeois indulgence and who occupies a troubled existence. Haller encounters the Magic Theatre in a pamphlet, which addresses him directly by name and tells him that his suicide is inevitable. Whether the Magic Theatre is symbolic or literal is unknown and increasingly irrelevant: Haller's search for the theatre leads him first to a dance hall and later to a true manifestation of the Magic Theatre, in which five doors separate fractions of the user's life. Hesse's novel dealt with the division and compartmentalization of self; the climax makes these divisions both physical and spiritual. Like many of Hesse's readers living in the widening gyre of twentieth-century disillusionment, Arthur Lipsett could readily identify with Harry Haller: Lipsett was, after all, an outsider who was, if not tormented by, at least highly aware of the ironies and hypocrisies of the society in which he lived. Hesse's Magic Theatre gave Lipsett another example to draw from of the anastomotic pathways of the universe—in this case, the various tributaries that flow into the whole individual, those doors that open onto transcendent interior realities. In extending the metaphoric function of the Magic Theatre, Lipsett writes of the mind as containing two rooms, an "order room" and a "chaos room," a distinction of faculties that bonds his intentions to several concurrent threads—the surreal, the absurd, the existential—a division between logic and instinct.[22] In this conception of the division of the self, Lipsett is again engaging a favourite theme of his: that of paired opposites.

As Lipsett developed his project, the role of magic—of good and evil reflected in white-and-black magic—assumed a prominent place in his notes. He described what he was doing as magic—specifically, a form of "psychical defense" magic.[23] Lipsett was not naive, nor is this a product of his illness; it was a complex metaphor that sobered up the comedy of his filmmaking. Where some in his audience had seen sardonicism or even cynicism, his rhythms, his juxtapositions, his dial tuning of sound and image might instead be good magic, protective spells, psychic defences against the soul murder of contemporary life. Lipsett's conception of psychic defence was also tied to other symbols—for instance, the decidedly practical Incan quipu, a string-based record-keeping system that could chronicle the calendars, debts, and other forms of data of an entire civilization, an arch-symbol of encoded knowledge, and, like John Sparks's Histomaps, a grand act of condensing the scale of information. In Lipsett's poetics, these values—magic, psyche, memory aids, and encoded knowledge—had become inextricable from one another. He had written to L.M. Kit Carson that, when he had made *21-87*, his sense of continuity involved a search for "the larger multi-reality situation [of] collective consciousness (or unconsciousness) of a civilization."[24] In planning *Strange Codes*, he found suggestions of that multi-reality in this relic of an ancient, codified system.

Lipsett also took inspiration from self-reflexive twentieth-century theatre, noting his contemporary Peter Brook, most strongly associated with the Royal Shakespeare Company but best known in North

America at the time for his production of Peter Weiss's controversial Brechtian play *Marat/Sade* (1963). In Weiss's play, the inmates of the Charenton Asylum, led by the Marquis de Sade, stage a performance of a play about the Revolution culminating in the assassination of Jean-Paul Marat. That this leads to prescient insights on the nature of revolution, theatre, and violence was less a recognizable influence on Lipsett's plans than the self-conscious novelty of actors playing characters who must become actors to play characters. The Bavarian clown Karl Valentin, best known for his influence on Weimar culture, is linked in Lipsett's notes to a "Theatre of the Unconscious," which is at once a concept from the writings of Sigmund Freud (on mental projection) and a parodic riff on the confrontational and metatextual inferences found in the theories of Bertolt Brecht (epic theatre) and Antonin Artaud (the theatre of cruelty).[25] Lipsett's "Theatre of the Unconscious" is more comic slogan than fully realized dramatic theory, suggesting at once the nocturnal operations of the mind and the absurd image of a theatre where both actors and audience are out cold.

When Lipsett was initially structuring *21-87*, he wrote of the "shock-state" into which the viewer entered and which they "must grapple with, continuously counter-check and question."[26] The shock-state, as he had conceived it, was a sudden elevation of anxiety in the spectator to provoke reflection. In Lipsett's plans for *Strange Codes*, he writes of "reality-slaps," a concept upon which he does not elaborate but which suggests an echo of the shock-state: to "slap" the audience in his Theatre of the Unconscious is to awaken them to new knowledge and new systems. Such reality-slaps existed in theatre and cinema in a breaking of the fourth wall, an invitation into the maker's confidence; in literature, such a "reality-slap" might take the form of self-reflexive awareness of the nature of texts, intertextual dependence, and the curious inheritances of language and communication systems. These "sudden reality-slaps" would serve to "position preceding phenomena"; like the shock-state, these reality-slaps were moments that forced the spectator into a state of self-interrogation.[27]

All of these influences take root in Lipsett's plans for *Strange Codes*, but he was also committed to occult and surreal processes, the unconscious associations that could emerge through automatic writing. On one page, in bright red marker, Lipsett writes, "messages from space."[28]

For Lipsett, making art was a subconscious process; this is why his flowcharts were, at least initially, born of a necessity that bordered on resentment when his superiors at the Film Board expected him to explain his work before it was even made. The process of making the work was an operation between the conscious and unconscious mind. At the NFB, his audience had been practical makers who saw their collective work as a combination of rational, logical continuity, visual storytelling, and governmental problem-solving. Lipsett came to them as a riddle, because his process was a gathering of elements that would inevitably surrender their arrangement to instinct. Lipsett's rhythmic digestion of images, achieved through editing, was a process he could rationalize after the fact but could hardly anticipate. His method, like the automatic processes of the Surrealists, was a revelation of soul and psyche.

In mid-1974, when Lipsett applied to the Canada Council for project funding to make this new film, he described the project as "psychic travels around the world investigating telepathic communication."[29] He would undertake these psychic travels "using the imagination, paper-image material, sounds, props, painted backdrops, constructed sets and kinetics, to conjure up moments in time."[30] In his notebooks, Lipsett writes of his pursuit of a code, but he specifies it as a "universal code," one that, like Surrealist automatism, could "pull-in" messages from beyond ordinary reality, a suggestion of divine sources, a spirit realm.[31] In this aspect, Lipsett's complex sourcebook departs from aesthetic inspiration and fixes itself into an occult territory, as he had previously explored, through layers of ironic formal commentary, in *Fluxes* and *N-Zone*. He would come to see *Strange Codes* as a "spirit theatre in miniature," a work that was obliquely instructive and that followed in the path of occult techniques, of which he gives the examples of automatic writing, planchette pointing (Ouija board), and a dowsing pendulum.[32] In his application to the Canada Council, Lipsett described these techniques as a means "to make contact with the forces that made men and events move."[33]

After Judith Sandiford had left the Belsize house, Lipsett invited Henry Zemel to collaborate as a cameraman on his new film. The men had stayed in touch: Henry Zemel would frequently send Lipsett and Sandiford postcards after their return from England. The postcards chart his journeys through the southwestern United States, with stays in California and Arizona, and later begin issuing from other metropolitan cities where he had set up to work on projects: London, New York, Montreal. Lipsett was himself an accomplished cinematographer, far more so than Zemel: his work on *21-87* and *Free Fall* indicate a distinctive style that had synthesized direct cinema with the abstraction of the New American Cinema. What he needed Zemel to fulfill was less a creative partnership and more a utilitarian task: Lipsett needed a camera operator because, this time, he would be appearing on screen throughout.

"At the present time I am working on ideas relating to Psychic Defense and will make sure of them in structuring the film," Lipsett explained to the Canada Council, "I will be constructing, shooting and editing the film from June 1st to November 30."[34] As supplemental material, he included a print of *Fluxes*, along with effusive letters of support from Tom Daly, Norman McLaren, and Robert Verrall, his colleagues from the National Film Board. His application was successful, and he would receive the funding in two payments—a new, transactional exchange for Lipsett after years of being salaried to make his films. The first payment came in July 1974, and on September 24, Lipsett reached out to Canada Council officer Penni Jacques to request the remainder of his grant, which he received the following week. By that time, shooting had been completed. The final print was delivered to the Canada Council on November 20; at that time, Lipsett was still negotiating music rights, but regardless of whether that was resolved, the film would remain unchanged. In a show of supreme conscientiousness, he would write them with his final budget and return a cheque for the difference, a sign of his careful accounting held over from his years as a civil servant.[35] The Canada Council was satisfied with the film, but in a letter of congratulations, Jacques warmly admitted some bewilderment. "I must say," she writes, "I feel it goes beyond me."[36]

*Strange Codes* takes place in Lipsett's rented house on Belsize Avenue in Toronto, but the space of the house is both labyrinth and proscenium, a tangle of rooms that are anonymous, discontinuous, and densely packed with imagery. Lipsett occupies these rooms in a variety of costumes: he plays himself, appearing unadorned in street clothes, a character that he describes as "the Archeologist" in his notes, a name he also assigns to his first disguise, that of a Shriner detective.

In this disguise, his head is topped with a Hellenic Association fez as he examines papers and objects with a large magnifying glass. He performs as a uniformed militant, which he refers to as "the Mongolian," described by Michael Dancsok as a Russian Cossack for his fur cap and double-breasted uniform. He becomes a scientist, or, as he calls it, a "lab coat," through a costume change achieved simply by putting on a lab coat over his street clothes. By wrapping himself in a kimono and putting on a feathered crown, Lipsett becomes a wizard, referred to in his notes as "the Magician." With the simple addition of a papier-mâché mask, he becomes the mischievous Monkey King of the Peking Opera. For his final disguise, as "the Egyptian," he is cloaked in a bedsheet, his head wrapped in a scarf.[37] Masks will play a major role in the events that occur in this space, from a cardboard cutout in the style of an Incan mask, worn by the Archeologist while holding a mirror up in the direction of the unseen cameraman, to a death mask that the Egyptian wears at the end, laid in state like a ruler.[38]

Lipsett's disguises were both self-aware performance and another form of animation, a summoning of figures from pictures. He writes that "characters (as cutouts) can come out of pictures and 'walk' about house," as if his disguises were cutout collage figures like those that had populated *Anything Can Happen on Channel 6* and the Khrushchev sequence of *Very Nice, Very Nice*.[39] The disguises also implicate *Strange Codes* in the repertory tradition of the Peking Opera, which features stock characters marked by their distinctive roles and voices. In all of these disguises, Lipsett is an explorer. His plans envision a comic, even ridiculous template for his explorer, noting, as he does, the influence of the destructive archeology of Heinrich Schliemann, the earnest intercultural commentary of André Gide, and, most integral of all, the explorations of Raymond Roussel, whose tour of Africa is eagerly imaginary, populated by carnivalesque guides.[40] In his enigmatic scenes and tableaux, Lipsett rotates through a series of guides, each of them representatives of order (the logical investigators) and chaos (magicians and mystics), each of them appearing as if drawn out from behind the doors of the Magic Theatre.

As the film begins, the camera surveys a wall-mounted collage: sarcophagi, graphic shapes, letters, and notes written in Lipsett's hand. Lipsett lays on the floor and stares at the ceiling, the camera viewing him from a low angle. When the credits appear, it is as if they are appearing from his perspective, on the ceiling, in defiance of gravity. On the soundtrack, a recording of the Peking Opera plays, alternating in a simple exchange with prolonged excerpts of Warren McCulloch describing the formation of information systems. McCulloch's speech is drawn from the same interview that Roman Kroitor conducted with him for *The Living Machine* (1961); it is a speech that Lipsett kept a transcription of in his records as far back as late 1965, which can be found among his notes for *Fluxes*, for it is where he had first encountered McCulloch's metaphor for an anastomotic model of information.[41] Lipsett had a plan for the film's structure prior to filming, that the early scenes would establish "the two main brains"—order and chaos—"before getting into summoning instructions."[42] He would abandon his plans for summoning instructions—on-screen directions to the viewer asking them to imagine images—but the desire to establish figures, themes, and energy patterns would remain through the introduction of symbols of order and chaos, the Archeologist and the Monkey King.

At both the beginning and the end of the film, Lipsett stands in a room, out of costume, shuffling with wooden boards that he leans up against a wall. On the wall is an eighteenth-century French blueprint of an equestrian sculpture, the horse's interior framework showing through the sculpted shell. The wooden frame suggests the Trojan Horse, that deceptive gift that allowed the Greeks to secret their soldiers through the gates of Troy and overpower the Trojans. As a framing device, these scenes suggest he is undertaking the monumental task of single-handedly building the Horse inside his living room. The task will not be completed, but the film itself was conceived to be like the Trojan Horse, a covert operation, albeit one that emerges from and deposits to the subconscious. The image of an individual single-handedly undertaking this Herculean task, and, at that, an individual who projects milquetoast bewilderment to the degree that Lipsett does with his blank gaze and timid smiles, is a picture of futility incarnate. The structuring role of this fable indicates the danger of these strange codes from space, these "messages from the future," an expression that, in the presence of this allusion, departs from Lipsett's interest in cybernetic futurity and seems instead a deliberate reference to the prophet Cassandra, whose warning that soldiers were hiding in the Horse was dismissed as madness.[43] Lipsett assumes multiple roles in the story of Troy that span across time from the ancient (as Epeus, as Cassandra) to the modern (as Schliemann, restorer and destroyer of Troy).

The Archeologist, equipped with fez and magnifying glass, pulls a roll of paper out of a cigar box, magnifying Latin words: *Umerus* (the ridge of a mountain); *Sator* (an ancient form of geometric palindromic word puzzle); *Partio* (party). The Monkey King retrieves and reads from a Latin-to-English/English-to-Latin dictionary, turning its pages backwards as if reading right to left, a gesture made all the more comic by the likelihood that Lipsett cannot read through the narrow eyes of the mask. Still, the presence of the translating dictionary suggests Lipsett anticipates a search for the meaning of the scroll. The Archeologist reads D.A. Alexander's *Secret Codes and Decoding*, a book published to coincide with the interest that had been generated in codification by the popular conception of the Turing machine in the spycraft of the Second World War. The Archeologist holds the magnifying glass in front of his eye, in a gesture that questions whether this decoding is aimed outward or inward. His cigar box roll now shows single frames from a comic book, pulled too fast to read in the bend of the magnifying glass. This gesture, of reviewing objects of plainly declarative meaning, whether comic panels, word lists, or handwritten notecards, seen too quickly to be understood, is a central gesture of Lipsett's performance. Lipsett establishes puzzle motifs early in the film with a Tower of Hanoi, a child's vertical stacking puzzle in which circles of different sizes are fitted over a series of poles. Other motifs emerge through cutaways to carvings and symbols—for instance, wooden toys depicting animals, as well as absurd disjunctions of scale, as when the filmmaker's eye is seen from the "wrong" side of a magnifying glass. Proscenium compositions of Lipsett in character break up scenes of him searching, and each of his disguises bears a different method of searching, a distinct performance of investigation. This is at its clearest in the Archeologist's Schliemann-esque search for clues as he flips through Lipsett's paperboard flowcharts. This search for clues, the thread that ties together these fragments into a cohesive sequence, bears another form of continuity in the central and constant presence of the artist.

Lipsett writes of a desire to invoke the "bizarre continuity" he perceives in both Nancy comic strips and John Coltrane's "Giant Steps," a mysterious, clever bridge of Coltrane's distinctive chromatic thirds chord progression and the surreal, elastic gags of Ernie Bushmiller.[44] This was some distance from the "treasure-hunt continuity" that he had conceived for *A Trip Down Memory Lane*, which imagined feeding the searching eyes of the spectator. It also departs dramatically from the psychophysical continuity that Lipsett had conceived of in making *Free Fall*. Lipsett's new "bizarre continuity" was differentiated from these earlier, highly deliberated approaches to cinematic continuity. "Giant Steps," with its cyclic progression, was a paradigm of continuity in mid-century music, but its translation to cinema, even a cinema of motifs, was not readily accessible as visual grammar. In effect, what made the continuity of *Strange Codes* so "bizarre" was its refusal of conventional sequence and the expectations that came with that. Lipsett had built an ensemble of disguises, like the stock characters in the Peking Opera, each improvising on a theme, each removed from another by a slight variation, trading fours. Added to this progression is the suggestion, by his motley costuming, that the boundaries of reality that separate past and present, East and West, have shattered.

The image had assumed a more complex continuity without the aid of a driving rhythm, but the sound–image relation had been simplified. In adopting a minimalist approach to sound design, Lipsett finally found a way to bear the lesson of John Cage's indeterminacy. Whether Warren McCulloch's statements align with Lipsett's actions by pure chance or by planned design, there is a sense that these alignments are loose enough to be spontaneous, as when McCulloch's first remarks about the "anastomotic type" of machine learning are met on screen by a stream of images: Lipsett playing with a "Tower of Hanoi" puzzle, then moving and stacking boxes, and, finally, in his Monkey Mask reading the Latin translating dictionary. The images resonate with McCulloch's presentation of the branching pathways of knowledge—the multiplicity of the stacking puzzles, the plenitude of these unelaborated boxes, translation between modern and ancient tongues—but such resonances might be found in any alignment of Lipsett's performances with McCulloch's remarks. The same could be said of the codification Lipsett's images receive when accompanied by the Peking Opera, untranslated, ecstatically foreign to the English-speaking viewer. Gone are the metric exchanges and comic punctuations of speech that had dominated his earlier films; in their place is this simple exchange, between McCulloch's visionary thought with its long view of history and a baroque collision of emotion and grace heard in the Peking Opera.

**FIGURE 9.1:** Arthur Lipsett as The Mongolian in *Strange Codes* (Arthur Lipsett, 1975)

Much of *Strange Codes* is pitched between what little can be seen and how much can be concealed, to the degree that viewing it becomes a strange game in which the odds of comprehension are stacked against the viewer. When Lipsett's Mongolian disguise is first introduced, McCulloch describes the sampling from which judgments are derived in anastomotic pathways. On screen is a black dot in the middle of a white background. As the camera zooms out, the Mongolian comes into view, wearing around his neck a large white circle that bears the dot. McCulloch's model depends upon the eye to recognize and compute information, and Lipsett offers information in a willingly deceptive way. His game is to supplant expectation, to give "reality-slaps." The Mongolian is dressed in a uniform that Michael Dancsok has described as that of a Russian Cossack.[45] Even so, the outfit is an odd parody, a double-breasted coat that looks more like a marching band costume than a military uniform and a pointed fur cap, nearer to a festive Santa

Claus cap than the fur hats of the Cossacks or the long-flapped loovuuz of the Mongolians. The camera zooms in on a bookcase from which the Mongolian retrieves a paper bag, a book on ancient Egypt, and a standee of James Mason's head. Lipsett smiles to the camera as he holds this strange assembly of pure mystery (the paper bag, its contents unknown), deliberated mystery (those of ancient Egypt), and the standee, itself a kind of absurd mask, a live-action staging of the comedy of disjunctive scale that Lipsett had encountered in the films of Stan VanDerBeek. The filmmaker is content to allow these collisions to emerge, live juxtapositions as a mysterious form of psychic defence.

The Archeologist continues to pull at his scroll of Latin words. Whether they have been plotted intentionally or at random is unclear, but the chosen words suggest the absurd and the mystical and provoke commentary on the film's elements and form, translating as follows: arise; Epeus (architect of the Trojan horse); antenna; naked; outside; born; Chinese; hidden. Taken as a sequence, it becomes semi-comprehensible as the basis of a myth. Far from the world of myth, Lipsett has changed his outfit again to become an archetype of modern knowledge, a Scientist: he wears a lab coat as he carries the standee of James Mason's face down a hallway, then down to the ground floor. Downstairs, Lipsett, out of costume, walks around a studio, searching for something. He sits wearing a cardboard cutout on his face, resembling an Incan mask. He grasps a mirror in his hand, moving it around for the camera, as if creating a portal to another dimension.

Meanwhile, the search continues: the Archeologist unfurls a comic strip from his cigar box scrolls and, in apparent frustration, stands up, casting it around the table, occasionally turning back to look at it with a magnifying glass too quickly to focus. The Mongolian, seated, holds a pair of binoculars to his eyes and searches the room, panning past the camera altogether. These characters search at a distance, the Archeologist examining clues from the past, exemplified in the makeshift ticker tape of the cigar box; the Mongolian in his imaginary watchtower interrogating a likewise imaginary landscape by panning his binoculars across a narrow space occupied only by himself and the camera operator. These somber figureheads of inquiry search for the concrete form of some invisible truth, but it is their counterpart, the Monkey King, a divine trickster, who takes the longest view of history and biology, as he opens a closet door to reveal a diagram of the stomach and musculature of a man, a turn inward to the organism. On the soundtrack, McCulloch interrupts the Peking Opera to make the simple remark that "what we lack is a logic of relations." As the music resumes its constant rapture, the Mongolian peers through a small telescope. In an edit that suggests his perspective, cardboard cutouts come into view, of the beak of a dodo and a can of Morton's salt. A pointing stick that traces the beak is revealed, by a subsequent cut, to be held by the Mongolian, who stands before Lipsett's "secret museum," his collages of text and image. McCulloch's remark on the logic of relations is embraced in this collage, which follows in the ideal of the Comte de Lautréamont, "the chance encounter of a sewing machine and an umbrella on an operating table."[46] The Mongolian's sudden teleportation from his watchtower to the collage, via the suggestion of the cut, is Lipsett's bizarre continuity in action, proof of his theatre as an imagined, interior space. With a pointer, the Mongolian lifts sheets of collage imagery to reveal further cutouts, and, in close-up, these juxtapositions are seen: historical photographs of Indigenous people are shown alongside a small box of Kellogg's Corn Flakes, as if they are two competing histories of America; a flap on an illustration of the human body lifts to reveal its interior; Mr. Peanut, mascot of Planters Peanuts, points to the scales of a fish while coolly leaning against a large X. The presence of Mr. Peanut may be a fleeting reference to Lipsett's contemporary, the Canadian performance artist Vincent Trasov, who performed from 1969 to 1974 as Mr. Peanut in a grotesque papier-mâché costume, even running for mayor in Vancouver in 1974, while being documented by painter and photographer Michael Morris. Through Trasov's performances, the absurd image of Mr. Peanut had gathered even greater absurdity, becoming a Canadian icon of radical postmodern costumed performance art.[47]

The Mongolian holds pieces of paper, as if he is in the midst of building this collage. The Scientist, seen only from the neck down, carries a top hat, a bird sculpture, and an oversized letter Z. The Mongolian, still seated with his binoculars in hand, pauses as if in reflection before holding them again to his face, as if this has all been seen at a distance, through his binoculars. Lipsett's manipulation of the sequential inference of the cut is much like his collaging of the quotidian and the profound; the secret museum had always been a copious inventory of fascinations, but these collages have reached a new level of 'pataphysical, pseudoscientific posturing, uproariously comic in the new functions they conceive for Mr. Peanut, disconcerting in the unelaborated presence of statesmen and tribesmen, of birds and fish and ancient knowledge. A portrait of nineteenth-century scientist and father of electromagnetism Michael Faraday will recur, as he holds a rod up in all the style with which twentieth-century vaudevillian Groucho Marx would later hold a cigar.

FIGURE 9.2: Arthur Lipsett as The Monkey King in *Strange Codes* (Arthur Lipsett, 1975)

Lipsett's hands are seen gathering materials and sifting through boxes of black oversized letters on white backgrounds. These letters, which have appeared throughout the film, are one of the readiest, most linear, and most recognizable of codes—the Modern English alphabet—but their appearances in his flowchart collages are chaotic and random, disavowing linearity or any other logical grouping. They become pure graphic form. The Monkey King holds a small globe in his hands and, later, reaches to grasp it from a shelf to admire it, slowly rotating it in front of the blank stare of the mask, another wilful hiccup in the linearity of Lipsett's performed actions. On the soundtrack, Warren McCulloch speaks of human perception and computation, the need to review and revisit images in order to understand them. As McCulloch speaks, the Mongolian, in close-up, opens the chest and stomach flap of the collaged human body, rapidly flipping it up and down, giving little glimpses to the human interior and, by chance or design, reinforcing McCulloch's remark through the repetition of this action. Henry Zemel, filming over Lipsett's shoulder as he moves the flap, captures Lipsett giddily laughing. For much of the film, Lipsett maintains a stone face, or at most a smirk, but this brief glimpse of joy is evidence of the pleasure he found in these absurd gags.[48]

The Scientist gathers a pair of hoops, an ornate vase, a pair of shoes, and a small bottle and sets them down before a vast collage that takes up much of a room, one part laid flat on the ground, another stood against a wall. Among the images on display are mandalas, astrological charts, lettering charts, anatomical charts, and books opened to image-rich pages. The Scientist squats to lay down some of the oversized letters, releasing them in an alphabetic order but seemingly laying them around the room at random. Lipsett, out of costume, opens a series of tea boxes that contain small texts written in Chinese logograms. Much of *Strange Codes* is less about symbols than it is about visual obscurity, with signs and texts either too fleeting or too blurred to comprehend. Even the disguises that he wears hold multiple meanings for him, only some of which are readily comprehensible. The codices, dictionaries, and recognizable systems are a red herring: the information that is being received is too plentiful and too slight in its registration to meet comprehension. *Strange Codes*, more than any of Lipsett's earlier films, is an arch expression of the copious inventory. Its inventory is not readily legible as that of a particular civilization, nor is it merely the horde of a pack rat. Like the stuff of cartoons, it is the overstuffed box that explodes, launching forth more than it could possibly have held. When the box explodes in the hands of the comic, the body rushing to contain it is more meaningful than all the data that is falling to the ground. The gesture of futility becomes universal just as the natural intimacy of this bursting stuff becomes universal.

Lipsett had planned the first half of the film to explore the paired opposites of order and chaos. This organizing principle remains present, however faintly, in his characterizations of searching intellect (the Archeologist) and unbridled impulse (the Monkey King). It had always been his intention to spend the remainder of the film dealing with "summoning." His original plan of offering the viewer instructions suggests that the film itself was to become an occult object, one that had to be viewed in a particular way, whether through half-shut eyes or through the imagination. Even with that approach abandoned, *Strange Codes* makes a noticeable transition into mysticism with Lipsett's next costume change. Putting on a feathered crown and a kimono, he becomes the Magician, a disguise cobbled from East and West, part medicine man, part priest, part wizard, part clown. Lipsett's sincerity in any of his roles is brought into question by virtue of his sense of humour, and when this ridiculous costume is paired with his stone-faced demeanour, his disguises reach their maximal comic impact. Whether he is earnest in his ritual is irrelevant; his notes offer that when Lipsett conceived of the Magician, he had another Chinese allusion in mind. He referred to this disguise as "Fu Manchu," a master criminal created and popularized in the racist pop fiction of British writer Sax Rohmer. In its originating context, the image of Dr. Fu Manchu was that of an evil other from a distant, ancient, and mysterious "Orient," whose criminal genius led him to concoct obscure schemes, puzzles that had to first be solved before they could be defeated. Lipsett's attraction to comics and pulp literature makes Fu Manchu a natural ideal of non-Western mysticism, but his synthesis of these ideas into the appearance of the Magician are a statement outright of the costume's ironic, absurd foundations. Lipsett formed *Strange Codes* out of allusions, and his references, if not his sources themselves, are largely comic, from his hapless suggestion of the "exotic" criminal genius, to his futile attempt at building the Trojan Horse, to the dedication he had originally intended for the film: "to Wolfgang Kohler who helped launch a washing machine into space."[49]

Although he had never been so present on screen in his earlier films, with *Strange Codes*, Lipsett revels in a role he had long played off screen, that of the Holy Fool, an archetype that became increasingly common among artists in postwar America, emerging out of a madcap performativity that was predominantly Jewish, revolutionary, and intellectual. The Holy Fool held that clowning is the sane response to an insane world. Arthur Lipsett played the Holy Fool at work for years. It won him the affection and bewilderment of his colleagues, and, in the end, it had made him easier to dispense with. Lipsett played the Holy Fool as, at the end of his long nights in the sound bullpen, he offered rolls of mag sound to his colleagues as if offering hors d'oeuvres, and, again later, as he danced in the street in Plattsburgh, New York, bragging to strangers that he and Robert Verrall were being detained by the FBI. As the Holy Fool, he had made six films, each increasing in their negative capability, their blank invitation to meaning, their uproarious portrait of the human condition.[50]

The Beats were the major Holy Fools to emerge in mid-century Western counterculture, products of a collision of deep reading, political and social disillusionment, and spontaneous insight. They were Gregory Corso's "mad children of soda caps," and their challenge resonated from the Omnist raps of Allen Ginsberg, to the poet-led satirical rock band The Fugs and the performances and publications of members Ed Sanders and Tuli Kupferberg, to the emergence of the Yippies and the courtroom theatrics of Jerry Rubin and Abbie Hoffman, to the nightclub, in the righteous and surreal sarcasm of Lenny Bruce and the uncanny double-talk of Professor Irwin Corey. These mad children of soda caps staged large-scale protests that bore the spirit of Holy Foolishness, as in 1967, when some of the Beats, the incipient Yippies, and others gathered to march on the Pentagon, performing a mock exorcism and attempting to levitate the building, the central brain of America's war machine.[51] A few months later, the Fugs, Allen Ginsberg, and others gathered in St. Mary's Parish Cemetery in Appleton, Wisconsin, to exorcise the grave of red-baiting, homophobic American senator Joe McCarthy.[52] The Holy Fool could parcel divine insight, Bardic citation, righteous outrage, and the happening. This archetype was first defined by Ginsberg in 1958 when he wrote of Gregory Corso as a poet who "wants a surface hilarious with ellipsis...what is he *saying*? Who cares?! It's said!"[53] The Holy Fools were a conduit for extemporized, seemingly divine acts of poetry, their improvised prayers scattered by laughter.

As he leans over the collage, the Magician lays down what appear to be a series of identical postcards of 14 Wall Street, home of the Bankers Trust—a building in need of an exorcism if ever there was one, a skyscraper topped with a pyramid. As cameraman Henry Zemel would say, "the triangle is upon us." The Magician stands to throw little homemade paper mandalas down at random, each the size of large coins. They fall among his books, cutouts, and markers. His tossing them is somewhere between the tossing of coins in consultation of the *I Ching*, and the rolling of a die, caught between predestination and chance, but in Lipsett's own notes, he gives some indication of how he perceives mandalas, speculating that they may be for "zeroing in on precise centers of attraction."[54] Thus, they are less an addition to his collage than an aleatoric path through it; and yet, they are also plentiful, some caught upright upon landing against the three-dimensional objects on his collage, an impractical surrender to chance. He allows them to simply "go together," following on the lesson John Cage had imparted to him. He describes this sequence as a "camouflage ceremony for those on the after-death plane."[55]

McCulloch tells the fable of the Brazen Head, credited to Friar Bacon and Friar Bungay as per Robert Greene's sixteenth-century play that bears their name. McCulloch recounts that "the first time it spoke, it said, time will be…and [then] it said time is…finally it said time has been." Each time the Head speaks, an impatient servant tasked to watch it dismisses these simple, profound statements as truisms; the Brazen Head, like Cassandra of Troy, is relaying messages from the future to fall on deaf ears. McCulloch's monologue coincides with the Magician adding to his collage a cut-out paper figure resembling Pierrot of the Commedia dell'arte, best known to modern audiences as Leoncavallo's Pagliacci, the tragic clown driven by jealousy and hopelessness to murder. The duelling symbolism of Pagliacci resonates with Lipsett's holy foolishness, a balance of levity and severity akin to the Beats. As the Magician admires and tenderly touches his mandalas, astrological charts, compasses, and other circular forms, Lipsett's clowning has traces of despair. Lapsing back into definitively comic strangeness, the Magician puts on a pair of glasses, gathers his pointing stick and a star-topped wand, and begins rolling dice on top of an image of a sculptural bust of Nefertiti. He places a pair of straw shoes on his collage, one next to a fortune teller's crystal ball, each on either side of the collage that now bears Haitian veves, curving symbols that serve as Vodou incantations. As McCulloch elaborates on his perceptual models, of what the eye and the brain communicate to each other, the Magician begins to draw a veve in magic marker, a summoning in action.

The Monkey King emerges from the closet, stepping out to reveal the anatomical diagram behind him, an implication that the trickster might enter and exit the "order room" of the body at will. This gives way to a rapid intercutting of the Magician flipping through a partially disassembled book of anatomical diagrams, placing new objects on top of it: an illustration of a bird, a homemade cut-out mandala, a stopwatch, and small black discs, possibly checker pieces, laid in a seemingly random pattern. He begins to assemble a human figure, combining various anatomical illustrations: an illustration of a child sticking their tongue out; triangular paper cutouts; a diagram of palm chakras; and an image of a man, his eyes blacked out with a panel, with bandages wrapped around his head, paired with an illustration of a sphere-headed, handless figure in the style of de Chirico. This figurative collage follows themes of corporeal being but decorates and extends the arrangement of the body with codes and complex, unstable metaphor. He adds various images that do not align with the corporeal metaphor of this figure—an X, a Japanese woodcut print. The last of the items the Magician applies to the figure is a stopwatch, which he begins to wind. The winding of the stopwatch acts as a final occult ritual, transforming the figure into a time machine that "winds" Lipsett into ancient time, and transforming the Magician into the Egyptian, Lipsett's final disguise.[56] As the Egyptian, Lipsett wears a creased bedsheet with a striped scarf bound over his head in the style of a turban. The Egyptian's first appearance is sudden and subtle, a reality-slap that casts doubt on the viewer's perception of the film's relation to the figure, space, and time. The Egyptian takes a piece of paper from the mouth of a mounted bird, one of the many sculptural facets of this final collage. Like the Archeologist's endless scroll, it bears a list of words that are unrelated save for their alternating metre: seer; opera; clear; Tokyo—messages from the future with rhyme but no reason. In a parallel action, the Archeologist continues to unspool discontinuous Latin words and Greek names from his cigar box scroll: *Protinus* (at once); *Aurae* (breeze); *Aurora* (the Greek goddess of dawn); *Ianthina* (violet); *Veho* (convey); *Virga* (shoot); *Translatio* (translation); *Usque* (always).

Returning to the Archeologist, his first disguise, Lipsett marks a shift into a rapturous climax. A series of actions serve to gather his characters: the Egyptian sifts through a pile of hand-drawn cards, settling on a drawing of the African continent, which he lays atop a mirror to the side of the collage; the Mongolian sits in his proscenium watchtower, and the camera zooms back into the dot on his chest, retreating; the Magician lays an inkwell and quill on the collage. The camera lingers on the crystal ball; the mandalas, orbs, and stopwatch are all mounted on the collage, his provisional time machine. Out of costume, Lipsett builds his Trojan Horse, pinning images to the wooden boards, arranging and deliberating on them. The Egyptian, with his final gesture, joins the collage: he lays down in it, with a cherubic mask on his face, like a pharaoh. Elsewhere, the Archeologist rapidly unspools the last of his Latin words: *Balineum* (bath); *Canis* (dog); *Diluvium* (flood); *Elevo* (lift); *Ligamen* (string); *Portento* (omen); *Quatio* (shake); *Queror* (lament); *Reditus* (revolve). Finally abandoning his scroll, the Archeologist instead picks up a photograph of a figure in a field and holds his magnifying glass to it. As the credits begin, tossed casually into a pile in the centre of the frame, other images intrude: Michael Faraday with his rod; the Archeologist's cigar box scroll; the eternal cool of Mr. Peanut leaning, a personification of elegance in top hat and monocle, which is soon concealed by a Japanese woodcut print of a demon. With a final cut, Lipsett inserts a fleeting, abstract glimpse of the Mongolian costume in close-up: the black dot at the midpoint of the circle, a distinctive imprint in the center of an absence.

After *Strange Codes* was completed, an opportunity arose for Lipsett to screen it on *Sprockets*, a CBC program that served as a showcase for independent films. The show was produced by filmmaker Julius Kohanyi and reflected the growing diversity of independent cinema in Canada, a shift away from the monopolizing influence of the National Film Board, one that had begun in the early- to mid-1960s with the growth of regional distribution services, local cooperatives, and other forms of federal support and tax incentives. Lipsett offered an explanatory note to Kohanyi and the *Sprockets* staff, introducing *Strange Codes* with an acknowledgement of his overarching presence as a conductor, calling the film "a gradual movement into the uncovering of clues by a character (the filmmaker) who keeps changing into different costumes."[57] Even in this, Lipsett makes clear that the film is not about different characters so much as it is about masks and costumes, a splintering of self akin to the corridor of the Magic Theatre: "He is searching for a certain kind of system. These costume changes help to get him into the correct mood for each stage of the film's development."[58] Lipsett offered Kohanyi a glimpse of the system that he discovered, "a visual network composed of movable objects and graphic elements, manipulated by the filmmaker in a progression of ritualistic actions."[59] The system he describes resembles the final moveable collage that is presented in the film, the makeshift figure and time machine through which he transforms from the Magician into the Egyptian. That collage is a collision of two-dimensional and three-dimensional objects, a network of loose, free-associative semiotic and historical relations that, in the end, becomes a tomb.

Lipsett gave Kohanyi a position from which to defend *Strange Codes*, a practical use for the film, as his work for the NFB had always required of him. He states that he is "attempting to discover new uses for these objects and graphic elements which will enable the building of a certain kind of game system and might be viewed as a game being constructed that could enable a human being to help make translations and connections from his inner world of feelings, to the world of day to day reality systems."[60] Lipsett points to codification, through which his film achieves a mischievous impenetrability, but it is all in the service of redeeming the broken contract between uncoordinated systems: between the ethereal and the corporeal, between the superstitious and the skeptical, between feeling and action, or even, as McCulloch would have it, between the eye and the brain: "The film is operating at a midway point between the primitive ritualized world and the world of logic and science. But perhaps it can be experienced simply as a strange play."[61] The film was broadcast on January 27, 1975, presented by one of Kohanyi's rotating hosts, filmmaker Michael Hirsch. The CBC described Lipsett's film as a "disjunctive, live-action portrait of the artist."[62]

It had been Lipsett's wish to place the film in distribution with Brandon Films, the largest collection of 16mm films circulating in the United States. Lipsett even notes his intention to send the film out for Brandon's consideration with a miniature Latin-to-English dictionary, a declaration of the film's codified nature made more eccentric by the implied obstacles of the miniature book as a consultation text.[63] Mark Slade, who had long been Lipsett's lone supporter in the distribution wing at the Film Board, attempted to convince the Film Board to distribute *Strange Codes* on the basis that clients may wish to acquire the entire body of a filmmaker's work.[64] That there was no interest seems only natural: the Film Board had long since lost interest in supporting Lipsett's work even as they were funding it, and his greatest opponents in his final years there had been Slade's colleagues. When Lipsett was on staff, they had spread rumours that his films were unprofitable. A cruel rumour had become a prophecy: despite having a national broadcast, *Strange Codes* did not find distribution, was the first of Lipsett's films to receive no press, and slipped into immediate obscurity.[65]

*Strange Codes* drew from Lipsett's long engagement in mysticism and in modern and postmodern art. His interests in Fluxus, energy fields, aleatoric methods, and Tibetan Buddhism were all present. One major distinction that separates this film from those that preceded it was the admission of magic as a part of the artist's process, an overt engagement with the occult that, in his earlier statements about his work, had often been subsumed into discussions of philosophy. In his notebook, Lipsett reflected on his declarations of magic, clarifying the sane course he was charting through unconventional sentiments that he knew might be met unkindly. "Of course I am approaching all of this from an artistic angle and do not wish to and never have wished to proclaim myself as some kind of wizard," he writes, "Naturally you are free to draw your own opinions. Nevertheless, I am more firmly on the side of good than ever."[66] He understood everything he planned, all of his staging, as being principally metaphoric. He was, at last and uneasily, exposing himself as the Holy Fool. He elaborates on his sense of the role of the artist in relation to these claims to magic and ESP: "Mature artists essentially are 'wizards' or good magicians who protect the community they live in, if only for personal self-defence."[67] Like the exorcisms of Ginsberg and company, Lipsett's mysticism was a beneficial service in a world that, like the world of Hesse's *Steppenwolf*, had become vacuous, severed from meaning and from the good. Lipsett's artist-wizards were the essential caretakers of the world because "not only can they send out corrective telepathic vibrations facilitated through their work but they are also very sensitive in receiving bad ones which they proceed to destroy."[68]

In the final moments of *Strange Codes*, as it builds to a rapture, the Peking Opera becomes overwhelming in its tinny rattles and in the elastic resonance of its steel percussion. Warren McCulloch interrupts the music one last time, repeating a statement regarding experiments involving the nervous response of a frog: "the minute you say 'ah,' you get an enormous response." With a final, ecstatic gasp, the Peking Opera's singer says, "ahhhh." It is a correspondence across cultures, across space and time, made possible by the film itself, which has become a time machine. Arthur Lipsett would never complete another film. His work had been so joyously defined by resonances between disparate parts, but this would be his final synthesis of call-and-response.

# TEN

# THE 10,000 THINGS

IN BUDDHIST PHILOSOPHY, "THE TEN THOUSAND THINGS" IS AN expression of the plenitude of worldly stuff, a hypothetical innumerability, a finite boundary on the infinite. One of the things that Arthur Lipsett had told Judith Sandiford early in their courtship that had struck her as beautiful was that everything had a sound.[1] It was a statement of his intensified perception, and a romantic translation of an idea that recurs throughout his notes, that everything has a vibration. Lipsett would return again and again to the notion that everything has a vibration, gleaned from Warren McCulloch, one of those ambiguities between science and mysticism that Lipsett had embraced as a biophysical theory, a governing moral tenet of Buddhism, and an explanation for his own visceral perception. Of his many conceptualized but unproduced films, one was titled *The 10,000 Things*, a final spilling-forth of all the contents of his overstuffed boxes.[2] The ten thousand things assumes a profound dimension in Lipsett's life and work, the life of a pack rat whose homes were overflowing with things, the labours of an artist whose work involved overstuffing boxes in joyous rhythm.

Not long after *Strange Codes* was completed, Lipsett moved from Toronto to Victoria, BC. As a confessed Anglophile, Lipsett may have imagined being at home in Canada's most British city. Friends who knew him there would recall him as a solitary figure, spending a lot of time at the beach.[3] "I'm here on vacation, doing some writing," he would say, "I've come here to regain my health and stay warm. I understand all those little old ladies now."[4] He spent much of 1975 and the early part of 1976 in Victoria, staying long enough for his presence to make the local entertainment news when he was the subject of a profile in Victoria's weekly *Monday Magazine*. The interviewer, Ellery Littleton, met him at the zero mile marker of the Trans-Canada Highway, a literal sign of starting, or starting over. Explaining his work to Littleton, Lipsett said that "the lines of reality can be extended. The drama comes in because everybody's going in a different direction."[5] Littleton perceived Lipsett's remarks as "mystical ramblings," but much of what he said was lucid, offered in defence of the willful difficulty of his films. Asked why his films are chaotic, Lipsett replied that they are highly structured: "They are like a soup that you swim in. You can get up any time and leave the room. Bring back a vomit bag or a nausea pill."[6] With his final question, Littleton asks why Lipsett always works in black and white, a potential sore point for the filmmaker who had attempted repeatedly to shift into colour and who had strong interests in the aesthetic potential of colour filmmaking. Lipsett, with characteristic wit, speaks of himself in the third person, in a stentorian style: "They said that he saw things in black and white. Dogs do, you know, it's a scientific fact. He was brought up in black and white."[7] It was not lost on Lipsett that so many of the critical responses his work received had reduced it to black-and-white moralizing. Even in Littleton's article, a sidebar finds an employee of the local NFB office, Linda Moore, describing Lipsett as "handing out indictments" with his filmmaking.[8] Lipsett's films were not indictments, but his statement to Littleton may well be: he was "brought up" as a dog in the National Film Board of Canada, and his work would always be marked by the unambiguous contrast of the institution.

While in Victoria, Lipsett corresponded with Tanya Ballantyne, later known as Tanya Tree, who had been a close friend and colleague of his at the NFB in the mid-1960s. Ballantyne decided she would travel to visit Lipsett and make a film about it. Mark Slade and Terry Ryan arranged for her to get production support from the British Columbia offices of the NFB, and she made the pilgrimage with a group of friends. The film would be titled *Blue and Orange*, and it plays out, much like *Strange Codes*, as a work of performance art: Ballantyne shaves her head, is reunited with Lipsett, and goes to Victoria's Provincial Parliament with him, where they hurl pages from the *I Ching* on its lawn. "We were really just playing," she would later recall, "It was a 'happening'...I think Arthur was desperately trying not to hurt people. So the idea was to show people the playfulness of life. And they don't have to take it all seriously."[9] That performative aspect of *Blue and Orange* was carrying forward from Lipsett's interest in Fluxus and Neo-Dada, and there at the provincial parliament, he could be a Holy Fool, after Ginsberg, with the social support of being, if not in a crowd, at least in the company of friends. Ballantyne's presence did not sanitize Lipsett's behaviour so much as it clarified the playful, performative, creative aspects of it. Although he was the major subject, Lipsett was merely a performer in Ballantyne's film, over which she asserted sole authorship, and when she shared it with her colleagues from the NFB, it was met with apprehension. She was resistant to Terry Ryan's suggestions that it be expanded or changed, and, as a result, it was never distributed.[10]

Shortly after shooting ended for *Blue and Orange*, Lipsett moved back to Toronto, this time to 94 Amelia Street in Cabbagetown. Knowing that he needed to find a way to support himself, he wrote to a number of people in government: both Tom Daly and Guy Glover received letters from him asking about employment, as did Pierre Juneau, who had been an executive at the Film Board during Lipsett's tenure there and who had since become the undersecretary of state. Lipsett even wrote to Prime Minister Pierre Trudeau asking if he might be given a grant to study "the new theatre."[11] Daly told Juneau that "if any need arises suited to (Arthur Lipsett's) special capabilities, you can be sure we will think of him."[12] His pleas for work were met with dispassionate nods. The community he had belonged to was moving on without him.

Judith Sandiford had been in touch with Lipsett sporadically but would see him for the last time in 1976. She had decided to take a road trip across Canada, heading west, and wanted to say goodbye before she left. She found him sitting in a park down the block from his Cabbagetown apartment. Lipsett led her back to his apartment, where they made love. Toward the end of their visit, he pointed to a bundle in the closet. He told her it contained a gun and that when he ran out of money, he intended to shoot himself.[13] Whether the threat was sincere or merely provocative is unknowable, but his reason given was not the worsening of his illness, but the hopelessness of his financial situation. He had come to realize, with the trickle of indifferent acknowledgements to his requests for work, that for him there was no returning to the Film Board. When he left, he had told Martin Lavut that it was a WASP organization and that, as a Jew, he never felt at home there.[14] Other indications of his hostility towards the NFB come through in remarks he gave in interviews, pointing out to Ellery Littleton that there was no work of his kind being made there and telling Terry Ryan that, upon his departure, "he's not sure if he intends to leave a forwarding address."[15] Now reduced to pursuing help from an organization that had met him with rumours, bullying, resentment, and incomprehension, he found himself unable to imagine an alternative. Fearing for his safety and acting out of love and selflessness, Sandiford cashed in a Canada Savings Bond and gave the money to Lipsett. To her relief, he used the money to take a cab from Toronto to Montreal in an act of desperate self-preservation. After six years away, he was finally going home.[16] When he arrived, he would return to where he had lived when his professional life had begun, the austerity of the Clifton Arms.

The Clifton Arms was one of several places that Lipsett lived, on and off, over the coming decade. When he was not there, he was a guest in the homes of friends, such as Tanya Ballantyne. With the difficulty of having no stable employment, and the meagre support of social assistance, aspects of Lipsett's lifestyle and creative work were strained. His days were listless, drifting, full of false starts as he continued his attempts to resume making art while coping with his illness. If the ten thousand things had been an easy metaphor for his crowded life and the plenitude of his art, it could double as a reminder of all that he had lost since leaving the house on Belsize, couch surfing with his few possessions and most of his collaging materials in storage in Toronto. In 1978, Lipsett gave an interview to Lois Siegel for *Cinema Canada*, the country's national film magazine. In characteristic generosity, he described the faces seen in *Very Nice, Very Nice* with a simple, empathetic aphorism: "there's so many ways of living lives."[17] His perception of those faces was in stark contrast to the grotesqueries that his colleagues had seen: the most grotesque face in the film, after all, was his own, contorted and lit from beneath to be consonant with the monster masks and skull effigies of the protestors.

He described his method as that of "holding time together," a means of provoking reflection, a new evolution on his old concepts of "shock-states" and "reality-slaps."[18] Lipsett had continued to pursue filmmaking as a means of survival: "I have no choice anymore...it's difficult for an artist to infiltrate the government to do something."[19] He reflected on the difficulties he'd faced as a filmmaker at the NFB for the uncommon form of his work: "there was very little work being done of the type I was doing...I always had a lot of pressure on me. It was difficult just to get the money to continue. There was always the question of the kind of film I wanted to make next."[20] At the time of the interview, Lipsett was waiting for a decision from the NFB about a series of five films for children that he had proposed, an extension of the *Discovery Film* series that he had first proposed in 1964.

When Lipsett did hear from the NFB, it was about an entirely different project. The Board had found a way to use Lipsett's special capabilities after all, inviting him to contribute a one-minute film to their Canada Vignettes series. Lipsett was asked to pitch a project to his old friend Robert Verrall and offered him an explanation that Verrall didn't quite understand, that it would be "all about corners," although whether he meant geometric vertices or street corners, is unclear.[21] Verrall would serve as executive producer alongside Dorothy Courtois as producer. The Canada Vignettes series had been initiated by the CBC, who were seeking short films to use as interstitials, in between programs, in lieu of commercials. This was a windfall for many NFB filmmakers, with more than 120 short films produced in a two-year period. The parameters could allow Lipsett to reintroduce himself to the NFB and represented a small expansion of the lengths of his early commercials for the CBC and the Montreal International Film Festival. Lipsett proposed *Traffic Flow* as "a study of interrelationships of visual signals in a setup in a room. Kinetic experiment of signal bounce around the room using 3-D object constructions."[22] Lipsett was expected to meet a tight schedule, shooting the film between March 3 and March 8, 1978, and cutting it over the following weeks, with a final delivery date in May.[23]

By September of that year, the film remained in an unfinished state. A conflict had arisen between Lipsett and Verrall that would cause a lasting rift. Lipsett wrote a letter of resignation, with an explanation that suggests his growing intolerance for bureaucracy: "I, Arthur Lipsett have developed a phobia of sound tape. Also my creative ability in the film field has disappeared. There is no way to explain this and the result is that I cannot continue to work for the government."[24] His claims to a phobia reinforce concerns about his declining mental health, his claim of losing creativity demonstrates his growing despair, but it is his final, defiant statement, that he "cannot continue to work for the government," that suggests that he could no more tolerate the bureaucracy of the Film Board than its bureaucracy could tolerate him. His phrasing resonates with an earlier act of resistance, when his Film Board colleague Derek Lamb invited him to teach a course at Harvard University, and he responded, "I cannot come to Harvard at this point in history."[25]

Thomas Schnurmacher's column in the *Montreal Gazette* deepens the questions about what happened to *Traffic Flow*. In July 1979, almost a year after Lipsett's resignation, an item ran declaring that Lipsett's archives were in the process of being seized: "Film-maker Arthur Lipsett's film archives are about to be seized in Toronto, where they have been kept in storage."[26] According to Schnurmacher, Lipsett "ran afoul of the National Film Board when he was $150 short in producing receipts for a film project."[27] The broken-telephone nature of entertainment journalism leaves ambiguous which project Schnurmacher might be referring to, but if true, it was more likely *Traffic Flow* than anything else: "The National Film Board cancelled his film for this reason, which is rather amazing when one considers that the NFB's annual maintenance budget approaches $1 million."[28] The implication that *Traffic Flow* was cancelled for purely bureaucratic reasons would indicate either vindictiveness on the part of the production staff or displeasure and embarrassment at what was being produced. Given the rumours encircling Lipsett the last time he had resigned and the hostility with which his work had been consistently met in his final years at the NFB, either scenario remains a possibility.[29]

The more urgent matter at hand in Schnurmacher's article was the case of Lipsett's secret museum, the storehouse of collages, writings, photographs, records, and other materials that he had placed in storage in Toronto, which he now needed to bail out. Having lived in close proximity to this piling archive in his Coronet Street apartment, he had stored the materials out of the desperation of no longer having anywhere to put them. A group of his friends—among them, poet Fortner Anderson and filmmakers Christopher Nutter and Robert Ditchburn—arranged for a fundraising screening that paired *Very Nice, Very Nice* with Stanley Kubrick's *A Clockwork Orange*.[30] During the screening, Lipsett stood and performed an interpretive dance.[31] To some in attendance, Lipsett's dance was a sign of his growing departure from reality, but it may also have been the natural direction his art had taken in abandoning the fixed forms of older media. The dance could be a renewal of Lipsett's "good magic," from the ossifying distance of 1961 to the immediate present, an endurance of the Magician and his time machine. When the trunks containing his secret museum were reclaimed, Lipsett had nowhere to put them; Ditchburn kept them in his basement for a decade, where Lipsett would dip into them occasionally to retrieve objects as needed, be they records, musical instruments, or books.

Many of Lipsett's old friendships faded. He lost touch with Sandiford and Lavut and had virtually no contact with his colleagues from the NFB, some of whom he had parted company with on bad terms. Even those colleagues who had continued to hold him in high regard, like Terry Ryan and Mark Slade, gradually lost touch with him as his illness worsened, and he came to resemble less a friend than a responsibility. John Max proved a unique exception; their long friendship weathered the difficulty because they were living similar lives, with their lifestyles and their temperaments rendering them increasingly reclusive and concerned for one another; likewise, Tanya Ballantyne became a strong supporter of Lipsett and another persistent link between his present and past life. Even through his nocturnal habits, his years at the Film Board had brought him warm, collegial relationships; with that gone, Lipsett cultivated a new social circle, connecting with Fortner Anderson and filmmakers Lois Siegel, Robert Ditchburn, Ryan Larkin, and Christopher Nutter.

Like Lipsett, Christopher Nutter had joined the Film Board as a young man, one of a group of young filmmakers that had arrived in the mid-1960s at a time when the organization was grappling with its identity: cinema vérité was supplanting the poetic constructions of Film Board documentaries, the organization was beginning to branch out further into dramatic filmmaking, and Lipsett was establishing the possibilities for underground filmmaking to the displeasure of his colleagues. Nutter's early credits at the Film Board were as a screenwriter for Morten Parker's docudrama *A Trumpet for the Combo* (1965) and Mort Ransen's *No Reason to Stay* (1966). *No Reason to Stay* had been an autobiographical account of Nutter's experience as a school dropout. He would make one film of his own, *Garden* (1971), an animated film that depicts a surreal garden, produced by Tom Daly. Nutter knew Lipsett then in passing and had long admired him, having seen *Very Nice, Very Nice* on television as a teenager, but they would only develop a close friendship in the mid-1970s, after Lipsett returned to Montreal. In the absence of Sandiford and Lavut, Nutter became a supportive figure in Lipsett's life. As Nutter explains in an interview with Michael Dancsok, "we wound up being kind of recluses together. We were sort of treading waters for a few years until Arthur sank." He would try to record their conversations: "Sometimes he would agree and then make me take the tape recorder off…he loved to listen to music. That's what we did."[32] Lipsett had a similar friendship with Fortner Anderson, the two listening for hours together to radio stations with the dial tuned between stations.

Following his second exit from the Film Board, Lipsett's agony was plain to see, even through his eccentricities. In the summers, he would wear a winter coat. Still the Holy Fool, he had devoted himself to making what he called "peering devices," tubes held to the eye, like a telescope or kaleidoscope. He would also carry around a small camera, simply to see the world through it. His friends doubted there was film in the camera. He became known and liked as a character on the Main, but his emotional struggle was no longer subtle.[33] Friends of his who knew him in this period remembered him as tortured, no longer cleaning or taking care of himself, and increasingly haunted by voices and sounds. He began to use gaffer tape to tie his hands up into mudras. When John Max and Lois Siegel went to check on him once, at his apartment at the Clifton Arms, they heard him inside and believed he had taped his mouth shut.[34] According to Tanya Tree, his mudra bindings also involved taping metal to his hands, and he would go for days without eating.[35] These gestures, like his impromptu dance at the fundraising screening, are ambiguous; what appeared to some as purely self-destructive madness may have been, for Lipsett, the new and natural extension of his performance art.

Lipsett eventually settled in as a regular guest in the home of his aunt, Etta Goldberg, on St. Kevin Street. Aunt Etta, his mother's sister, had an affectionate relationship with Lipsett and took care of him, allowing him to sleep on her couch. Despite Lipsett's chaotic life, his aunt's home remained organized, with his chaos confined in one drawer of a side table next to the couch where he slept.[36] He was first admitted to the Jewish General Hospital in Montreal in 1982, and Nancy Carpenter became his outpatient doctor in January 1983. She knew him as charming and intelligent, despite his struggles. He was considered either a chronic schizophrenic or a paranoid schizophrenic, a discrepancy of diagnosis based on his doctors being unable to pin down when precisely his problems began. "He had auditory hallucinations, which were sometimes a great comfort to him when they were nice," Carpenter recalled. "He loved them."[37] When they were not kind to him, they tormented him for being Jewish. Carpenter would give him medications, which he hated to take. He would often stop taking his medications. Occasionally, he would take too much, attempting suicide. He would tell Lois Siegel that these fluctuating doses—from all to nothing—were "little experiments."[38] In the years that Carpenter knew him, he was not doing creative work; he had left that behind him. In her words, he was trying to decide whether to live or die. He related to her that he considered hope to be a trickster. According to her, he would wander the streets, paranoid, and get beaten up by cops and rednecks. Once in a while, he would tell her that he was ready to make a film, and she would encourage him to speak to his former colleagues, and he would return to chastise her for having encouraged him, "because it won't work. I'm no good. I don't have it."[39]

In his final months, Lipsett severed contact with most of his friends and began to experience a series of downward, depressive spirals. His illness was becoming more severe, as was his poverty. His aunt, who had been ill and hospitalized for a time while they were living together, found that she could no longer care for him. During his last hospitalization, Lipsett was warm, funny, and charming. Dr. Carpenter would come to believe that he had been putting on a show in order to convince the staff to discharge him. He left the hospital with two bags of clothing, bought the rope he would use to hang himself, and moved, for the last time, into the Clifton Arms.

Arthur Lipsett was buried in Montreal's Hawthorn-Dale Cemetery, and his interment was paid for by the city. Christopher Nutter gave his eulogy to a small audience of family, friends, and former colleagues. In the months after Nancy Carpenter discovered his body, Lipsett was the subject of a wide-ranging retrospective memorial article written by Lois Siegel, who, in the course of interviewing him in the late 1970s, befriended him and became a facilitator during his brief return to the NFB. Siegel interviewed many of Lipsett's closest collaborators and friends, including Judith Sandiford, Lipsett's sister Marian, and his former colleagues. Those who had supported him at the Film Board were content to remember him only as a tragic figure, one whose films, considered in retrospect, revised their memories of him as a person, his strangeness shifting from charming and funny to paranoid and miserable. The sad circumstances of his death cast a pall on his work that it could not shake off; only eight years earlier, Lipsett had expressed empathy with the faces of *Very Nice, Very Nice*, commenting that "there's so many ways of living lives," but now, for those too desperately seeking an explanation for his sad end, they saw instead a gallery of taunting, leering creatures, a malicious and cruel society. The absurd dimensions of his work had never been easily understood, but considerations both critical and casual would increasingly depend upon the context of suicide to interpret work made at the height of his joyous, comic wit.

Lipsett was not entirely forgotten at the Film Board. After his death, the staff eventually posted a notice on a bulletin board that read, "Arthur Lipsett took his own life about ten days ago."[40] Animator Jacques Drouin was the only member of the Film Board staff other than Lois Siegel to pay a public tribute to Lipsett, whom he did not know, but in whose work he saw only an immensity of suffering. "I know few works as disturbing as his," Drouin wrote, "How not to think of Arthur Lipsett when I hear news on the radio about the Chernobyl disaster or when television repeatedly sends us insane images of the Challenger explosion."[41] Drouin's tribute bore a pithy title that casually and tellingly invoked the superficiality with which Lipsett's death was met: "Very sad, very sad." His accompanying filmography for Lipsett pointedly excludes both *N-Zone* and *Strange Codes*.

At the time of Lipsett's death, he and his father were both patients at the Jewish General Hospital but were unaware of this. Solomon Lipsett had been suffering from Alzheimer's for years and had moved into a Jewish retirement home in 1983.[42] He would die on November 21, 1986, only seven months after his son. Their circumstance is symbolic of the isolation that Arthur Lipsett found himself in during those final months, when his disconnection from others became so total as to seem like a blindness, the passing of distant ships. Lipsett's intense privacy made him an enigma in the minds of many of his friends, who knew only fragments of his story that, combined with myths, made the facts of his life even more evasive. In the aftermath of his death, his secret museum, the copious inventory of his life as a collector that had been kept in four steamer trunks, was reclaimed from Robert Ditchburn's basement and brought to the Cinémathèque québécoise, where it formed the bulk of their comprehensive archival collection of Lipsett materials.

By the turn of the twenty-first century, Arthur Lipsett had attracted the advocacy of public admirers, with recurrent acknowledgement from influential fans like Hollywood filmmaker George Lucas, who was inspired by *21-87* to conceive of "the force," the invisible, mystical energy that drives his *Star Wars* universe.[43] Lipsett's impact on commercial culture, be that impact real or imagined, would come to eclipse his own films, from the advocacy he had received from Lucas and Stanley Kubrick, to the various claims that his style had an impact on music videos, a bloodthirsty chorus aimed just as frequently at Stan Brakhage and other experimental filmmakers whose work was decidedly, and often ideologically, non-commercial.[44] The NFB staff had been evasive in the 1980s, but they would later attempt to adopt a conciliatory tone in the interest of maintaining control over Lipsett's story and exploiting the tragedy of his death. They would be involved in two documentaries about Lipsett: the first, co-produced with TV Ontario, was *Remembering Arthur* (2006), an intimate and thorough inquiry into Lipsett's life made by his friend Martin Lavut and driven primarily by the affecting presences of Judith Sandiford and Christopher Nutter. The second, Eric Gaucher's *The Arthur Lipsett Project: A Dot on the Histomap* (2007), was produced fully in-house by the Film Board and is a defensive film featuring only NFB staff who gloss over the complexity of Lipsett's films in order to justify the institution's entrenched hostility toward him, an act of clucking sympathy over a prodigy who lost his talent.[45]

Arthur Lipsett was not a doomed prodigy, predestined to misery because of his genius; he was an outsider with an extraordinary mind whose wit and creativity was in step with the best of his generation. He was stuck in the wrong venue for too long and became habituated to it. He was an aesthetic visionary who had continued to evolve his craft until his illness and a lack of support and opportunity made it impossible for him to continue. His illness was not the first obstacle he had encountered in his professional life: before that, the rumours had already been spreading, that the pale, shy man at the wastebasket had been lionized before his time, that his films were unprofitable, that he was weird. He found bastions for shelter: a theory for anastomotic art; paired opposites and flowlines; novel modes of continuity ranging from the psychophysical, to the "treasure-hunt," to the bizarre—the foolish wonder of the copious inventory, the bursting suitcase, the overflowing box, the failing container.

In 1968, Mark Slade pled Lipsett's case in the pages of the *Montreal Gazette*, arguing that there was "a generation of young people whose own survival is linked with the survival of Arthur Lipsett."[46] The generation he spoke of was born against the glow of the atomic bomb. They were coming of age in the shadow of the Viet Nam War. They had grown up absurd, in a vortex of social and technological change. They asked questions and made demands about their roles in society. For those young people, the absurdity of Lipsett's films became an invitation, a promise of a new kind of continuity, whether dancing together into the apocalypse, wrestling with automatons, plummeting through flowlines into a state of grace, digging up time capsules to set them reeling, or stuffing one's mouth with foreign prayers. It was only after Slade's declaration that Lipsett treaded deeper into his own process, summoning supernovas, stuffing and emptying boxes, curating secret museums. Arthur Lipsett died almost twenty years after Slade made his plea, but long before that, that generation had changed. It had learned to survive the loss of people like Arthur Lipsett: by going straight, like every other generation.

The films of Arthur Lipsett are evidence of his resilience. His life was difficult despite his ability to find joy and humour in his difficulty; it was marked by loss and alienation, and, even at the best of times, he was under pressure to clarify and justify the way that he saw the world. But when he was making films, he was able to expand his complex vision of the world. Hope was a trickster, but oftentimes, so was he. His art was fragmentary, but that fragmentation was just an emerging continuity in the interesting times of his most rewarding years. Even through the fragmentation, purposeful obscurity, and strained humanism of his art, he was developing universal codes, in rhythms that transcended the narrow margins of any one language, in symbols that resonated across distant cultures and epochs. From his final films, he had at last emerged: the lost visionary in the human landscape.

# NOTES

## Introduction

1. The first public account of Lipsett's illness came in the form of a prolonged feature article that doubled as a eulogy: Lois Siegel's "A Clown Outside the Circus," *Cinema Canada* 134 (October 1986), 10–14.
2. The NFB was predated in this role by the Canadian Government Motion Picture Bureau (CGMPB), formed in 1918 to advertise the Canadian landscape and its resources. While it was a unique organization at its outset—the first government film production organization in the world—by the 1930s, its standing was in decline partly due to the inability on the part of the CGMPB to keep up with the technological evolutions of film sound. For a thorough accounting of the CGMPB, see Peter Morris, *Embattled Shadows: A History of Canadian Cinema 1895–1939* (Montreal: McGill–Queens University Press, 1978).
3. A discussion of the tragicomic facets of experimental film can be found in David Sterritt, "Wrenching Departures: Morality and Absurdity in Avant-Garde Film," in *The Last Laugh: Strange Humors of Cinema*, ed. Murray Pomerance (Detroit: Wayne State University Press, 2013), 93–108.
4. Ron Rice, "Foundation for the Invention and Creation of Absurdist Movies," *Film Culture* 39 (Winter 1965): 117. Rice's essay is less a manifesto than a droll self-portrait of the outsider and a record of the attitude with which he and poet Taylor Mead collaborated, a tacit boast of the proud informality of "underground knowledge."
5. Of the collage filmmakers who predate Lipsett, even British propagandist Charles A. Ridley, working within a conservative institutional context, made work with absurdist qualities. In Ridley's *Schichlegruber—Doing the Lambeth Walk* (1942), sequences from Leni Riefenstahl's *Triumph of the Will* (1936) are re-edited so that Nazi soldiers are shown performing the popular dance craze of the title. The elasticity of their movements is ridiculous: agents of evil become puppets of pleasure.

6   Alfred Jarry conceived of 'pataphysics as a parody of science, a mock inquiry into the nature of natures, an investigation of things even further removed from reality than the metaphysical. Aaron Hillyer has described the 'pataphysician in these terms, as one who "seeks to initiate a new world on the grounds of a tenuous unreality." Aaron Hillyer, *The Disappearance of Literature: Blanchot, Agamben, and the Writers of the No* (New York: Bloomsbury, 2013), 34. Arthur Lipsett's notes and proposals, interpreted at length in the coming pages, drift from tangible symbols to perceptible states of reflection to utter ineffability.

7   Bert Cardullo, *Theories of the Avant-Garde Theatre: A Casebook from Kleist to Camus* (Lanham, MD: Scarecrow Press, 2013), 31.

8   Sparks's Histomaps represent a close precursor to contemporary data visualization, but they also follow in a long line of synchronoptic graphs, cartographical flowcharts that began in the mid-eighteenth century with the work of Thomas Jeffreys. A thorough accounting of these efforts can be found in Jankel Myrdal, "On source criticism in world history," in *Methods in World History: A Critical Approach*, eds. Arne Jarrick, Jankel Myrdal, and Maria Wallenberg Bondesson (Lund: Nordic Academic Press, 2016), 50. The flowchart became a central form in Lipsett's thinking, a form he often used to plan and sequence his films due to how readily it leant itself to paper collage.

9   In a letter to the Frameworks listserv, dated October 25, 1998, critic Fred Camper argues that "Lipsett cannot see humour because he cannot stand outside of his footage," a claim that unduly diminishes Lipsett and renders his films "deadly serious," in contrast to the amused process of Bruce Conner: "For Lipsett, this footage *is* the world." Camper's reflections are an effort at distinguishing Lipsett's ontological presence in his footage from the materialist comedy of Bruce Conner, but they also indulge in a psychological interpretation of Lipsett's process that discounts—or simply does not recognize—the often riotous tone of his films.

10   This parallel between Lipsett and the player piano is not in reference to the latter's use as a transcription device, but it is evident in the work of Western composers, beginning with Nancarrow and later taken up by James Tenney, manually punching piano rolls to perform impossible feats.

11   Robert S. Dupree, "The Copious Inventory of Comedy," in *The Terrain of Comedy*, ed. Louise Cowan (Dallas: Dallas Institute of Humanities and Culture, 1984), 163–94. I come to Dupree's concept, which dominates my analysis, thanks to Cameron Moneo's doctoral dissertation, "Dissertation in Which There Appears Lost Punchlines, Dreadful Puns, Low Resolution, Etc.: On the failure of humour in avant-garde film and video" (Ph.D. diss., York University, 2019), to my knowledge the only book-length treatment of comedy in avant-garde film.

12   Mallarmé's original remark, "Le monde est fait pour aboutir dans à un beau Livre," given in an interview with Jules Huret (*Revue Blanche*, 1891), is commonly translated as the expression given here.

13   A notable exception to this is William Wees's 2007 lecture "From Compilation to Collage: The Found-Footage Films of Arthur Lipsett," in which Wees dares to take Lipsett's work seriously for its contradiction to the broader context of National Film Board production without undue attention to the tragic circumstances of the artist's life. Wees makes particularly effective use of I.A. Richards's theorization

of the literary metaphor—specifically, the distinction between vehicle and tenor—in outlining the formal directions of the Film Board in general. Such a lens inevitably situates Lipsett's films in a circuit of logical fallacies and a discourse of comprehensible ironies, one that is worthier than the sentimental readings given to Lipsett's films but nonetheless reductive. William Wees, "From Compilations to Collage: The Found-Footage Films of Arthur Lipsett," *Canadian Journal of Film Studies* 16, no. 2 (Fall 2007): 2–22.

14  Antonin Artaud, "Van Gogh, the Man Suicided by Society," in *Antonin Artaud, Selected Writings*, ed. Susan Sontag (New York: Farrar, Straus and Giroux, 1976), 483–512. The history of artists and poets whose deaths might be attributed to being "suicided by society" invites the most melancholy of copious inventories, from A for Arbus to Z for Zürn. The term is a misnomer in its exclusion of the soul murder of poets, a topic that resonates with Artaud's outrage and Lipsett's decline and is treated at length by Kenneth Rexroth in his 1953 poem "Thou Shalt Not Kill," written in memory of Dylan Thomas.

## One: The Stranger

1  Nancy Carpenter, interview by Michael Dancsok, July 11, 1997, transcript.
2  Carpenter, interview.
3  Judith Sandiford, Arthur Lipsett's partner from 1962 to 1973, has assembled a remarkable account of the Lipsett family history. For further reading, see https://artword.net/lipsett/.
4  My account of Lipsett's origins and family life is indebted to Judith Sandiford's research, as well as to that offered in Michael Dancsok, "Transcending the Documentary: The Films of Arthur Lipsett" (master's thesis, Concordia University, 1997) and in Amelia Does, *Do Not Look Away: The Life of Arthur Lipsett* (London, ON: Amelia Does, 2012).
5  The home, still standing today, is much unchanged when compared with family photographs: a stone foundation with a chimney and a brick second storey, an archetypal example of Montreal residential architecture of the early- to mid-twentieth century.
6  See Ira Robinson, "Reflections on Antisemitism in French Canada," *Canadian Jewish Studies* 21 (2014): 90–122.
7  Robinson, "Reflections," 99.
8  Arcand's writings—hysterical, fearmongering, and founded on rhetorically self-confirming irrationalism—remain in print and circulated by an anonymous devotee in Montreal. A comprehensive account of Arcand's publishing activities can be found in Hugues Théorêt, "The Rise and Fall of Adrien Arcand: Antisemitism in 20th Century Quebec," *Antisemitism Studies* 3, no. 2 (Fall 2019): 231–72.
9  Ira Robinson, *A History of Antisemitism in Canada* (Waterloo, ON: Wilfrid Laurier University Press, 2015), 96.
10  Arcand's imprisonment is thoroughly accounted in Jean-François Nadeau's *The Canadian Führer: The Life of Adrien Arcand* (Toronto: James Lorimer & Co., 2011).

11  Does, *Do Not Look Away*, 30.
12  These claims about the nature of Lipsett's relationship with his father are well-documented in interviews with Lipsett's sister Marian Arnold, his friend Christopher Nutter, and his therapist Nancy Carpenter. Marian Arnold, in particular, has given accounts of the harsh atmosphere of their family home to Dancsok and Does, albeit much of it recalled from a distant and difficult childhood.
13  Does, *Do Not Look Away*, 27.
14  Does, 26. The household cleaner is identified in various accounts as "rat poison"; however, what precisely she ingested is unknown. Judith Sandiford adds to the verifiable information a strong but apocryphal image that she formed from Arthur Lipsett's account: that his mother had taken the poison and then went out into the snow. Martin Lavut, dir., *Remembering Arthur* (Toronto: Public Pictures, 2006), DVD.
15  This detail, highlighted in conversation with Amelia Does, provides insight into Marian Arnold's own pain over her upbringing. It also indicates the subjectivity of her account of family life in the Lipsett household, offered with wounds showing.
16  Lavut, *Remembering Arthur*.
17  In contradiction to claims that Solomon Lipsett did not support his son's interest in the arts, Arthur Lipsett would later tell a journalist that his father "sent [him] to art school with his blessings." Dusty Vineberg, "A 'Short' Story: Waste-basket to Potential Oscar," *Montreal Star*, February 24, 1962, 5.
18  Lismer's introduction to this community is accounted in Ross King, *Defiant Spirits: The Modernist Revolution of the Group of Seven* (Vancouver: Douglas & McIntyre, 2010), 60–63.
19  Angela Nairne Grigor, *Arthur Lismer, Visionary Art Educator* (Montreal: McGill–Queen's University Press, 2002), 304.
20  Grigor, *Arthur Lismer*, 198.
21  Northrop Frye, *Northrop Frye on Canada*, eds. Jean O'Grady and David Staines (Toronto: University of Toronto Press, 2003), 542.
22  Arthur Lismer, "Comment on the Fine Arts," undated (circa 1950s), File A22, Arthur Lismer Fonds, Museum of Fine Arts Archives, Montreal.
23  Grigor, *Arthur Lismer*, 203.
24  Arthur Lismer, "Art in the Atomic Age," transcript of lecture given on CBC radio, 1953, File C7, Arthur Lismer Fonds, Montreal Museum of Fine Arts Archives, Montreal, Quebec.
25  "Arthur Lipsett Best Student in Art School," *Gazette* (Montreal), April 4, 1955, 12.
26  "Marina Greciano Captures Museum's Top Art Standing," *Gazette* (Montreal), April 8, 1957, 9.
27  John Grierson, "A Film Policy for Canada," *Canadian Affairs* 1, no. 11 (June 1944): 11.
28  Grierson's subsequent testimony reveals much of his character, insisting that a civil servant must be, by training, neutral. A full account of these events can be found in D.B. Jones, *Movies and Memoranda: An Interpretative History of the National Film Board of Canada* (Ottawa: Canadian Film Institute, 1981), 49–50.

29  John Grierson, "First Principles of Documentary," *Cinema Quarterly* 1, no. 2 (Winter 1932): 67–72.
30  D.B. Jones, "Tom Daly's Apprenticeship," *Film History* 3, no. 3 (1989): 266.
31  Jones, *Movies and Memoranda*, 24.
32  The second volume of Gary Evans's study of the Film Board decidedly begins in 1949 on the eve of the National Film Act, even taking its title, *In the National Interest*, from the wording of the act, which indicates how transformative this event was. For a full account, see Gary Evans, *In the National Interest: A Chronicle of the National Film Board from 1949 to 1989* (Toronto: University of Toronto Press, 1991), 15–17.
33  The unit system was a simplification of an organizational model recommended by Grierson years earlier. The particularities of the unit system are offered in Jones, *Movies and Memoranda*, 60–61.
34  McLaren's autonomy within the Film Board was due to a number of factors: having been enlisted by Grierson, he represented continuity and Grierson's legacy within the NFB; he is credited for having dictated the emphasis on art school graduates for enlistment, thus becoming responsible, directly or indirectly, for an incoming generation of Film Board administrators; his work was modest, a relatively light expense in terms of board resources, and intimate; and the esteem with which his work was held internationally, and the positive attention it brought the Film Board, led to him requiring no oversight.
35  Biographical profile of Arthur Lipsett, undated, National Film Board Archives, Montreal, Quebec.
36  Low's description of Lipsett's enthusiasms is worth dwelling upon: Low would recall Lipsett's explanations as "clear and straightforward," a sign of the didactic, discursive expectations that defined the culture of the NFB. Eric Gaucher, *The Arthur Lipsett Project: A Dot on the Histomap* (Montreal: The National Film Board of Canada, 2007), DVD.
37  Arthur Lipsett, public lecture, McMaster University, circa 1967, tape provided by Brett Kashmere from the collection of Henry Zemel.
38  Roman Kroitor is given sole credit as the screenwriter, and the text takes dramatic licence to condense the detail-rich accounts given in Berton's book to the format of the film.
39  For *City of Gold*, Roman Kroitor developed the eponymous "Kroitorer," "a machine that enabled one to shoot the photographs as if a hand-held camera had been there at the time," essentially a method to allow the optical camera to follow a charted path, to mirror the movements of a human operator. Kroitor's clever engineering is evidence of the interdisciplinary skills of Unit B filmmakers. Evans, *In the National Interest*, 75. Low's technique was a ready shorthand at the NFB within a few years, as evidenced in animated films like Gerald Budner and Robert Verrall's *A is for Architecture* (1960). Not only was the technique influential, but it typifies experimentation at the Film Board: formal innovation in the service of storytelling.
40  Gaucher, *The Arthur Lipsett Project*.
41  "Storyboards covered the walls, masking every inch." This description is offered by Derek Lamb to Lois Siegel in Siegel, "A Clown Outside the Circus," *Cinema Canada* 134 (October 1986): 13.

42   Lipsett's contribution to *Men Against the Ice* is substantial: an opening narration describes the origins of oceanic exploration, as profile images of ancient explorers glide through a black world map in chalky white forms. This conventional animation is performed using fades and simple transitions. Throughout the film, historical illustrations of polar exploration are edited in an interweaving montage, with an emphasis on the *City of Gold* effect, the camera guided through static images to emphasize scale or detail.

43   Franz Schulz-Reichel, known professionally as Crazy Otto, was a classically trained pianist who became a popular novelty performer thanks to two techniques that gave him a distinctive sound: one was his detuning the piano to become a "tipsy wire box"; the other was his insistence on playing the melody on bass keys and rhythm on treble keys. The aggression with which he played, paired with these approaches, results in a mad variation on the style of Scott Joplin.

44   Lipsett's mechanization of Gould anticipates Gould's mechanization of himself: Gould became a national icon and international star for his celebrated interpretations of Johann Sebastian Bach's *The Goldberg Variations*, and his retirement from public performance in the 1960s coincided with his dedication to perfectly machined recordings. In a sense, Gould's appearance in the feet clip reveals Lipsett's recognition of how mechanization took command in modern art. Both Lipsett and Gould had their creativity and technique expanded by electromechanical technology, each—in their own way—extending the legacy of musique concrète: Lipsett in his films, Gould in his "contrapuntal radio" sound collage documentary *The Idea of North* (1967).

45   These films are held in the archives of the Cinémathèque québécoise. The use of Baby Dodds in the Montreal Film Festival trailer is particularly telling as an indication of what kind of music Lipsett responded to and influenced his percussive editing style. Dodds's drum improvisations, often dealing with both pitch and rhythm, assume a hypnotic structure, mirroring the dynamic invention of ragtime, with a ratcheting, metallic timbre not unlike the mechanical aggression of the ragtime pianist.

46   In these roles, Lipsett was co-credited. As an animator on Bobet's series, he worked with (and likely under the supervision of) Evelyn Lambart, a pioneer of the NFB's animation department; on *The Rough Road to Freedom*, Lipsett was part of an animation team that included Roy Nolan and Pierre L'Amare. This demonstrates both the mentorship system that existed for Lipsett in Unit B and the topics he was exploring through service work: conflict, emancipation, and education.

47   *Opening Speech* is also a notable example of the alien reverberation of the sound effects used in many NFB films of its time, here perfectly synchronized and densely layered by Karl du Plessis; and yet, those sounds are full of a distinctively artificial presence. Such percussive effects—panting, slamming, footsteps, and clattering—would be mirrored, if not fractured and reused, in Lipsett's own films to a similar effect of comic punctuation.

48   Arthur Lipsett, "Fly Little Bird" (proposal), June 1960, Box VI #15, Tom Daly Collection, National Film Board Archives, Montreal, Quebec.

## Two: Revelation

1. This anecdote, offered by Derek Lamb, is further evidence that Lipsett maintained an absurdist affect and that he found humour in a premise others might find bizarre, like eating magnetic tape. Eric Gaucher, *The Arthur Lipsett Project: A Dot on the Histomap* (Montreal: The National Film Board of Canada, 2007), DVD.
2. The portrayal of Lipsett as an artist toiling in the wastebaskets of the institution was initiated in an article in early 1962 in which Lipsett described his process as "collecting scrap from the wastage." Dusty Vineberg, "A 'Short' Story: Waste-basket to Potential Oscar," *Montreal Star*, February 24, 1962, 5.
3. Among other tasks, Lipsett edited an episode of Donald Brittain and Stanley Clish's *Canada at War* (titled *Cinderella on the Left*, 1962), a successor to Legg's series. Lipsett was thus involved in the production of conventional compilation films.
4. "Arthur Lipsett," press release, Arthur Lipsett Collection, Cinémathèque québécoise Archives, Montreal, Quebec.
5. Michael Dancsok, "Transcending the Documentary: The Films of Arthur Lipsett" (master's thesis, Concordia University, 1997), 25.
6. Schaeffer, as a primary instigator of radiophonic poetics, led the discourse around sound art in the 1950s. His philosophical credo *In Search of a Concrete Music* was published in French in 1952. In 1960, when Lipsett was beginning his sound collage work, Schaeffer's would have been a dominant text that Lipsett likely encountered.
7. Questions have persisted regarding the precise materials that Lipsett used in making the sound collage of *Very Nice, Very Nice*: the rumour that Lipsett's work emerged from rubbish bins around the building led many to believe that he was working with 16mm magnetic stock. Archivist and artist Steven Woloshen confirms to the author via email (April 25, 2023) that, because the film was initially developed as an audio essay, a workprint on quarter-inch tape would likely exist.
8. The precise setting of Lipsett's labours within the NFB building is unclear, but in *A Dot on the Histomap: The Arthur Lipsett Project*, Derek Lamb guides the filmmakers to a hallway, suggesting that Lipsett's work was being performed in provisional spaces, outside of the controlled environment of the building's conventional sound studio. Gaucher, *The Arthur Lipsett Project*.
9. Arthur Lipsett, "Fly Little Bird" (proposal), June 1960, Box VI #15, Tom Daly Collection, National Film Board Archives, Montreal, Quebec.
10. Lipsett, "Fly Little Bird."
11. Lipsett, "Fly Little Bird."
12. Lipsett uses the phrase "flowlines" when describing the means by which sequences are reconciled into a coherent whole within his work. The notion of an arc of gathering and dispersing energy would likewise run through his engagements with his colleagues, illustrated in the charts that accompanied his proposals and resonating with concepts of forces and fields governing natural and electroacoustic phenomena that preoccupied him in subsequent years. Arthur Lipsett, public lecture, McMaster University, 1967, tape provided by Brett Kashmere from the collection of Henry Zemel.

13   Arthur Lipsett, "Strangely Elated" (chart), circa 1961, Production file 61-205 (*Very Nice, Very Nice*), National Film Board Archives, Montreal, Quebec. This and other planning documents were also printed with an introduction in Michael Dancsok, "Ciné-Documents: An Introduction to Notes and Proposals by Arthur Lipsett," *Canadian Journal of Film Studies* 7, no. 1 (Spring 1998): 43–46.
14   Siegfried Kracauer, *Theory of Film: The Redemption of Physical Reality* (New York: Oxford University Press, 1960), 46–57.
15   Lipsett, "Strangely Elated."
16   Lipsett, "Fly Little Bird."
17   This proposal demonstrates Lipsett's allegiance to Lismer's belief that artists maintain the disposition of a curious child. Lipsett's later, unsuccessful proposals for projects on childhood and creativity indicate that this would remain an ongoing concern for him.
18   The images that Lipsett took during his summer travels were not the only images of his used in the film. According to his colleague Neil Shakery, many of the images were taken during earlier trips to England. Amelia Does, *Do Not Look Away: The Life of Arthur Lipsett* (London, ON: Amelia Does, 2012), 45.
19   The rocket launch was sourced from Fox Newsreels. The image of the hydrogen bomb explosion came from the NFB's own stock inventory. Doris Tennant, Memorandum to Bill Galloway, November 30, 1961, Production file 61-205 (*Very Nice, Very Nice*), National Film Board Archives, Montreal, Quebec.
20   Roland Barthes, "The World of Wrestling," in *Mythologies*, trans. Annette Lavers (New York: Hill and Wang, 1972), 17.
21   Rathburn, director of the NFB's Music Department, is the subject of James K. Wright and Allyson Rogers's meticulous study *They Shot, He Scored: The Life and Music of Eldon Rathburn* (Montreal: McGill–Queen's University Press, 2019).
22   Whalley's line is taken from an NFB documentary about Inuit sculpture, John Feeney's *The Living Stone* (1959).
23   This is a celebrated postcard image of New York City. *Sunset over New York City* is found in "Flug und Wolken," Manfred Curry, Verlag F. Bruckmann, München (Munich), 1932.
24   Aerial films purchased from Aerofilms & Aero Pictorial Ltd. D.F. Smith, Letter to Colin Low, November 24, 1961, Production file 61-205 (*Very Nice, Very Nice*), National Film Board Archives, Montreal, Quebec.
25   Robert S. Dupree, "The Copious Inventory of Comedy," in *The Terrain of Comedy*, ed. Louise Cowan (Dallas, TX: Dallas Institute of Humanities and Culture, 1984), 163–94.
26   Vineberg, "A 'Short' Story," 5.
27   Lawrence Lipton, *The Holy Barbarians* (New York: Julian Messner, 1959), 7.
28   Our understanding of Lipsett's consumption of experimental films is largely informed by accounts given by his partner, Judith Sandiford, of what Guy L. Coté would screen for them from his collection.
29   Peter Harcourt, "The Innocent Eye: An Aspect of the Work of the National Film Board of Canada," *Sight and Sound* 34, no. 1 (Winter 1964–65): 21.
30   John Keats, *The Complete Poetical Works and Letters of John Keats* (Cambridge: Houghton, Mifflin and Company, 1899). My use of the term descends from R.

Bruce Elder's writings on Stan Brakhage, in which he characterizes negative capability, by way of both Keats and Charles Olson, as "a valuable antidote to our culture's tendency toward rationalization." R. Bruce Elder, *The Films of Stan Brakhage in the American Tradition of Ezra Pound, Gertrude Stein, and Charles Olson* (Waterloo, ON: Wilfrid Laurier University Press, 1999), 463.

31  Martin Lavut, *Remembering Arthur* (Toronto: Public Pictures, 2006), DVD.
32  Derek Hill, "Short and Sharp," *Observer* (London), December 24, 1961, 21.
33  G.F. Noble, Memorandum to Tom Daly, March 22, 1962, Production file 61-205 (*Very Nice, Very Nice*), National Film Board Archives, Montreal, Quebec.
34  Canadian Embassy (Tokyo, Japan), Letter to the Under-Secretary of State for External Affairs (Ottawa, Canada), November 14, 1962, 2017.0055.61.AR, Professional Correspondence, Arthur Lipsett Collection, Cinémathèque québécoise Archives, Montreal, Quebec.
35  Lipsett, "Fly Little Bird." Emphasis is Lipsett's.
36  Harris and Lipsett struck up a brief but warm correspondence, owing in part to Harris's friendship with Guy Glover, Norman McLaren's partner who was himself an animator and producer at the NFB. Hilary Harris, Letter to Arthur Lipsett, April 22, 1963, 2005.0080.26.AR, Personal Correspondence, Arthur Lipsett Collection, Cinémathèque québécoise Archives, Montreal, Quebec. Harris writes of being engaged in a film about the population crisis—likely *The Squeeze* (1964)—and how he "can't seem to get away from a Very Nice influence."
37  Stanley Kubrick, Letter to Arthur Lipsett, May 31, 1962, 2017.0055.61.AR, Professional Correspondence, Arthur Lipsett Collection, Cinémathèque québécoise Archives, Montreal, Quebec. A subsequent offer to edit the soundtrack to Kubrick's *Dr. Strangelove, or, How I Learned to Stop Worrying and Love the Bomb* (1962) is purported to have been made; apocryphal though this story may be, the trailer that Kubrick later commissioned from Pablo Ferro bears the influence of *Very Nice, Very Nice*.
38  Lois Siegel, "A Clown Outside the Circus," *Cinema Canada* 134 (October 1986): 13.
39  Siegel, "A Clown Outside the Circus," 13.

### Three: A Personal Vision

1  Ernest Callenbach, "The Films of Stan Brakhage," *Film Quarterly* 14, no. 3 (Spring 1961): 47–48.
2  This changed across Canada through cinema societies at universities in the mid-1960s when such groups began to integrate underground movie showings into their programming. Such programs were helped along by mixing the films of American underground filmmakers with those acquired from the NFB, made by Lipsett, McLaren, Guy Glover, and others. For further discussion of this context, see Stephen Broomer, *Hamilton Babylon: A History of the McMaster Film Board* (Toronto: University of Toronto Press, 2016).
3  The complex history of distribution for underground cinema in America and, in particular, the conflict that resulted in the founding of the co-op demonstrate why this art form is so imbricated with American experience. Excellent accounts

of the conflict between Mekas and Cinema 16 founder Amos Vogel can be found in David E. James, *To Free the Cinema: Jonas Mekas & the New York Underground* (Princeton, NJ: Princeton University Press, 1992) and in Scott MacDonald, *Cinema 16: Documents Toward a History of the Film Society* (Philadelphia: Temple University Press, 2002).

4   This drought would end in the mid-1960s through the founding of two services: Willem Poolman's Film Canada, a commercial distributor that specialized in distributing European art cinema, and the Canadian Filmmakers Distribution Centre, which specialized in Canadian underground cinema.

5   For an extensive history of the Coté collection and its influence on the Canadian art cinema circuit, see Pierre Hébert, "Procès d'une collection," *Objectif* 32 (Spring 1965): 3–16.

6   Guy L. Coté, *A Private Collection of Experimental Abstract Poetic Personal Amateur Animation Films* (St. Laurent, QC: Guy Coté, July 1960).

7   Amelia Does, *Do Not Look Away: The Life of Arthur Lipsett* (London, ON: Amelia Does, 2012), 45. Like Lipsett, Millar had an interest in world cultures, which had led to his other assignment of 1962, four films for the NFB's *Great Religions* series, written by philosopher George Grant and directed under the supervision of producer James Beveridge.

8   Arthur Lipsett and David Millar, "Experimental Film-Makers – A Personal Vision" (proposal), July 18, 1962, Production file 62-213 (*The Experimental Film*), National Film Board Archives, Montreal, Quebec.

9   Lipsett and Millar, "Experimental Film-Makers."

10  Lipsett and Millar, "Experimental Film-Makers."

11  McLaren's methods had already been the subject of a self-portrait, *Pen Point Percussion* (1951), made a decade earlier for the NFB.

12  It is worth acknowledging in this context that, in addition to being an accomplished animator in his own right prior to assuming the responsibilities of a producer, Glover was also McLaren's life partner. Their relationship is detailed in Nichola Dobson's *Norman McLaren: Between the Frames* (New York: Bloomsbury, 2018).

13  Lipsett and Millar are doing this out of sheer utility, based on what would read best on black-and-white television sets, but it has an analytical effect, another way of seeing McLaren's craft and of relating it, however subtly, to Breer's.

14  The quotation, potentially apocryphal, has been reported widely and in various translations in the past century. Ernst's work, and his whole conception of collage art, had a massive impact on Joseph Cornell, whose efforts in experimental collage filmmaking anticipate Lipsett and Conner by twenty years but strongly resemble their work.

15  Comte De Lautréamont, *Les Chants de Maldoror*, trans. Guy Wernham (New York: New Directions, 1965), 263.

16  The imagery that VanDerBeek creates often suggests the great subversions of reality that occur in the paintings of René Magritte. VanDerBeek's admirer and most famous imitator, Terry Gilliam, would carry this aspect of VanDerBeek's collage practice forward in his work as a member of British comedy troupe Monty Python.

17  VanDerBeek's work in this area is accounted in Gloria Sutton, *The Experience Machine: Stan Vanderbeek's Movie-Drone and Expanded Cinema* (Boston, MA: MIT Press, 2015).
18  Hébert, "Procès d'une collection," 13–14.
19  A detailed account of Conner's experience in making *A Movie* is given in Amelia Does, "'Worthwhile Insanity': On Collage Filmmaking and Arthur Lipsett, an Interview with Bruce Conner," *INCITE!: Journal of Experimental Media* 2 (Spring–Fall 2010): 62–72.
20  Michael Dancsok, "Transcending the Documentary: The Films of Arthur Lipsett" (master's thesis, Concordia University, 1997), 44.
21  Bob Gardiner, "Televiews," *Ottawa Citizen*, November 21, 1962, 35.
22  Terry Ryan, Memo sent to distribution staff at the National Film Board, October 25, 1967, 2005.0080.36.AR, *The Experimental Film* (Text), Arthur Lipsett Collection, Cinémathèque québécoise Archives, Montreal, Quebec.
23  Martin Lavut, *Remembering Arthur* (Toronto: Public Pictures, 2006), DVD.
24  At the time, Lavut's creative work included an appearance in Julian Roffman's beatnik horror movie *The Mask* (1961), and Lavut would begin to make independent films of his own a few years later with *At Home* (1968). He would become a staple director of dramatic and documentary fare for the CBC through the 1970s and '80s.
25  Does, *Do Not Look Away*, 45. Amelia Does has done an excellent job in laying out the warmth and depth of the friendships Lipsett had at the NFB, drawn from the memories of those she interviewed, as did Lavut in his 2006 documentary *Remembering Arthur*. Does adds the detail here that Lipsett's new apartment had formerly been rented by colleague Neil Shakery and his wife Karin, which suggests the sense of fellowship that Lipsett had found in the small community of Unit B.
26  Lavut, *Remembering Arthur*.
27  Lavut, *Remembering Arthur*.

## Four: Processional

1  Arthur Lipsett, "*21-87*" (handwritten note), circa 1963, Production file 62-206 (*21-87*), National Film Board Archives, Montreal, Quebec.
2  Lipsett speaks about his interest in paired opposites at length in a recorded talk given at McMaster University in 1967, tape provided by Brett Kashmere from the collection of Henry Zemel.
3  Receipt from Simon's Cameras Inc., March 14, 1962, 2005.0055.41.AR, Professional Correspondence, Arthur Lipsett Collection, Cinémathèque québécoise Archives, Montreal, Quebec.
4  Martin Lavut, *Remembering Arthur* (Toronto: Public Pictures, 2006), DVD.
5  Lipsett's use of a Bolex camera was unusual in the context of Unit B, where the bulk of production was done using sync-sound cameras with large magazine capacities and even, in some cases, in-camera sound-recording options, like the Auricon camera. Practicalities aside, this was another gesture of aligning himself with the

American underground for whom Bolex cameras were essential tools and were, by the early 1960s, central to the work of Stan Brakhage and Jonas Mekas, both of whom proselytized on behalf of the intimacy and mechanics of the instrument.

6 Arthur Lipsett, "*Processional*" (proposal), circa 1962, Production file 62-206 (*21-87*), National Film Board Archives, Montreal, Quebec.
7 Lipsett, "*Processional*."
8 Lipsett, "*Processional*."
9 Lipsett, "*Processional*." Lipsett's emphasis.
10 Outtakes from *Lonely Boy*, outtakes from *The Living Machine*, and agreement with NASA are detailed in various memoranda present in the National Film Board archives. Tom Daly, Memorandum to Lois Dooh, June 7, 1962; Tom Daly, Memorandum to Lois Dooh, June 13, 1962; Donald Swartz, Letter to Tom Daly, October 31, 1963; Tom Daly, reply, December 2, 1963, Production file 61-205 (*Very Nice, Very Nice*), National Film Board Archives, Montreal, Quebec.
11 The exception to this is that Lipsett does allow for particular sound effects to interact with the image. For example, a repeating mechanical bleat becomes a structuring element for the first cuts in the film. Likewise, his music cues tend to coincide with edits.
12 The histories of these automatons have been charted in Gaby Wood's *Living Dolls: A Magical History of the Quest for Mechanical Life* (London: Faber, 2003).
13 John Bray's account of Dodsley's collection deals in part with its provenance and claims to Eastern wisdom. John Bray, "The Œconomy of Human Life: An 'Ancient Bramin' in Eighteenth-Century Tibet," *Journal of the Royal Asiatic Society, Third Series* 19, no. 4 (2009): 439–58.
14 Lipsett, "*Processional*."
15 Gernsback never comments directly on the phenomenon, despite often giving longwinded explanations for various inventions throughout the text. The closest he comes to elucidating the name pattern is in the opening of the novel—"He was Ralph 124C 41+, one of the greatest living scientists and one of the ten men on the whole planet earth permitted to use the Plus sign after his name"—and in its conclusion, when the protagonist's lover, Alice 212B 423, remarks that she now understands him to be "one to foresee for one!" Hugo Gernsback, *Ralph 124C 41+: A Romance of the Year 2660* (New York: The Stratford Company, 1925).
16 Lipsett, "*Processional*."
17 A comprehensive overview of the subgenre of the mock epic can be found in Ritchie Robertson, *Mock-Epic Poetry from Pope to Heine* (Oxford: Oxford University Press, 2009). My use of the term in reference to *21-87* is to denote the filmmaker's ability to cast a profound atmosphere over such trivialities.
18 Judith Sandiford describes John Max's sharing of his prayer as a gift to Lipsett, a demonstration of something highly personal to him that he would only perform in private.
19 Lipsett, "*21-87*."
20 Lipsett, "*21-87*."
21 Arthur Lipsett, Letter to L.M. Kit Carson, undated (circa 1966), 2005.0055.39.SC, *21-87* (documents), Arthur Lipsett Collection, Cinémathèque québécoise Archives, Montreal, Quebec.

22  Lipsett, Letter to L.M. Kit Carson.
23  Lipsett was one of many experimental filmmakers to take inspiration from the *Bardo Thodol*. In America, the influence of the beat movement and the psychedelic movement in creating a generation of Western Omnist-Buddhists succeeded also in producing a massive body of cinema that drew broad connections between states of being and Evans-Wentz's articulation of the Bardo plane. While Lipsett was working on *21-87*, Vancouver poet and filmmaker Sam Perry was drawing from the *Bardo Thodol* in his attempt to make an epic film cycle, only fragments of which survived his suicide in 1966. The only completed epic film cycle in the history of Canadian cinema to date, R. Bruce Elder's thirty-six-hour *The Book of All the Dead* (1975–94), likewise bears influence from themes of the *Bardo Thodol*.
24  Arthur Lipsett, untitled script (*21-87*), undated, 2005.0055.39.SC, *21-87* (documents), Arthur Lipsett Collection, Cinémathèque québécoise Archives, Montreal, Quebec.
25  Lipsett, untitled script (*21-87*).
26  Lipsett, "*21-87*."

### Five: The Green Fuse

1  William York Tindall, *A Reader's Guide to Dylan Thomas* (London: Thames and Hudson, 1962), 39.
2  Dylan Thomas, Letter to Pamela Hansford Johnson, November 5, 1933, in *The Collected Letters*, ed. Paul Ferris (London: J.M. Dent, 1985), 39.
3  Ralph Maud, *Where Have the Old Words Got Me? Explication of Dylan Thomas's Collected Poems* (Montreal: McGill–Queen's University Press, 2003), 237.
4  Jean-Claude Pilon, "Sept films canadiens / *21-87*, film canadien d'Arthur Lipsett," *Objectif* 23–24 (October–November 1963): 41. Author's translation.
5  It was also a title shared with a Jimmy Giuffre trio album released that March; Lipsett, as an avid collector of modern jazz records, would have encountered it prior to proposing his film that July. A particularly radical record in its time, *Free Fall* features entire cuts of unaccompanied clarinet.
6  The term pixilation was purportedly coined by Lipsett's colleague Grant Munro when he collaborated with Norman McLaren on *Neighbors* (1952), and the technique had been used by McLaren extensively in *Two Bagatelles* (with Munro, 1953) and *A Chairy Tale* (with Claude Jutra, 1957). Pixilation had been with cinema since the beginning of the twentieth century, as early as Segundo de Chomón's *Hôtel électrique* (1908) and Émile Cohl's *Jobard ne peut pas voir les femmes travailler* (1911). Lipsett was developing his approach, which was more violent and abstract and bore a distinctively strained continuity, at the same time that similar approaches were emerging from the New American Cinema, including the films of Stan Brakhage, Marie Menken's *Go! Go! Go!* (1962–64), and the first chapters of Jonas Mekas's *Walden* (1964–68). Norman McLaren and Grant Munro may have served as a more local example of pixilation filmmakers, but their use of pixilation was in support of dramatic structures and in the interest of simple comedies and allegories. The difference

between these approaches can be situated in the context of Dylan Thomas's "force": when Menken or Mekas use pixilation, exposing one frame at a time on changing subjects, this allows minutes to collapse into seconds, time-lapse as a tool for violent abstraction and defamiliarization of movement, a gesture symbolic of hungry synapses with a gluttonous appetite for the passing moment. McLaren and Munro's pixilation, by contrast, casts simple illusions, often held on actors attempting stillness as objects are artificially animated around them—a process that bears the very image of death: a purely synthetic manipulation of the living subject.

7   Laura Kuhn speculates in *The Selected Letters of John Cage* that Lipsett had misunderstood the compositional methods of *Indeterminacy*. It is possible that he heard the record and perceived a conflict of elements, as opposed to a kind of sonic naturalism. However, I speculate in turn that, as Cage's notes on the Folkways release are very clear, Lipsett's predicament was social rather than intellectual, in that he had to balance courting Cage with the difficulty of pitching this collaboration to his colleagues. John Cage, *The Selected Letters of John Cage*, ed. Laura Kuhn (Middletown, CT: Wesleyan University Press, 2016), 288n529.

8   Arthur Lipsett, "*Free Fall*" (second proposal), September 6, 1963, Production file 63-213 (*Free Fall*), National Film Board Archives, Montreal, Quebec.

9   Lipsett, "*Free Fall*" (second proposal).

10  Arthur Lipsett, "*Free Fall*" (first proposal), July 16, 1963, Production file 63-213 (*Free Fall*), National Film Board Archives, Montreal, Quebec. Lipsett's emphasis.

11  Arthur Lipsett, "*21-87*" (handwritten note), circa 1963, Production file 62-206 (*21-87*), National Film Board Archives, Montreal, Quebec.

12  Lipsett, "*Free Fall*" (first proposal).

13  John Cage, *Silence: Lectures and Writings* (Middletown, CT: Wesleyan University Press, 1961), 12.

14  Lipsett, "*Free Fall*" (second proposal).

15  When McLaren's film was at last completed, it was without Balanchine's participation. The final film was choreographed by Canadian ballet dancer Ludmilla Chiraeff, a sign that the rigidity of the NFB did not lend itself to collaborations with modern artists.

16  John Cage, Letter to Arthur Lipsett, October 12, 1963, 2017.0055.61.AR, Professional Correspondence, Arthur Lipsett Collection, Cinémathèque québécoise Archives, Montreal, Quebec.

17  Cage, Letter to Arthur Lipsett.

18  Cage's final letter to Lipsett maintained a cordial optimism that they may yet find a way to work together, a time when "we could start from scratch knowing from the outset that we would not be knowing where we are going." John Cage, Letter to Arthur Lipsett, November 29, 1963, 2017.0055.61.AR, Professional Correspondence, Arthur Lipsett Collection, Cinémathèque québécoise Archives, Montreal, Quebec.

19  Vostell's conception of the reconciliation of destruction and creation in art is recounted at length in Benjamin Lima, *Violence in Concrete: Wolf Vostell's Art and Germany After 1945* (New York: Peter Lang, 2016).

20  The painting illustrates the eternal slumber of Endymion, brought about by his

lover, Titan goddess Selene, a reversal of the Pygmalion myth in that, rather than a wish to bring stone to life, Selene's wish is to suspend Endymion in sleep. Its presence here is another sign that Lipsett views the present moment as revealed through paired opposites, with Selene's wish operating between desire and destruction, and casting her beloved into an eternal life that resembles death; further to that, Lipsett's inclusion is, like his use of images of sleeping children, a declaration of a world asleep.

21 The use of *Four-Line Conics* was solicited by Bill Galloway on Lipsett's behalf. Doris Tennant, Memorandum to Bill Galloway, May 7, 1965, Production file 63-213 (*Free Fall*), National Film Board Archives, Montreal, Quebec.

22 The image in question is an advertising image for Professor E.J. Mack's "chin reducer and beautifier no. III," dated 1909.

23 The man's head is unidentified, but the street scene contained inside of the face is Sabine Weiss's "Running Man, Paris" (1953). Lipsett would license other images of Weiss's for use in his next film.

24 The image of Lavut with false eyes may be a reference to Man Ray's *Emak-Bakia* (1926), in which Kiki de Montparnasse is shown with stylized eyes painted on her eyelids, which open to reveal her real eyes beneath. Man Ray's gesture illuminates the symbolism of the eye as a deceptive site of transit between waking life and the stupor of a dream.

25 Tom Daly, Letter to Ross Buskard, November 22, 1963, Production file 63-213 (*Free Fall*), National Film Board Archives, Montreal, Quebec.

26 It might be noted, in light of this discussion of Lipsett's efforts in constructing sound, that his soundtracks have been treated as autonomous since his death—for example, with the 2005 Global A Records release of his soundtracks (GLOBAL 007LP).

27 Lipsett would later present an inscription of the energy pattern of *Free Fall* at the Cinémathèque canadienne on September 29, 1964: a pair of illustrations, close in composition, that elaborate on the shape of an arrow pointing to the upper right, as if charting a rise in a graph. The illustrations, one in black-and-red ink on lined notebook paper, the other in green-and-black marker on card stock, are furious concentrations of curving lines falling away from the incline of an arrow. Inverse to the arrow is a stick figure, head to the lower left, arms spread as if in free fall. It is described by Lipsett, tongue in cheek, as a "representation of the dramatic approach of the film." Author's translation from French. Arthur Lipsett, "*Free Fall*" (drawing), circa 1964, 1992.0153.AN, *Free Fall*, Arthur Lipsett Collection, Cinémathèque québécoise Archives, Montreal, Quebec.

28 D.B. Jones, *Movies and Memoranda: An Interpretative History of the National Film Board of Canada* (Ottawa: Canadian Film Institute, 1981), 113.

29 Jones, *Movies and Memoranda*, 113. So central is this concept of artistic dictatorship to Jones that his eighth chapter is titled for it.

30 Arthur Lipsett, "The Formation of Verbal and Visual 'Language' in Young Children," July 27, 1964, Box XVI #8, Tom Daly Collection, National Film Board Archives, Montreal, Quebec.

## Six: Time-Capsule

1 Nick Yablon, *Remembrance of Things Present: The Invention of the Time Capsule* (Chicago: University of Chicago Press, 2019), 3.
2 The theme of mutuality and empathy in Buber is of special significance to Lipsett, whose interest in Buber's writings stemmed from the latter's conceptions of loneliness and alienation, the salve for which is social communion and, through communion, a sense of belonging with other beings or within a greater continuity. Religiosity, Buber's term for the spiritual fount that escapes the narrows of dogma and denomination, resonates with Lipsett's Omnism, that reconciliation of ecstatic parts first felt in *Free Fall*. Lipsett encountered these themes in Martin Buber, *Between Man and Man*, trans. Ronald Gregor Smith (London: Kegan Paul, 1947).
3 For a thorough and posthumous account of Donald Brittain's career, see Brian Nolan, *Donald Brittain: Man of Film* (Amherstview, ON: Digiwire, 2004). Nolan's account is primarily biographical; to that same end, and to have the subject in his own words, consult Kent Martin's feature documentary *Donald Brittain: Filmmaker* (1992).
4 The quotation is drawn from an archival interview with Brittain, who died in 1989. Eric Gaucher, *The Arthur Lipsett Project: A Dot on the Histomap* (Montreal: The National Film Board of Canada, 2007), DVD.
5 Brittain's standing among his colleagues, and the political cachet he held at the NFB during this period of transition, is elaborated in D.B. Jones's *Movies and Memoranda: An Interpretative History of the National Film Board of Canada* (Ottawa: Canadian Film Institute, 1981), 112–13.
6 The antisocial characterization of Lipsett that has been advanced from this story deserves to be contested: the equipment in question is dependent upon elements that go through wear and tear, such as lightbulbs and blades, and in an environment where equipment would frequently change hands, it is likely that Lipsett was simply habituated to the equipment he used daily. Accounts of Lipsett's behaviour may paint him as paranoid or unwilling to share, but they also show someone with a discerning eye for reliable equipment working to avoid the distraction of fixing and readying different equipment each day.
7 Buber, *Between Man and Man*, 73.
8 Arthur Lipsett, notes to Donald Brittain "in order to communicate to him some basic thinking on our film Time Capsule," December 25, 1964, Arthur Lipsett Collection, Cinémathèque québécoise Archives, Montreal, Quebec, 4.
9 Lipsett, notes to Donald Brittain, 1.
10 The Dostoyevsky quote comes via B.F. Skinner's phrasing in *Cumulative Record: A Selection of Papers* (New York: Appleton-Century-Crofts, 1961), 5.
11 Lipsett, notes to Donald Brittain, 1.
12 Lipsett, notes to Donald Brittain, 2.
13 I must note that, while Lipsett wrote in broad philosophical terms about world events, these claims assume highly specific meaning in his use of newsreel imagery. There is no evidence that his proposal was conceived in relation to specific events or images; however, there are considerable memoranda dealing

with the licensing of stipulated footage, confirming that, while Lipsett's work was anchored in exploratory research, his collages were built with clear intention.

14  The long history of compilation filmmaking at the NFB, dating back to its origins and the celebrated work of Stuart Legg, meant that the institution was at its most comfortable navigating such solicitations of non-original footage; to have Lipsett doing so more closely resembled the labour the NFB had come to expect of its filmmakers, and there is no evidence that he was ever denied expense requests for the acquisition of footage.

15  Lipsett had solicited this material from Grant McLean, it having first been licensed from Parthenon by the NFB for Theodore Conant's series *The Child of the Future* (1964). Lipsett flips the orientation of the image from its original and excludes the more triumphant climax of these experiments in which a miniature rocket is launched. Lipsett had also requested footage of Marshall McLuhan, host of *The Child of the Future*, but the footage of McLuhan was left unused. Arthur Lipsett, Letter to Grant McLean, January 21, 1965, Production file 64-623 (*A Trip Down Memory Lane*), National Film Board Archives, Montreal, Quebec.

16  Memoranda related to Project Mercury, the behaviours of the rhesus monkeys, and the associated controversies around animal testing and subject origins are presented in John M. Logsdon, *Exploring the Unknown: Selected Documents in the History of the U.S. Civil Space Program, Volume 7* (Washington: NASA, 1995). The contemporaneous account by James M. Grimwood (*Project Mercury: A Chronology*, Washington: NASA, 1963), issued by NASA's Office of Scientific and Technical Information, is likewise useful in forming a full vision of the space monkey program.

17  The photographs are drawn from the mid-century documentary art photography movement; the image of the Black man is W. Eugene Smith's portrait of a Haitian man in a trance, "Mad Eyes" (1959), and the image of the old woman is an untitled piece by Sabine Weiss (1957), whose work Lipsett had previously drawn from for a collage in *Free Fall*. Lipsett had also approached Henri Cartier-Bresson with a request to use material from his journey to Castro's Cuba but was refused.

18  George McLain was a pioneering pension advocate of interwar-era California, best known for running in the 1960 presidential primary; an obscure figure by 1965, the presence of his image here is purely semiotic, an intercourse of slogan and symbol.

19  Dusty Vineberg, "Television and Radio: Drama Schedule Poses Problem," *Montreal Star*, May 15, 1968, 16.

20  For a further account of the mondo genre, see Mark Gooddall, *Sweet & Savage: The World Through the Shockumentary Film Lens* (London: Headpress, 2006).

21  The history of the compilation film had, coincidentally, been mapped out in the same year as *A Trip Down Memory Lane* was produced, in Jay Leyda's *Films Beget Films: A Study of the Compilation Film* (New York: Hill and Wang, 1964).

22  Lipsett's interest in behaviourism is established in his proposal for *A Trip Down Memory Lane* and intersects with many of his ideas around human agency within a technocracy from *21-87* onward. He was immersed in this material: like many young intellectuals in the 1960s, he would have encountered behavioural psychology through newspapers, magazines, and pop culture, and he is likely

to have read the influential texts of B.F. Skinner; in addition, his partner Judith Sandiford was a former student in the McGill Department of Psychology.
23  Gaucher, *The Arthur Lipsett Project*.
24  Michael Posner, *Leonard Cohen, Untold Stories: The Early Years* (New York: Simon & Schuster, 2020), 313.
25  Biggs's antagonism to Lipsett is well-recorded: Joseph Koenig attributes to him a remark, provoked by the enthusiasm for Lipsett's films from Swedish officials visiting the NFB, that "we only need one Norman McLaren, there's not room for another guy like that; we don't need Arthur Lipsett." Gaucher, *The Arthur Lipsett Project*.
26  *Imperial Sunset* information sheet, circa 1967, Production file E-28-66 (*Imperial Sunset*), National Film Board Archives, Montreal, Quebec.
27  Arthur Lipsett, Editing notes for *Commonwealth* (*Imperial Sunset*), circa 1967, Production file E-28-66 (*Imperial Sunset*), National Film Board Archives, Montreal Quebec.
28  A.M. Saltarelli, Letter to Arthur Lipsett, December 22, 1966, 2005.0080.26.AR, Personal Correspondence, Arthur Lipsett Collection, Cinémathèque québécoise Archives, Montreal, Quebec.

## Seven: Print-Out

1  Lipsett's charts of his recordings are held at the Cinémathèque québécoise. Arthur Lipsett, "Découpage sonore de *Fluxes*," December 6, 1965, 1999.0089.AR, *Fluxes* (script document), Arthur Lipsett Collection, Cinémathèque québécoise Archives, Montreal, Quebec.
2  In Lois Siegel's 1986 article on Lipsett's life and death, his Film Board colleague Gordon Martin comments on his work that it anticipated the then-contemporary "world of moving images we know today, where we can flip back and forth on the TV between 30 channels." Lois Siegel, "A Clown Outside the Circus," *Cinema Canada* 134 (1986): 10–14. Lipsett's conception of rapid televisual modulation was following a current in the broader culture in the 1960s, where such modulation could be glimpsed in video art and in strange exceptions, as when the fictional David Holzman (L.M. Kit Carson) shoots a time-lapse of his television set in *David Holzman's Diary* (1967).
3  Arthur Lipsett, Stock shots used in *Print-Out* (*Fluxes*), circa 1968, Production file A-70-67 (*Fluxes*), National Film Board Archives, Montreal, Quebec.
4  Arthur Lipsett, "Notes for *Fluxes*" (proposal), November 12, 1965, 2005.0055.32.SC, *Fluxes* (scenario), Arthur Lipsett Collection, Cinémathèque québécoise Archives, Montreal, Quebec.
5  Lipsett, "Notes for *Fluxes*."
6  Lipsett, "Notes for *Fluxes*."
7  Lipsett, "Notes for *Fluxes*."
8  George Maciunas, *Purge Manifesto* (*Fluxus Manifesto*) (New York: George Maciunas, 1963).
9  The informal membership of the Fluxus movement in the 1960s included Dick Higgins, Jackson Mac Low, George Brecht, Nam June Paik, Al Hansen, La Monte

Young, and Yoko Ono. Formed from the initial influence of John Cage, their orientalist fascinations grew in the mid-1960s, in another parallel to Lipsett's preoccupations with East Asian spirituality. Thomas Kellein and Jon Hendricks, *Fluxus* (London: Thames and Hudson, 1995).

10 Arthur Lipsett, "Strangely Elated" (chart), circa 1961, Production file 61-205 (*Very Nice, Very Nice*), National Film Board Archives, Montreal, Quebec.

11 Arthur Lipsett, "*Fluxes*" (transcript of Warren McCulloch as interviewed by Roman Kroitor, circa 1961), Lipsett's transcription dated December 9, 1965, 2017.0055.62.AR, *Fluxes* (text document), Arthur Lipsett Collection, Cinémathèque québécoise Archives, Montreal, Quebec.

12 Arthur Lipsett, "*Fluxes* Ideas Page" (loose-leaf sheets), undated, 2005.0055.23.AR, Holographic notes, Arthur Lipsett Collection, Cinémathèque québécoise Archives, Montreal, Quebec.

13 Lipsett, "*Fluxes* Ideas Page."

14 Gérard Bertrand, Memorandum to Frank Spiller and Frank Keyes, November 26, 1968, Production file A-70-67 (*Fluxes*), National Film Board Archives, Montreal, Quebec.

15 Bertrand, Memorandum to Frank Spiller and Frank Keyes.

16 Frank Spiller, Memorandum to Tom Daly, November 29, 1968, Production file A-70-67 (*Fluxes*), National Film Board Archives, Montreal, Quebec.

17 Tom Daly, Letter to Arthur Lipsett, December 4, 1968, 2005.0055.32.SC, *Fluxes* (scenario), Arthur Lipsett Collection, Cinémathèque québécoise Archives, Montreal, Quebec. Daly's enduring support of Lipsett is evident in the letter, calling the film "a succès fou."

18 Arendt argues that Eichmann's disavowal of responsibility was a result of a poisonous bent of law-abiding conformity. Hannah Arendt, *Eichmann in Jerusalem: A Report on the Banality of Evil* (New York: Viking Press, 1963), 135. Arendt's text brings together two of Lipsett's recurrent interests: behaviourist psychology and the perils of fascism. Much of *Fluxes* is a response to Arendt, as the film takes "following orders" as one of its central themes.

19 Lipsett, "*Fluxes* Ideas Page."

20 Linda S. Godfrey and Richard D. Hendricks, *Weird Wisconsin: Your Travel Guide to Wisconsin's Local Legends and Best Kept Secrets* (New York: Sterling Publishing Company, 2005), 135.

21 This might be taken as a play on the production culture of the NFB with its simultaneity of working, production, and release titles; the state of the object itself becomes freed up by these declarations of incompleteness, which throws willful doubt on Lipsett's careful montage, casting it as a kind of patchwork exercise.

22 The figure appears to have facial hair and is dressed in flaming rags that may have been a robe. Again, the case of Thich Quang Duc's self-immolation is brought to mind, but the casual saunter of the figure is unusual and disturbing. The figure is deeply ambiguous: some see the figure as a grown man, others as a child. Mark Slade, a friend of Lipsett's based in the NFB's distribution division, who wrote an article praising *Fluxes* upon its release, mistakes them for two completely separate figures: "In an early Lipsett film a clean-shaven monk sets fire to himself. He burns. Lipsett's latest film, *Fluxes*, shows a boy on fire. Jellied flames cling to the child's

flesh; he struggles to his feet and stumbles across the jungle paddy, out of frame, to seek help." Slade's perplexing reading of this shot is in keeping with the long history of viewers projecting actions and emotions onto Lipsett's shots that are not present within them. Mark Slade, "Arthur Lipsett: The Hyper-Anxious William Blake of Modern Cinema," *Gazette* (Montreal), December 7, 1968, 21.

23  Francis M. Cornford, *Plato's Cosmology: The Timaeus of Plato* (London: Routledge, 1935), 225.
24  To this, Mark Slade adds that the icosahedron "aptly replaces the beauty of a rose, say, or a human smile." Like these generalities, the icosahedron dangled before Zemel's face also conceals identity and transforms the figure into pure symbol. Slade, "Arthur Lipsett," 21.
25  Arthur Lipsett, "*Fluxes*" (notecards and loose-leaf papers), undated, 2005.0080.22. AR, *Fluxes* (notebook), Arthur Lipsett Collection, Cinémathèque québécoise Archives, Montreal, Quebec. Lipsett does not attribute the quote.
26  Lipsett, "*Fluxes*."
27  In David Millar's *Buddhism* (1962), this footage is an introduction to the order of monks and the role of education in Buddhism. Lipsett's substitution of the teacher's speech for this pithy, disconnected, absent lesson deepens the comedy of the affair, a lampooning of what Western converts to Buddhism might expect to hear.
28  Lipsett, "*Fluxes*."
29  Lipsett, "*Fluxes*."
30  Lipsett uses this expression in his flowchart collages for *Fluxes*: Arthur Lipsett, passages of prayers covering body; the storage and movement of information, self-programming unit teaching; the glass box: a film construction; Pound—the mock epic. These collages are intact in the Cinémathèque québécoise archives. The collages contain many aesthetic ideas that are absent from the final film but that demonstrate Lipsett's evolving thinking around sound–image relationships. These charts also contextualize *Fluxes* within a range of Lipsett's inspirations, from Masaki Kobayashi's *Kwaidan* (1965), in which a priest covers the body of a blind musician in the text of the Heart Sutra to protect him from evil spirits, to Charles Mingus's "Ecclusiastics" (Atlantic Records, 1962), in which the band's harmonizations are met with the composer's extemporized wails of gospel fervour.
31  Slade, "Arthur Lipsett," 21.
32  Arthur Lipsett, notes to Donald Brittain "in order to communicate to him some basic thinking on our film Time Capsule," December 25, 1964, Arthur Lipsett Collection, Cinémathèque québécoise Archives, Montreal, Quebec, 4.
33  Arthur Lipsett, "The Search," November 22, 1967, Box VI #18, Tom Daly Collection, National Film Board Archives, Montreal, Quebec.
34  Lipsett, "The Search."
35  Alan Watts, *The Wisdom of Insecurity: A Message for the Age of Anxiety* (New York: Pantheon, 1951), 19.
36  Slade, "Arthur Lipsett," 21.
37  Arthur Lipsett, Memorandum to NFB Production Staff, January 23, 1968, 2005.0055.41.AR, Professional Correspondence, Arthur Lipsett Collection, Cinémathèque québécoise Archives, Montreal, Quebec.

38  Even this is based on only partial records: Lipsett is reporting information from the Montreal Distribution Office, which only accounted for bookings made with their own collection, the Municipal Library, and Loyola's Vanier Library.

### Eight: Landscapes

1   Michael Posner, *Leonard Cohen, Untold Stories: The Early Years* (New York: Simon & Schuster, 2020), 313.
2   Add to this list the "girls at the lab," whom Judith Sandiford recalls as a focus of Arthur Lipsett's gratitude and camaraderie. The female workforce that ran the Film Board's in-house lab were generous with Lipsett. As informal collaborators, they were the central resource for many filmmakers at the NFB but remain uncredited on the films that they processed, printed, and made opticals for.
3   Arthur Lipsett, "Landscapes" (proposal), September 4, 1968, Production file B-101-68 (*N-Zone*), National Film Board Archives, Montreal, Quebec.
4   Amelia Does speculates that the NFB's shift away from candid observation by the late 1970s caused Lipsett strain on a future project, *Traffic Flow*. Amelia Does, *Do Not Look Away: The Life of Arthur Lipsett* (London, ON: Amelia Does, 2012), 92. It is arguable that this change was already coming by 1968, beginning with the hostile reception with which Hubert Aquin's *À St-Henri le cinq septembre* (1962) was met, but was dramatically compounded by the more recent condemnation of Tanya Ballantyne's *The Things I Cannot Change* (1967). Lipsett's departure from shooting candid material, as stated in his proposal, was in keeping with looming legal apprehensions regarding cinema vérité.
5   Lipsett, "Landscapes."
6   Zemel himself disavows any authorial participation in the film in *Remembering Arthur* (2006), suggesting that his credit as co-writer was more a matter of an evolving discourse between the men than an organized collaboration. Martin Lavut, *Remembering Arthur* (Toronto: Public Pictures, 2006), DVD.
7   Arthur Lipsett, "Towards Purification" (loose-leaf sheets), undated, 2005.0055.23.AR, Holographic notes, Arthur Lipsett Collection, Cinémathèque québécoise Archives, Montreal, Quebec.
8   Lipsett, "Towards Purification."
9   Lipsett, "Towards Purification."
10  Program Committee Meeting Minutes, September 24, 1968, 2005.0055.14.SC, *N-Zone* (*Landscapes*), Arthur Lipsett Collection, Cinémathèque québécoise Archives, Montreal, Quebec.
11  Secret Museum of Mankind, "World's Greatest Collection of Strange & Secret Photographs" (advertisement), *Keen Magazine*, July 1942.
12  Arthur Lipsett, "The Mundane (Sangsāra) vs. Nirvana: A Farewell to the Material World" (flowchart), undated, 1999.0090.AR, Arthur Lipsett Collection, Cinémathèque québécoise Archives, Montreal, Quebec.
13  Lipsett, "The Mundane (Sangsāra) vs. Nirvana." That these Buddhist trappings are also Omnist is made clear among the loose-leaf papers when Lipsett notes that "Jesus said 'I am the door,'" a statement that, among Lipsett's aphoristic loose-leafs,

assumes the ambiguity of being at once a profound definition of prophethood and a claim as absurd as "I am the eggman."

14  Arthur Lipsett, "*N-Zone*" (diagram), undated, 2005.0040.AR, *Strange Codes* (mixing document), Arthur Lipsett Collection, Cinémathèque québécoise Archives, Montreal, Quebec.

15  The triangles that represent both the thesis and the climax are rooted with great intention in what Lipsett referred to as his "theory of the universe." He explained his theory to a class at McMaster University in 1967: "A thought I had today was that the universe is all composed of male elements and female elements," Lipsett recalled, "and I was asking Henry whether this would hold up, and he said that 'the triangle is upon us.'" For Lipsett and Zemel, the triangle represents an alternative to dualities and contraries, a broadening of objecthood and presence beyond the immediacy of perception. It suits Lipsett's 'pataphysical sensibility as a silly but authoritative declaration of ill-defined meaning in itself. Arthur Lipsett, public lecture, McMaster University, 1967, tape provided by Brett Kashmere from the collection of Henry Zemel.

16  Leah Dickerman, *Dada: Zurich, Berlin, Hannover, Cologne, New York, Paris* (Landover, Maryland: The National Gallery of Art, 2005), 159.

17  Lipsett, "*N-Zone*" (diagram).

18  Lipsett, "Landscapes."

19  Lipsett speaks about Alan Watts specifically in a talk at McMaster University in 1967. Lipsett paraphrases Watts's discussion of the roots of tantra in weaving, from *The Two Hands of God* (1963), as a means of explaining his approach to the search for meaning in his work and in the world at large: "As there is no woven cloth without the simultaneous interpenetration of warp and woof, there is no world without both the exhalation and inhalation of the Supreme Self." Lipsett takes Watts's explanation of the tantra as a checkerboard model for art-making, the mapping of complex energy patterns. Lipsett, public lecture.

20  One of the readiest examples among Canadian artists, coming in the same years as Lipsett's secret museums, is Joyce Wieland's *Reason Over Passion* (1968–69), a multiform work that exists as a 16mm film and two quilts, one featuring the phrase in English, the other in French.

21  Arthur Lipsett, Letter to Frank Spiller, July 25, 1969, Box VI #8, Tom Daly Collection, National Film Board Archives, Montreal, Quebec.

22  Tom Daly, Memorandum to Desmond Dew and Ron Birch, December 31, 1969, Production file B-101-68 (*N-Zone*), National Film Board Archives, Montreal, Quebec.

23  It has been suggested by several observers, including Zemel himself, that Lipsett was assuming Zemel's family as a surrogate family because of problems in his own family life. However, it might also be argued that Lipsett was not trying to become Zemel and assume his specific life—rather, he was seeking to give concrete form to the camaraderie of his soon-to-be post-NFB life, an act of replacing what he had lost in the collapse of Unit B. For this reason, *N-Zone* counts among its participants his new friends (Henry Zemel and Israel Charney), his oldest friends (John Max and Martin Lavut), and his partner (Judith Sandiford).

24  This is the closest Lipsett will come to an explicit declaration of allegiance to the Neo-Dada impulses present in the art of his era, and it gives added credence

to those claims that *Fluxes* takes its inspiration from the Fluxus movement. In his editing chart, Lipsett even refers to it as "fluxes book," further suggesting a possible lack of differentiation he saw between his chosen term of "fluxes"—the fluxes of an anastomotic metaphor—and "fluxus," the stylized name of the Fluxus group.

25  An extended version of this monologue is on a tape recording, care of Henry Zemel by way of Brett Kashmere, which Lipsett introduces as *Readings from the Instruction Box*. The recording begins with Lipsett reading an article from the New York Times; thereafter, the provenance of his text is uncertain, but much of it seems plainly autobiographical, as when he says, "I use my walls as a kind of note board; the apartment is a kind of think factory."

26  This music is drawn from the Lyrichord album *Buddhist Drums, Bells and Chants*. Arthur Lipsett, Letter to Lyrichord Discs, Inc., April 8, 1969, Production file B-101-68 (*N-Zone*), National Film Board Archives, Montreal, Quebec.

27  Arthur Lipsett, "*N-Zone*" (flowchart), undated, 1999.0088.AR, *N-Zone* (script document), Arthur Lipsett Collection, Cinémathèque québécoise Archives, Montreal, Quebec.

28  Lipsett, "*N-Zone*" (flowchart).

29  By coincidence, not long after Lipsett made *N-Zone* but before it was released, trepanation enjoyed a brief renewal of interest through the strange case of Amanda Feilding, a British student who trepanned her own forehead with a dentist's drill as an act of advocacy for the practice. The act was captured on film in her documentary *Heartbeat in the Brain* (1970).

30  A full account of the Parti Rhinocéros is given in Munroe Eagles, James P. Bickerton, Alain-G. Gagnon, and Patrick J. Smith (eds.), *The Almanac of Canadian Politics* (New York: Oxford University Press, 1995).

31  The rhinoceros is also a potent image in then-recent Absurdist theatre: in Eugene Ionesco's *Rhinocéros* (1959), a satire of the conformity that preceded the Second World War, the population of a small French village become rhinoceroses.

32  Lipsett, "*N-Zone*" (diagram).

33  Lipsett, "*N-Zone*" (flowchart).

34  Sheila Melvin and Jindong Cai, *Rhapsody in Red: How Western Classical Music Became Chinese* (New York: Algora Publishing, 2004), 262.

35  Arthur Lipsett, Memorandum to Tom Daly, June 25, 1970, Production file B-101-68 (*N-Zone*), National Film Board Archives, Montreal, Quebec.

36  Lipsett, "*N-Zone*" (flowchart).

37  Lipsett, public lecture.

38  Lipsett, "*N-Zone*" (notebook, loose-leaf, unpaginated). Arthur Lipsett Collection, Cinémathèque québécoise Archives, Montreal, Quebec.

39  Lipsett, "*N-Zone*."

40  Lipsett, "*N-Zone*."

41  Lipsett, "*N-Zone*."

42  Lipsett, "*N-Zone*."

43  Lipsett, "*N-Zone*" (flowchart).

44  Lois Siegel, "A Clown Outside the Circus," *Cinema Canada* 134 (October 1986): 12–13.

45  Terry Ryan, "Six Filmmakers in Search of an Alternative," *Artscanada* (April 1970): 25.
46  Ryan, "Six Filmmakers in Search of an Alternative."
47  Henry Zemel, "*N-Zone* Continued," *Artscanada* 158/159 (August–September 1971): 56–57.
48  Paul Gaffney, "Six Lipsett Films Get Tedium Rating," *Ottawa Journal*, October 23, 1970, 41. Critic Paul Gaffney's hostility towards the films is at least partly aimed at Zemel, whose efforts to interpret Lipsett he describes as "vague stabs." One might counter this: how else to stab at such dense, rich, and mystical work but vaguely? Of Lipsett's films, Gaffney addressed their comprehensibility in the dismissive populism of the day: "if you don't happen to be Arthur Lipsett, your chances of following most of his films are indeed thin."
49  Zemel, "*N-Zone* Continued," 57. By virtue of its titling, "*N-Zone* Continued" suggests the influence of Barbara Rubin's *Christmas on Earth Continued* (1967), a multiform work that was a music festival, a film proposal, and a party, offered as an extension of her controversial film *Christmas on Earth* (1963). Like Zemel's piece, *Christmas on Earth Continued* refuses to be bound by the container of the film, building an impossible sequel in text that is both a proposal for future art and a paracinematic extension in itself.
50  *N-Zone* information sheet, circa 1970, Production file B-101-68 (*N-Zone*), National Film Board Archives, Montreal, Quebec.
51  *N-Zone* information sheet.
52  Siegel, "A Clown Outside the Circus," 11.

### Nine: Messages from Space

1  Judith Sandiford, interview by author, February 19, 2022.
2  Tom Daly, Letter to Arthur Lipsett, August 19, 1970, 2005.0055.14.SC, *N-Zone* (*Landscapes*), Arthur Lipsett Collection, Cinémathèque québécoise Archives, Montreal, Quebec.
3  For a comprehensive account of the events leading up to the October Crisis, see D'Arcy Jenish, *The Making of the October Crisis: Canada's Long Nightmare of Terrorism at the Hands of the FLQ* (Toronto: Doubleday, 2018).
4  Arthur Lipsett, Letter to Tom Daly, October 19, 1970, Production file B-101-68 (*N-Zone*), National Film Board Archives, Montreal, Quebec.
5  Arthur Lipsett, Letter to Tom Daly, February 5, 1971, Production file B-101-68 (*N-Zone*), National Film Board Archives, Montreal, Quebec.
6  Arthur Lipsett, "*Strange Codes*" (application to the Canada Council for the Arts), file A74-0475, Canada Council for the Arts Archives. Provided to the author by Brett Kashmere.
7  The area in which Lipsett and Sandiford were living was considerably removed from where independent filmmaking activity was becoming established in the city. At this time, in the early- to mid-1970s, much of this scene was anchored in the city's downtown, and there is no evidence of any exchange between himself and the city's experimental filmmakers, many of whom idolized Lipsett and none

of whom seem to have been aware that Lipsett was present in the city at the time. This offers a fine parallel to his life in Montreal, isolating himself in the Clifton Arms, far from the trendier areas where his colleagues were living.

8   Sandiford, interview by author.
9   Sandiford, interview by author.
10  Sandiford, interview by author.
11  Amelia Does, *Do Not Look Away: The Life of Arthur Lipsett* (Amelia Does, 2012), 84.
12  Charlotte Nadeau, Letter to Arthur Lipsett, April 22, 1969, 2005.0055.41. AR, Professional Correspondence, Arthur Lipsett Collection, Cinémathèque québécoise Archives, Montreal, Quebec.
13  The Canada Council 14th Annual Report, 1970–71 (Ottawa: CCA, 1971), 37.
14  The Canada Council 15th Annual Report, 1971–72 (Ottawa: CCA, 1972), 31.
15  There is extensive documentation in the Cinémathèque québécoise archives that details Lipsett's search for information about appropriate pastes and glues for affixing paper to plywood. Arthur Lipsett, Letter to M. Taylor, April 30 (year unknown, circa 1971), 2005.0080.26.AR, Personal Correspondence, Arthur Lipsett Collection, Cinémathèque québécoise Archives, Montreal, Quebec.
16  Arthur Lipsett, "Composition Notes," undated, 2005.0055.23.AR, Holographic notes, Arthur Lipsett Collection, Cinémathèque québécoise Archives, Montreal, Quebec.
17  Lipsett, "Composition Notes."
18  Lipsett, "Composition Notes."
19  Arthur Lipsett, "*Strange Codes*" (notebook), undated circa 1973, 2005.0049.AR, *Strange Codes* (notes), Arthur Lipsett Collection, Cinémathèque québécoise Archives, Montreal, Quebec. This document, the densest and most intact of Lipsett's research notebooks, is unpaginated.
20  Arthur Lipsett, *Strange Codes* loose-leaf notes, undated, 2005.0055.23.AR, Holographic notes, Arthur Lipsett Collection, Cinémathèque québécoise Archives, Montreal, Quebec. In the mid-1960s, Lipsett would frequently refer to Rimbaud's text as a source for *Free Fall*, and, according to his colleague Mark Slade, Lipsett came to see the film as a transit from Dylan Thomas's metaphoric invisible force to Rimbaud's enigmatic reflections on love, mortality, and failure. Mark Slade, interview with Amelia Does, as referenced in Does, *Do Not Look Away*, 65. Rimbaud's prose poem is a work of bald intimacy the likes of which does not exist in Lipsett's work; its title phrase may instead have been, for Lipsett, a ready metaphor for tortuous experiences and, at the same time, an expression so absurd, so out of context, so overtly romantic, as to undermine its complaint—much like that tortured soul, benighted in love, who becomes a fabulous opera.
21  Lipsett, "*Strange Codes*" (notebook).
22  Lipsett, "*Strange Codes*" (notebook).
23  Lipsett, "*Strange Codes*" (notebook).
24  Arthur Lipsett, Letter to L.M. Kit Carson, undated (circa 1966), 2005.0055.39.SC, 21-87 (documents), Arthur Lipsett Collection, Cinémathèque québécoise Archives, Montreal, Quebec.
25  A significant part of Valentin's legacy is his influence on Brecht's conception of epic theatre—in particular, providing inspiration for Brecht to integrate chalked

face paint onto his actors as a metaphor for fear. Walter Benjamin, *Understanding Brecht*, trans. Anna Bostock (London and New York: Verso, 1983), 115.

26  Arthur Lipsett, "*21-87*" (handwritten note), circa 1963, Production file 62-206 (21-87), National Film Board Archives, Montreal, Quebec.

27  Lipsett, "*Strange Codes*" (notebook).

28  Lipsett, "*Strange Codes*" (notebook).

29  Lipsett, "*Strange Codes*" (application).

30  Lipsett, "*Strange Codes*" (application).

31  Lipsett, "*Strange Codes*" (notebook).

32  The phrase "spirit theatre in miniature" first appears in Lipsett's notebook for *Strange Codes*; it seems a culmination of his ideas about epic theatre and the theatre of cruelty, a further evolution of his theatre of the unconscious, and its new name gives it the impression of being at once epic and fugitive, like a mural depicting some greater force in the universe.

33  Lipsett, "*Strange Codes*" (application).

34  Arthur Lipsett, "*Strange Codes*" (application to the Canada Council for the Arts), file A74-0475, Canada Council for the Arts Archives. Provided to the author by Brett Kashmere.

35  The full exchange, from the notification of his successful application to Jacques's letter in receipt of the repayment, is chronicled in a series of letters between Lipsett, Jacques, and Timothy Porteous (Associate Director to the Canada Council), dated July 1974 to February 1975, which can be found in file A74-0475, Canada Council for the Arts Archives, provided to the author by Brett Kashmere.

36  Penni Jacques, Letter to Arthur Lipsett, December 6, 1974, file A74-0475, Canada Council for the Arts Archives. Letter provided to the author by Brett Kashmere.

37  These character "names" are given in Lipsett's annotated shot list, found in his notebook for the film.

38  The theatricality of Lipsett's approach is elaborated in his notebook, which includes a dramatis personae under the heading "to invent a new kind of theatre dialogue." His characters for an earlier version of the film are there named as Bruck Nuber, Maltrane Quantry, Missy Hassee, Howzer Souzer, Chinee Ché, and Pineapple Parfain, names that recall the surreal, evocatively psychedelic names found in the pseudonyms of Captain Beefheart's Magic Band or in the novels of Thomas Pynchon. Lipsett, "*Strange Codes*" (notebook).

39  Lipsett, "*Strange Codes*" (notebook).

40  Lipsett, "*Strange Codes*" (notebook).

41  Arthur Lipsett, "*Fluxes*" (transcript of Warren McCulloch as interviewed by Roman Kroitor, circa 1961), Lipsett's transcription dated December 9, 1965, 2017.0055.62. AR, *Fluxes* (text document), Arthur Lipsett Collection, Cinémathèque québécoise Archives, Montreal, Quebec.

42  Lipsett, "*Strange Codes*" (notebook).

43  That Lipsett is building a Trojan horse is easily overlooked because of the tightness of Zemel's compositions and the subtlety of the presence of the blueprint. However, in his shot list, Lipsett clearly notes that this sequence focuses on the construction of the Trojan horse. The French blueprint remains in the collection of Cinémathèque québécoise.

44　Lipsett, "*Strange Codes*" (notebook).
45　Michael Dancsok, "Transcending the Documentary: The Films of Arthur Lipsett" (master's thesis, Concordia University, 1997), 61.
46　Comte De Lautréamont, *Les Chants de Maldoror*, trans. Guy Wernham (New York: New Directions, 1965), 263.
47　Trasov and Morris's Mr. Peanut project is commemorated in a video produced with Byron Black, *My Five Years in a Nutshell* (1975), described by the artists as "a three dimensional anthromorph." Peter Steven, *Brink of Reality: New Canadian Documentary Film and Video* (Toronto: Between the Lines, 1993).
48　This is not a spontaneous improvisation of camera operator Zemel; Lipsett notes his own laughter in his shot list and its inclusion is an intentional breaking of the fourth wall.
49　Lipsett, "*Strange Codes*" (notebook).
50　In American experimental film, Lipsett had holy fools as his contemporaries—chiefly, George Landow (later known as Owen Land), who in *Wide Angle Saxon* (1975) did to *The Confessions of Saint Augustine* what Lipsett had done to *Steppenwolf*. Like *Strange Codes*, *Wide Angle Saxon* offers no ready key to its signification, with the filmmaker miming madrigals in an angelic medieval costume.
51　A thorough accounting of this event is offered by Jeffery W. Fenn, whose book is named for the event: *Levitating the Pentagon: Evolutions in the American Theatre* (Newark: University of Delaware Press, 1992).
52　Accounts of these happenings can be found in Michael Schumacher, *Dharma Lion: A Critical Biography of Allen Ginsberg* (New York: St. Martin's Press, 1992), 497–501.
53　Allen Ginsberg, introduction to Gregory Corso, *Gasoline* (San Francisco: City Lights, 1958), 13.
54　Lipsett, "*Strange Codes*" (notebook).
55　Lipsett, "*Strange Codes*" (loose-leaf notes).
56　In Lipsett's notebook, he makes frequent references to Gustav Meyrink's *The Golem*, a haunting modern novel that explores the mental stability of its protagonist and draws from the legend of the Golem—a creature animated by a Rabbi to wreak vengeance and serve the course of justice, to defend the Prague ghetto from antisemites and pogroms. Lipsett's conceits are indebted to Meyrink, in whose novel memories and dreams can be exchanged with the swap of a hat. There is also a sense that all of Lipsett's various disguises are Golems of legend, animated by his spells to perform magical defense. His act of making a two-dimensional collaged human has its roots in the legend of the Golem, but also in the first of the Gothic horrors: Dr. Victor Frankenstein's Creature. The Golem of legend is an agent of vengeance and justice, but Lipsett's collage is more like Frankenstein's Creature, a defiant experiment. The human body itself is the original time machine.
57　Arthur Lipsett, Letter to the producers of *Sprockets* "concerning the screening of *Strange Codes*," undated, Arthur Lipsett Collection, Cinémathèque québécoise Archives, Montreal, Quebec.
58　Lipsett, Letter to the producers of *Sprockets*.
59　Lipsett, Letter to the producers of *Sprockets*.

60 Lipsett, Letter to the producers of *Sprockets*.
61 Lipsett, Letter to the producers of *Sprockets*.
62 Entry for *"Sprockets,"* January 27, 1975, CBC Archives website.
63 The most famous such books are mass-produced miniature Bibles, whose density made their portable scale less a solution than a challenge, an amusing disconnect between form and function; in then-recent memory, the miniature book was popularized through pocket-sized editions of *Quotations from Chairman Mao Tse-tung*, which was more aphoristic and useful.
64 Lois Siegel, "A Clown Outside the Circus," *Cinema Canada* 134 (1986): 11.
65 Between 2017 and 2019, I undertook a digital restoration of *Strange Codes* in partnership with the Cinémathèque québécoise. In lieu of proper elements, the only non-print materials available are Lipsett's cutting copy of the soundtrack and negatives belonging only to his outtakes. There is only one print of the film, which is archived under the care of the Cinémathèque québécoise.
66 Lipsett, *"Strange Codes"* (notebook).
67 Lipsett, *"Strange Codes"* (notebook).
68 Lipsett, *"Strange Codes"* (notebook).

## Ten: The 10,000 Things

1 Lois Siegel, "A Clown Outside the Circus," *Cinema Canada* 134 (1986): 11.
2 Lipsett's unproduced concepts for films appear throughout his notes, which should often be taken lightly as the passing thoughts and jokes of a great and restless wit. His concept for *The 10,000 Things* appears to have been that of a feature-length colour fiction film, distinct in its debts to Jewish Europeans in serving as a reverse journey to that of Franz Kafka's *Amerika* (1927), which would become an "underground Nosferatu" dealing with, among other things, "the Golem of Prague," to be scripted by Lipsett and Zemel. Many other concepts are detailed in a loose, undated sheet of paper stored in the Cinémathèque québécoise archives. Titled "List of Film Ideas," the list does not provide insight into Lipsett's process, but it does testify to Lipsett's cheerful, creative restlessness, with some ideas reduced to just a title: "Walker Evans—journey across Canada with still camera"; "film on stone-memories, possibly shot in Rome"; "Environmental Soup (Breer - 'conversation' film)"; "De-fusing the Technological Bomb"; "Unfolding Heart"; "Monkey-School."
3 Amelia Does, *Do Not Look Away: The Life of Arthur Lipsett* (London: Amelia Does, 2012), 86.
4 Ellery Littleton, "Lipsett: A Tour with a Film Revolutionary," *Monday Magazine* 1:11 (September 1975): 8.
5 Littleton, "Lipsett," 8.
6 Littleton, "Lipsett," 8.
7 Littleton, "Lipsett," 8.
8 Littleton, "Lipsett," 8.
9 Michael Dancsok, "Transcending the Documentary: The Films of Arthur Lipsett" (master's thesis, Concordia University, 1997), 63. Further to Tree's admission that

Lipsett was trying not to hurt people, friends of Lipsett's have claimed that, in the 1970s, he became paranoid about the potential for his art to be weaponized. However, so many of the claims about Lipsett's paranoia seem impossible to distinguish from accounts of his sense of humour. Beyond the paranoia of unknowingly making cinematic war machines, there is also the implication that he may have been struggling with violent impulses, as when Judith Sandiford witnessed him chopping up their chair. There is no record that Arthur Lipsett ever behaved violently toward anyone.

10   Terry Ryan, interview by Michael Dancsok, November 22, 1996, transcript.
11   Pierre Juneau, Letter to Arthur Lipsett, May 26, 1976, Box XVI #8, Tom Daly Collection, National Film Board Archives, Montreal, Quebec.
12   Tom Daly, Letter to Pierre Juneau, June 1, 1976, Box XVI #8, Tom Daly Collection, National Film Board Archives, Montreal, Quebec.
13   Judith Sandiford, interview by author, February 19, 2022.
14   Does, *Do Not Look Away*, 85.
15   Terry Ryan, "Six Filmmakers in Search of an Alternative," *Artscanada* (April 1970): 25.
16   This story has become a leering, pitiless facet of Lipsett lore—that he paid for a cab from Toronto to Montreal. It was offered to Lois Siegel by Henry Zemel with the only context being that Lipsett was "frustrated by some incident." It has been used to demonstrate his instability, his detachment from reality, his impracticality, his eccentricity. Sandiford has no regrets about giving him the money, and the suicide threat he had made has never been part of the various accounts of his cab ride. With his environmental sensitivities and the strain of his anxieties, that taxi must have been the only means Lipsett could imagine to get back home.
17   Lois Siegel, "Arthur Lipsett: A Close Encounter of the Fifth Kind." *Cinema Canada* 44 (February 1978): 10.
18   Siegel, "Arthur Lipsett," 10.
19   Siegel, "Arthur Lipsett," 10.
20   Siegel, "Arthur Lipsett," 10.
21   Martin Lavut, *Remembering Arthur* (Toronto: Public Pictures, 2006), DVD.
22   Arthur Lipsett, "Traffic Flow" (program committee information sheet), February 16, 1978, Production file 42-015 (*Traffic Flow / Canada Vignette*), National Film Board Archives, Montreal, Quebec.
23   Lipsett, "Traffic Flow."
24   Arthur Lipsett, Letter of resignation to the National Film Board, September 21, 1978, Production file 42-015 (*Traffic Flow / Canada Vignette*), National Film Board Archives, Montreal, Quebec.
25   Eric Gaucher, *The Arthur Lipsett Project: A Dot on the Histomap* (Montreal: The National Film Board of Canada, 2007), DVD.
26   Thomas Schnurmacher, "Lipsett's archives being seized," *Gazette* (Montreal), July 19, 1979, 51.
27   Schnurmacher, "Lipsett's archives being seized," 51.
28   Schnurmacher, "Lipsett's archives being seized," 51.
29   Christopher Nutter, who had made a sign for the project, relates to Michael Dancsok that the disputed amount was ultimately paid to the Film Board by Lipsett's aunt, Etta Goldberg; according to Nutter, "Arthur was trying to release some

money for artists who had already done work for the project and should be paid." Christopher Nutter, interview by Michael Dancsok, March 16, 1997, transcript.
30 Schnurmacher, "Lipsett's archives being seized," 51.
31 Does, *Do Not Look Away*, 96.
32 Christopher Nutter, interview by Michael Dancsok, March 16, 1997, transcript.
33 Fortner Anderson, interview by Michael Dancsok, March 14, 1997, transcript.
34 Lois Siegel, interview by Michael Dancsok, February 7, 1997, transcript.
35 Lavut, *Remembering Arthur*.
36 Fortner Anderson, interview by Michael Dancsok, March 14, 1997, transcript.
37 Nancy Carpenter, interview by Michael Dancsok, July 11, 1997, transcript.
38 Lois Siegel, interview by Michael Dancsok, February 7, 1997, transcript.
39 Nancy Carpenter, interview by Michael Dancsok, July 11, 1997, transcript.
40 Jacques Drouin, "Very sad, very sad," *Asifa Canada* 14:2 (September 1986), 14.
41 Drouin, "Very sad, very sad," 14.
42 Does, *Do Not Look Away*, 101.
43 Lucas's first films, produced while he was a student at the University of Southern California, were heavily influenced by experimental cinema. The inspirations he took from Lipsett—not formal, but merely referential—appear as early as his first feature, the dystopian fantasy *THX 1138*, in which human beings are known by numbers, and again in *Star Wars: A New Hope*, wherein a jail cell in which Princess Leia is being held is labelled cell "2187." Lucas's reverence for Lipsett was never profound, but it loomed sufficient in his mind to be superficially stitched into his movies.
44 Brakhage himself, it might be noted, learned of Lipsett only after his death, on a trip to Vancouver in 1988. Shortly after encountering his work for the first time, Brakhage bemoaned in a public lecture that "the Canadian Film Board didn't seem to respect him at all. In fact, I've had confirmation that they're dumping all his films. They're throwing them out in the trash! The print that I'm showing you right now comes from the trash, thanks to Richard Kerr." Stan Brakhage, "Ciné-Document: On Canadian Painting and Film," *Canadian Journal of Film Studies* 14:1 (Spring 2005): 94–95. This author's own prints of Lipsett's films likewise came from the trash. Contrary to myth, Arthur Lipsett's films were not assembled from scraps in the National Film Board's rubbish bins: they were tossed there.
45 The National Film Board's attempt at conciliatory treatment of Lipsett was further undermined in 2010 when their animation division produced Theodore Ushev's *The Lipsett Diaries*, a purely speculative, poorly researched, and maudlin film that dramatizes a lurid fantasy of Lipsett's tragedy. It prominently features filmmaker Xavier Dolan narrating a histrionic script in which a fictional Lipsett howls with resentment at the memory of his mother. The film ends with a cowardly disavowal of its own veracity, admitting ominously that "his diaries have never been found" and, further, that "this film is not a biography of the filmmaker Arthur Lipsett," that it "is not based on real diaries," that it "is the product of the authors' imagination and free interpretation," evidence of the enduring disrespect with which Lipsett's memory was held at the Film Board. There is no evidence that Arthur Lipsett ever kept a diary.
46 Mark Slade, "Arthur Lipsett: The Hyper-Anxious William Blake of Modern Cinema," *Gazette* (Montreal), December 7, 1968, 21.

# FILMOGRAPHY

### Arthur Lipsett as director, 1960-75

*Anything Can Happen on Channel 6* (1960, b&w, 60s, National Film Board of Canada [NFB])
*Very Nice, Very Nice* (1961, b&w, 7m01s, NFB)
*Experimental Film* (1962, b&w, 27m26s, NFB)
*21-87* (1963, b&w, 9m38s, NFB)
*Free Fall* (1964, b&w, 9m32s, NFB)
*A Trip Down Memory Lane* (1965, b&w, 12m39s, NFB)
*Fluxes* (1968, b&w, 24m06s, NFB)
*N-Zone* (1970, b&w, 45m24s, NFB)
*Strange Codes* (1975, b&w, 23m18s, Giraffe Productions)

### Arthur Lipsett as animator and co-animator, 1960-61

*Men Against the Ice* (dir. David Bairstow, 1960, b&w, 28m05s, NFB)
*Les femmes parmi nous* (dir. Jacques Bobet, 1961, b&w, 29m30s, NFB)
*The Conquest of Freedom* (pr. James Beveridge and Marcel Martin, 1961, b&w, 27m53s, NFB)

### Arthur Lipsett as editor and co-editor, 1961-68

*Collège contemporain* (dir. Pierre Patry, 1961, b&w, 20m18s, NFB)
*Regards sur l'occultisme* (dir. Guy L. Coté, 1965, b&w, 116m18s, NFB)

*The Continuing Past* (dir. Stephen Ford, 1966, col., 24m03s, NFB)
*Imperial Sunset* (dir. Josef Reeve, 1967, b&w, 17m58s, NFB)
*The Invention of the Adolescent* (dir. Patricia Watson, 1967, b&w, 28m13s, NFB)
*Data for Decision* (dir. David Millar, 1968, col., 22m15s, NFB)
*North* (dir. Josef Reeve, 1968, col., 14m36s, NFB)

## Arthur Lipsett as photographer, 1962

*À Saint-Henri le cinq septembre* (dir. Hubert Aquin, 1962, b&w, 41m36s, NFB)

# ARCHIVAL SOURCES

Cinémathèque québécoise Archives, Montreal, Quebec.
Collection of Michael Dancsok, Regina, Saskatchewan. Interview transcripts.
Collection of Brett Kashmere, Oakland, California.
Collection of Judith Sandiford, Hamilton, Ontario.
Montreal Museum of Fine Arts Archives, Montreal, Quebec.
National Film Board Archives, Montreal, Quebec.

# BIBLIOGRAPHY

Arendt, Hannah. *Eichmann in Jerusalem: A Report on the Banality of Evil.* New York: Viking Press, 1963.

Artaud, Antonin. "Van Gogh, the Man Suicided by Society." In *Antonin Artaud: Selected Writings*, edited by Susan Sontag and translated by Helen Weaver, 483–512. New York: Farrar, Straus and Giroux, 1976.

"Arthur Lipsett Best Student in Art School." *Gazette* (Montreal), April 4, 1955, 12.

Barthes, Roland. *Mythologies.* Translated by Annette Lavers. New York: Hill and Wang, 1972.

Benjamin, Walter. *Understanding Brecht.* Translated by Anna Bostock. London and New York: Verso, 1983.

Brakhage, Stan. "Ciné-Document: On Canadian Painting and Film." *Canadian Journal of Film Studies* 14, no.1 (Spring 2005): 84–100.

Bray, John. "The Œconomy of Human Life: An 'Ancient Bramin' in Eighteenth-Century Tibet." *Journal of the Royal Asiatic Society* 19 (third series), no. 4 (2009): 439–58.

Broomer, Stephen. *Hamilton Babylon: A History of the McMaster Film Board.* Toronto: University of Toronto Press, 2016.

Buber, Martin. *Between Man and Man.* Translated by Ronald Gregor Smith. London: Kegan Paul, 1947.

Cage, John. *The Selected Letters of John Cage.* Edited by Laura Kuhn. Middletown, CT: Wesleyan University Press, 2016.

Cage, John. *Silence: Lectures and Writings.* Middletown, CT: Wesleyan University Press, 1961.

Callenbach, Ernest. "The Films of Stan Brakhage." *Film Quarterly* 14, no. 3 (1961): 47–48.

Cardullo, Bert. *Theories of the Avant-Garde Theatre: A Casebook from Kleist to Camus*. Lanham, MD: Scarecrow Press, 2013.

Cornford, Francis M. *Plato's Cosmology: The Timaeus of Plato*. London: Routledge, 1935.

Corso, Gregory. *Gasoline*. San Francisco: City Lights, 1958.

Coté, Guy L. *A Private Collection of Experimental Abstract Poetic Personal Amateur Animation Films*. St. Laurent, QC: Guy L. Coté, 1960.

Curry, Manfred and Verlag F. Bruckmann. *Flug und Wolken*. Munich: München, 1932.

Dancsok, Michael. "Ciné-Documents: An Introduction to Notes and Proposals by Arthur Lipsett." *Canadian Journal of Film Studies* 7, no. 1 (Spring 1998): 43–46.

Dancsok, Michael. "Transcending the Documentary: The Films of Arthur Lipsett." Master's thesis, Concordia University, 1997.

Dickerman, Leah. *Dada: Zurich, Berlin, Hannover, Cologne, New York, Paris*. Landover, MD: The National Gallery of Art, 2005.

Dobson, Nichola. *Norman McLaren: Between the Frames*. New York: Bloomsbury, 2018.

Does, Amelia. *Do Not Look Away: The Life of Arthur Lipsett*. London, ON: Amelia Does, 2012.

Does, Amelia. "'Worthwhile Insanity': On Collage Filmmaking and Arthur Lipsett, an Interview with Bruce Conner." *INCITE!: Journal of Experimental Media* 2 (2010): 62–72.

Drouin, Jacques. "Very sad, very sad." *ASIFA Canada* 14, no. 2 (1986): 14.

Dupree, Robert S. "The Copious Inventory of Comedy." In *The Terrain of Comedy*, edited by Louise Cowan, 163–94. Dallas, TX: Dallas Institute of Humanities and Culture, 1984.

Eagles, Munroe, James P. Bickerton, Alain-G. Gagnon, and Patrick J. Smith, eds. *The Almanac of Canadian Politics*. New York: Oxford University Press, 1995.

Elder, R. Bruce. *The Films of Stan Brakhage in the American Tradition of Ezra Pound, Gertrude Stein, and Charles Olson*. Waterloo, ON: Wilfrid Laurier University Press, 1999.

Evans, Gary. *In the National Interest: A Chronicle of the National Film Board from 1949 to 1989*. Toronto: University of Toronto Press, 1991.

Fenn, Jeffery W. *Levitating the Pentagon: Evolutions in the American Theatre.* Newark, DE: University of Delaware Press, 1992.
Frye, Northrop. *Northrop Frye on Canada.* Edited by Jean O'Grady and David Staines. Toronto: University of Toronto Press, 2003.
Gaffney, Paul. "Six Lipsett Films Get Tedium Rating." *Ottawa Journal,* October 23, 1970, 41.
Gardiner, Bob. "Televiews." *Ottawa Citizen,* November 21, 1962, 35.
Gaucher, Eric, dir. *The Arthur Lipsett Project: A Dot on the Histomap.* Montreal: The National Film Board of Canada, 2007. DVD.
Gernsback, Hugo. *Ralph 124C 41+: A Romance of the Year 2660.* New York: The Stratford Company, 1925.
Godfrey, Linda S., and Richard D. Hendricks. *Weird Wisconsin: Your Travel Guide to Wisconsin's Local Legends and Best Kept Secrets.* New York: Sterling Publishing Company, 2005.
Gooddall, Mark. *Sweet & Savage: The World Through the Shockumentary Film Lens.* London: Headpress, 2006.
Grierson, John. "A Film Policy for Canada." *Canadian Affairs* 1, no. 11 (1944): 3–15.
Grierson, John. "First Principles of Documentary." *Cinema Quarterly* 1, no. 2 (1932): 67–72.
Grigor, Angela Nairne. *Arthur Lismer, Visionary Art Educator.* Montreal: McGill-Queen's University Press, 2002.
Grimwood, James M. *Project Mercury: A Chronology.* Washington: NASA, 1963.
Harcourt, Peter. "The Innocent Eye: An Aspect of the Work of the National Film Board of Canada." *Sight and Sound* 34, no. 1 (Winter 1964–65): 19–25.
Hébert, Pierre. "Procès d'une collection." *Objectif* 32 (1965): 3–16.
Hesse, Herman. *Steppenwolf.* New York: Henry Holt and Company, 1929.
Hill, Derek. "Short and Sharp." *Observer* (London), December 24, 1961, 21.
Hillyer, Aaron. *The Disappearance of Literature: Blanchot, Agamben, and the Writers of the No.* New York: Bloomsbury, 2013.
James, David E. *To Free the Cinema: Jonas Mekas & the New York Underground.* Princeton, NJ: Princeton University Press, 1992.
Jenish, D'Arcy. *The Making of the October Crisis: Canada's Long Nightmare of Terrorism at the Hands of the FLQ.* Toronto: Doubleday, 2018.
Jones, D.B. *Movies and Memoranda: An Interpretative History of the National Film Board of Canada.* Ottawa: Canadian Film Institute, 1981.
Jones, D.B. "Tom Daly's Apprenticeship." *Film History* 3, no. 3 (1989): 259–73.

Keats, John. *The Complete Poetical Works and Letters of John Keats*. Cambridge: Houghton, Mifflin and Company, 1899.

Kellein, Thomas, and Jon Hendricks. *Fluxus*. London: Thames and Hudson, 1995.

King, Ross. *Defiant Spirits: The Modernist Revolution of the Group of Seven*. Vancouver: Douglas & McIntyre, 2010.

Kracauer, Siegfried. *Theory of Film: The Redemption of Physical Reality*. New York: Oxford University Press, 1960.

Comte De Lautréamont, *Les Chants de Maldoror*, trans. Guy Wernham. New York: New Directions, 1965.

Lavut, Martin, dir. *Remembering Arthur*. Toronto: Public Pictures, 2006. DVD.

Leyda, Jay. *Films Beget Films: A Study of the Compilation Film*. New York: Hill and Wang, 1964.

Lima, Benjamin. *Violence in Concrete: Wolf Vostell's Art and Germany After 1945*. New York: Peter Lang, 2016.

Lipton, Lawrence. *The Holy Barbarians*. New York: Julian Messner, 1959.

Littleton, Ellery. "Lipsett: A Tour with a Film Revolutionary." *Monday Magazine* 1, no. 11 (1975): 8.

Logsdon, John M. *Exploring the Unknown: Selected Documents in the History of the U.S. Civil Space Program*, Volume 7. Washington: NASA, 1995.

MacDonald, Scott. *Cinema 16: Documents Toward a History of the Film Society*. Philadelphia: Temple University Press, 2002.

Maciunas, George. *Purge Manifesto (Fluxus Manifesto)*. New York: George Maciunas, 1963.

"Marina Greciano Captures Museum's Top Art Standing." *Gazette* (Montreal), April 8, 1957, 9.

Maud, Ralph. *Where Have the Old Words Got Me? Explications of Dylan Thomas's Collected Poems*. Montreal: McGill–Queen's University Press, 2003.

Melvin, Sheila, and Jindong Cai. *Rhapsody in Red: How Western Classical Music Became Chinese*. New York: Algora Publishing, 2004.

Moneo, Cameron. "Dissertation in Which There Appears Lost Punchlines, Dreadful Puns, Low Resolution, Etc.: On the failure of humour in avant-garde film and video." Ph.D. diss., York University, 2019.

Myrdal, Jankel. "On source criticism in world history." In *Methods in World History: A Critical Approach*, edited by Arne Jarrick, Jankel Myrdal, and Maria Wallenberg Bondesson, 45–83. Lund: Nordic Academic Press, 2016.

Nadeau, Jean-François. *The Canadian Führer: The Life of Adrien Arcand.* Toronto: James Lorimer & Co., 2011.
Nolan, Brian. *Donald Brittain: Man of Film.* Amherstview, ON: Digiwire, 2004.
Pilon, Jean-Claude. "Sept films canadiens / *21-87*, film canadien d'Arthur Lipsett." *Objectif* 23–24 (1963): 40–41.
Posner, Michael. *Leonard Cohen, Untold Stories: The Early Years.* New York: Simon & Schuster, 2020.
Rice, Ron. "Foundation for the Invention and Creation of Absurdist Movies," *Film Culture* 39 (1965): 117.
Robertson, Ritchie. *Mock-Epic Poetry from Pope to Heine.* Oxford: Oxford University Press, 2009.
Robinson, Ira. *A History of Antisemitism in Canada.* Waterloo, ON: Wilfrid Laurier University Press, 2015.
Robinson, Ira. "Reflections on Antisemitism in French Canada," *Canadian Jewish Studies* 21 (2014): 90–122.
Ryan, Terry. "Six Filmmakers in Search of an Alternative." *Artscanada* 142/143 (1970): 25–27.
Schaeffer, Pierre. *In Search of a Concrete Music.* Translated by Christine North and John Dack. Berkeley: University of California Press, 2012.
Schnurmacher, Thomas. "Lipsett's archives being seized." *Gazette* (Montreal), July 19, 1979, 51.
Schumacher, Michael. *Dharma Lion: A Critical Biography of Allen Ginsberg.* New York: St. Martin's Press, 1992.
Siegel, Lois. "Arthur Lipsett: A Close Encounter of the Fifth Kind." *Cinema Canada* 44 (1978): 9–10.
Siegel, Lois. "A Clown Outside the Circus." *Cinema Canada* 134 (1986): 10–14.
Skinner, B.F. *Cumulative Record: A Selection of Papers.* New York: Appleton-Century-Crofts, 1961.
Slade, Mark. "Arthur Lipsett: The Hyper-Anxious William Blake of Modern Cinema." *Gazette* (Montreal), December 7, 1968, 21.
Sterritt, David. "Wrenching Departures: Morality and Absurdity in Avant-Garde Film." In *The Last Laugh: Strange Humors of Cinema*, edited by Murray Pomerance, 93–108. Detroit: Wayne State University Press, 2013.
Steven, Peter. *Brink of Reality: New Canadian Documentary Film and Video.* Toronto: Between the Lines, 1993.
Sutton, Gloria. *The Experience Machine: Stan Vanderbeek's Movie-Drone and Expanded Cinema.* Boston, MA: MIT Press, 2015.

Théorêt, Hugues. "The Rise and Fall of Adrien Arcand: Antisemitism in 20th Century Quebec." *Antisemitism Studies* 3, no. 2 (Fall 2019): 231–72.

Thomas, Dylan. *The Collected Letters*. Edited by Paul Ferris. London: J.M. Dent, 1985.

Tindall, William York. *A Reader's Guide to Dylan Thomas*. New York: Noonday Press, 1962.

Vineberg, Dusty. "A 'Short' Story: Waste-basket to Potential Oscar." *Montreal Star*, February 24, 1962, 5.

Vineberg, Dusty. "Television and Radio: Drama Schedule Poses Problem." *Montreal Star*, May 15, 1968, 16.

Watts, Alan. *The Two Hands of God: The Myths of Polarity*. New York: George Braziller, 1963.

Watts, Alan. *The Wisdom of Insecurity: A Message for the Age of Anxiety*. New York: Pantheon, 1951.

Wees, Wiliam. "From Compilations to Collage: The Found-Footage Films of Arthur Lipsett." *Canadian Journal of Film Studies* 16, no. 2 (Fall 2007): 2–22.

Wood, Gaby. *Living Dolls: A Magical History of the Quest for Mechanical Life*. London: Faber, 2003.

Wright, James K., and Allyson Rogers. *They Shot, He Scored: The Life and Music of Eldon Rathburn*. Montreal: McGill–Queen's University Press, 2019.

Yablon, Nick. *Remembrance of Things Present: The Invention of the Time Capsule*. Chicago: University of Chicago Press, 2019.

Zemel, Henry. "*N-Zone* Continued." *Artscanada* 158/159 (1971): 54–57.

# INDEX

*21-87* (Lipsett), 56–69, 72–74, 76, 79–80, 83, 88, 90–91, 94, 101, 103, 110, 113, 120, 129–30, 143, 148, 160–61, 163, 191, 211–12n22
*23 Skidoo* (Biggs), 104, 125

*A is for Architecture* (Budner and Verrall), 80, 199n39
*A La Mode* (VanDerBeek), 49–50
*The Abduction of a Sabine Woman* (Giambologna), 20
Academy Awards, 39, 42, 104
*Achooooo Mr. Kerrooschev* (VanDerBeek), 49–50
Adenauer, Konrad, 98–99
Alexander, D.A., 166
*American Bandstand* (series), 146
*The Americans* (Frank), 35
*Amerika* (Kafka), 222n2
Anderson, Fortner, 187–88
Anger, Kenneth, 102
*Angkor: The Lost City* (Blais and Parker), 78
*Animal Altruism* (Lipsett), 102
*Antikythera Philosopher*, 20
*Anything Can Happen on Channel 6* (Lipsett), 19–21, 27, 29–30, 34, 37, 53, 77–78, 83, 107, 135, 164. *See also* Hors-d'oeuvre
Aquin, Hubert, 22, 215n4

Arcand, Adrien, 9–10, 22–23
Arendt, Hannah, 111, 118
Armstrong, Louis, 31
Arnold, Marian (née Lipsett), 8, 10–11, 190
Art Association of Montreal, 10–12. *See also* School of Art and Design
Artaud, Antonin, 6, 161
*The Arthur Lipsett Project: A Dot on the Histomap* (Gaucher), 192, 201n8
*At Home* (Lavut), 205n24

Bach, Johann Sebastian, 200n44
*Bardo Thodol*, 68–69
Bairstow, David, 19
Balanchine, George, 75
Balfour, Arthur (Baron Riverdale), 98, 100
Ballantyne (Tree), Tanya, 182–84, 187, 189, 215n4
*Ballon Vole* (Dasque), 39
Barthes, Roland, 31
Bartlett, Richard, 2
*Beautiful Losers* (Cohen), 104
*Beauty and the Beast* (Cocteau), 82
Beckett, Samuel, 2–3, 29
Béliveau, Jean, 20
Berton, Pierre, 18, 27
Bertrand, Gérard, 110–11
Bessette, André (Brother André), 58

*Bethune* (Brittain), 89
Beveridge, James, 22, 116, 204n7
Bierstadt, Albert, 34
Biggs, Julian, 34, 212n25
Blackburn, Maurice, 82
Blais, Roger, 78
Blake, William, 71
*Blazes* (Breer), 45
*Blinkity Blank* (McLaren), 43–44, 47
*Blood and Fire* (Macartney-Filgate), 30
*Blue and Orange* (Ballantyne), 183
Bobet, Jacques, 22
*Book of Revelations*, 27, 61
Borowczyk, Walerian, 45–46
Bosch, Hieronymus, 57
Boyko, Eugene, 151–52
Brakhage, Stan, 202–3n30, 41, 43, 47, 191, 205–6n5, 207–8n6
Brandon Films, 178-79
Brecht, Bertolt, 161
Brecht, George, 212–13n9
Breer, Robert, 44–47, 77, 148
*Bringing Up Father* (comic strip), 120
Brittain, Donald, 89–92, 108, 201n3
Brook, Peter, 160–61
Broughton, James, 2
Bruce, Lenny, 32, 35, 174
Buber, Martin, 86, 88, 90
Buddhism, 4, 56, 65, 67, 69, 117, 121, 130–31, 139–41, 158, 179, 181
*Buddhism* (Millar), 214n27
Budner, Gerald, 199n39
Buñuel, Luis, 39
Burwash, Cecily, 103
Bush, Vannevar, 98
Bushmiller, Ernie, 167

Cadieux, Fernand, 44–46
Cage, John, 73–75, 108–9, 130, 138, 158, 167, 175
Callenbach, Ernest, 41
Cameron, Julia Margaret, 34
Camper, Fred, 196n9
Camus, Albert, 2–3, 29
*Canada at War* (series), 201n3
*Canada Carries On* (series), 25–26

Canada Council for the Arts, 157–58, 162–63
*Canada Vignettes* (series), 185
Canadian Federation of Film Clubs, 42–43
Canadian Filmmakers Distribution Centre, 42n4
Canadian Government Motion Picture Bureau, 15, 195n2
*The Candid Eye* (series), 16, 51
Carmichael, Franklin, 12
*Carmina Burana* (Orff), 80, 82
Carpenter, Nancy, 7, 198n12, 189–90
Carson, L.M. Kit, 68, 160, 212n2
Cartier-Bresson, Henri, 17, 35, 211n17
Cavalcanti, Alberto, 14
Cavara, Paolo, 100
Chagall, Marc, 147
*A Chairy Tale* (McLaren and Jutra), 207–8n6
*Les Chants de Maldoror* (Lautréamont), 48
Charney, Israel, 134–37, 144–45, 147
*The Child of the Future* (series), 211n15
Chiraeff, Ludmilla, 208n15
Chomón, Segundo de, 207–8n6
*Christmas Cracker* (Hale, Munro, Potterton and McLaren), 82
*Christmas on Earth* (Rubin), 218n49
Cinema 16, 203–4n3
Cinémathèque québécoise, 43, 191, 200n45, 209n27, 212n1, 214n30, 219n15, 220n43, 222n65, 222n2
*City of Gold* (Koenig and Low), 18, 27, 37, 80, 200n42
Clarke, Arthur C., 121
Clarke, Shirley, 43
Clarke Institute of Psychiatry, 156
Clifton Arms (Montreal), 19, 36, 43, 53, 156, 184, 189–90
Clish, Stanley, 201n3
*A Clockwork Orange* (Kubrick), 187
Cocteau, Jean, 82
Cohen, Leonard, 102, 104, 150
Cohl, Émile, 207–8n6
Coltrane, John, 166–67
Conant, Theodore, 211n15

*Concert for Piano and Orchestra* (Cage), 73
Conger Belson, Jane, 37
Conner, Bruce, 195n9, 44, 48, 50–51, 112
*The Continuing Past* (Ford), 103
Corey, Irwin, 174
Cornell, Joseph, 204n14, 138
*Corral* (Low), 149
Corso, Gregory, 174
*Cosmic Ray* (Conner), 50–51
Coté, Guy L., 37, 42–43, 50, 101, 123
Courtois, Dorothy, 185
Crosby, Bing, 93, 97
*The Crossroads of the World* (series), 22
Crowley, Aleister, 101
Crypt of Civilization, 87
Cunningham, Andrew, 119
cybernetics, 4, 56, 63, 110, 165. *See also* Warren McCulloch

dada, 2, 132
D'Avino, Carmen, 43
Dalai Lama, 117
Daly, Tom, 16–17, 27, 43, 52–53, 68, 84, 108, 111, 129, 133, 154–55, 163, 183, 188
Dancsok, Michael, 51, 164, 168, 188
Dasque, Jean, 40
*Data for Decision* (Millar), 116, 124
*David Holzman's Diary* (McBride), 212n2
*A Day in the Night of Jonathan Mole* (Brittain), 89
*The Days Before Christmas* (Macartney-Filgate, Jackson and Koenig), 32
de Chirico, Giorgio, 110, 114, 176
décollage, 76, 78–79. *See also* Wolf Vostell
Deren, Maya, 46
Diefenbaker, John, 131
Dinh Diem, Ngo, 65
*The Discovery Film* (proposal), 85–86, 88, 131, 185
Ditchburn, Robert, 187, 191
*Dr. Cyclops* (Schoedsack), 119
*Dr. Strangelove, or, How I Learned to Stop Worrying and Love the Bomb* (Kubrick), 203n37
Dodds, Baby, 21–22

Dodsley, Robert, 60
Does, Amelia, 198n15, 205n25, 215n4
Dolan, Xavier, 224n45
*Dom* (Borowczyk and Lenica), 45–46
*Donald Brittain: Filmmaker* (Martin), 210n3
Dostoyevsky, Fyodor, 90
*Dreams of Empire* (posterboard collage), 131
Drew, Les, 115
Drouin, Jacques, 190–91
du Plessis, Karl, 200n47
Dunning, George, 44–45
Dupree, Robert S., 5
Dürer, Albrecht, 142

*The Œconomy of Human Life* (Dodsley), 60
Eichmann, Adolf, 5, 111–12, 114–15, 119
Einstein, Albert, 99
Eisenhower, Dwight D., 20, 30, 34, 98
Elder, R. Bruce, 202–3n30, 207n23
Eldridge, Roy, 20
*Emak-Bakia* (Ray), 209n24
epic theatre, 161, 220n32
Ernst, Max, 48–49, 51
Evans, Gary, 199n32
Evans, Walker, 222n2
Evans-Wentz, Walter, 4, 68, 207n23, 130
*The Experimental Film* (Lipsett), 43–53, 55, 148

*The Face of Jesus* (Gage), 40
Falkner, Suki, 155
Faraday, Michael, 171, 177
Feeney, John, 202n22
Feilding, Amanda, 217n29
Fermi, Enrico, 101
Ferro, Pablo, 203n37
Ferron, Jacques, 142
*Fields of Sacrifice* (Brittain), 89
Film Canada, 204n4
Flaherty, Robert, 15
Fletcher, Trevor, 79
*Fluxus* (Lipsett), 5, 108–24, 130, 133–34, 139, 149, 155, 158, 162–63, 165

Fluxus (movement), 108–9, 136–37, 179, 183
*Fly Little Bird* (proposal), 27–29, 39. See also Very Nice, Very Nice
Focillon, Henry, 86
Folkways (record label), 4, 208n7
*Fontana Mix* (Cage), 73
Ford, Stephen, 103
*Four-Line Conics* (Fletcher), 79
Frank, Robert, 3, 35–37
*Free Fall* (Lipsett), 72–85, 88, 90–91, 94, 101, 103, 124–25, 129–30, 133, 155, 163, 167, 211n17, 219n20
Freud, Sigmund, 161
Freund, Karl, 79
Front de liberation du Québec, 154
Frye, Northrop, 13, 31, 34–35
The Fugs, 174

Gaffney, Paul, 218n48
Gage, Merrell, 40
Gall, Franz Joseph, 113
*Garden* (Nutter), 188
Gardiner, Bob, 52
Gaucher, Eric, 192
General Post Office (GPO) film unit, 14, 16
George VI, 34
Gernsback, Hugo, 63
Giambologna, 20
Gide, André, 164
Gilliam, Terry, 204n16
Gilmour, Clyde, 44–48, 51
Ginsberg, Allen, 174, 179, 183
Girodet de Roussy-Trioson, Anne-Louis, 78
Giroux, Lionel "Little Beaver", 31
Giuffre, Jimmy, 207n5
Global A Records (record label), 209n26
Glover, Guy, 44-48, 103, 108, 183, 203n36, 203n2
*Go! Go! Go!* (Menken), 207–8n6
Goldberg, Etta, 189, 223–24n29
Goldberg, Rube, 111, 115
*The Goldberg Variations* (Bach), 200n44
*The Golem* (Meyrink), 221n56
Gould, Glenn, 20
Grant, George, 204n7, 116

Greaves, William, 116
Greene, Robert, 175
Grierson, John, 14–16, 18, 23, 42, 45, 152, 199n34
Griffith, D.W., 15
Groves, Leslie, 98

Hale, Jeff, 19, 82
Halsman, Philippe, 99
Hansen, Al, 212–13n9
Harcourt, Peter, 37–38
Hartman, David, 138
Harris, Hilary, 39
Hayward, Stan, 44–45
*Heartbeat in the Brain* (Feilding), 217n29
Hebb, D.O., 102
*Helicopter Canada* (Boyko), 151
*Hen Hop* (McLaren), 18
Herschel, John, 34
Hesse, Herman, 159–60, 179
Higgins, Dick, 212–13n9
Hillyer, Aaron, 196n6
Hindenburg (dirigible), 95–96, 101
Hinduism, 68–69, 78
Hirohito, 99
Hirsch, Michael, 178
Histomap, 4, 6, 105, 123, 160
Höch, Hannah, 48
Hoffman, Abbie, 174
the holy fool, 6, 173–75, 179, 183, 188
Honzik, Karel, 86
*Hors-d'oeuvre* (Hale, Lamb, Lipsett, Pindal, Potterton and Verrall), 19, 21. See also Anything Can Happen on Channel 6
*Hôtel électrique* (Chomón), 207–8n6
*How Do You Say Hello* (series), 146

*I Ching*, 175, 183
Ibsen, Henrik, 108, 123
*The Idea of North* (Gould), 200n44
*Imperial Sunset* (Reeve), 103–4, 125, 152
*Impressions of Africa* (Roussel), 159
*In Search of a Concrete Music* (Schaeffer), 201n6
*Inauguration of the Pleasure Dome* (Anger), 101

*Indeterminacy* (Cage), 73
intercutting (editing technique), 20, 44, 64, 66, 79, 82, 92, 112, 114–15, 121, 135–36, 138, 142–46, 176
*The Invention of the Adolescent* (Watson), 103–4
Ionesco, Eugene, 2–3, 217n31
Ireland, Jill, 92

J.T. Donald and Company, 8
Jackson, Stanley, 30
Jacob, Henry, 37
Jacob, Thornwell, 87
Jacopetti, Gualtiero, 100
Jacques, Penni, 163
Jarry, Alfred, 2–3
Jeffreys, Thomas, 196n8
Jewish diaspora (Quebec), 8–10
Jewish General Hospital (Montreal), 7, 189, 191
Jiggs (comic strip character), 120
*Jobard ne peut pas voir les femmes travailler* (Cohl), 207–8n6
*The Jolifou Inn* (Low), 18, 80
Jones, Chuck, 45
Joplin, Scott, 200n43
Judaism, 10–11, 138
*Judoka* (Reeve), 103–4
Juneau, Pierre, 183
Jutra, Claude, 207–8n6

Kafka, Franz, 2–3, 57, 222n2
Keats, John, 38
Kempelen, Wolfgang von, 60
Kennedy, John F., 34, 99
Kennedy, Robert F., 129
Kerouac, Jack, 37
Kerr, Richard, 224n44
Khrushchev, Nikita, 34, 49–50, 82, 164
Kierkegaard, Søren, 69
King Jr., Martin Luther, 129
Kobayashi, Masaki, 214n30
Koenig, Joseph, 102–3, 124, 129, 212n25
Koenig, Wolf, 16, 18, 27, 59, 84, 102, 129
Kohanyi, Julius, 177–78
Kohler, Wolfgang, 173

Kowalski, Wladek "Killer", 31
Kracauer, Siegfried, 28, 56, 73, 147
Kramer, Eva, 11
Kramer, Renée, 11
Kramer, Zoltan, 11
Krieghoff, Cornelius, 18
Kroitor, Roman, 4, 16, 37, 58–60, 63–64, 67–68, 72, 88, 124, 165, 199n38, 199n39
Kubrick, Stanley, 40, 187, 191
Kuhn, Laura, 208n7
Kupferberg, Tuli, 174
*Kwaidan* (Kobayashi), 214n30

L'Amare, Pierre, 200n46
*La lutte* (Carriere, Brault, Fournier and Jutra), 31
LaLanne, Jack, 34
Lamb, Derek, 19, 52, 84, 186, 201n1, 201n8
Lambart, Evelyn, 16, 200n46
Land, Owen (George Landow), 221n50
*Landscapes* (working title), 129. *See also* N-Zone
Laozi, 148
Laporte, Pierre, 154
Larkin, Ryan, 187
*The Last of the Buffalo* (Bierstadt), 34
Lauterman, Dinah, 14
Lautréamont, Comte de, 48, 170
Lavut, Martin, 52–53, 82, 84, 112, 137, 142–43, 147, 155–57, 184, 187–88, 192
Lawrence, D.H., 86
Leach, Paul, 129
Legg, Stuart, 16, 25, 100, 211n14
Lenica, Jan, 44–46
Leoncavallo, Ruggero, 175
Leslie, Alfred, 37
Lincoln, Abraham, 34
Linder, Carl, 2
Lipchitz, Jacques, 20
*The Lipsett Diaries* (Ushev), 224n45
Lipsett, Norma, 8, 10–11
Lipsett, Solomon, 8, 10–11, 23, 191
Lipton, Lawrence, 36
Lismer, Arthur, 12–14, 17, 22–23, 28–29, 86

Littleton, Ellery, 182, 184
*Lively Arts* (series), 43
*The Living Machine* (series), 58-60, 63, 65, 67, 72-73, 95, 124, 165
*The Living Stone* (Feeney), 202n22
*Logos* (Conger Belson), 37
*Lonely Boy* (Koenig and Kroitor), 59, 67
Lorentz, Pare, 15
Low, Colin, 16-18, 27, 38, 52, 68, 84, 88, 103, 108, 129, 149-50
Lowy, Samuel, 86
Lucas, George, 191
Lye, Len, 14-15

Mac Low, Jackson, 212-13n9
Macartney-Filgate, Terence, 30, 32
*Macbeth* (Verdi), 114
MacDonald, J.E.H., 12
Maciunas, George, 108-9
Maclaine, Christopher, 2
*Mad Love* (Freund), 79
*The Magic Christian* (Southern), 159
Magritte, René, 204n16
Mallarmé, Stephane, 5
*A Man and His Dog Out for Air* (Breer), 45
*Man's Psychic Evolution* (posterboard collage), 131
The Manhattan Project, 98-99
Mao Zedong, 141, 144
Marais, Jean, 82
*Marat/Sade* (Weiss), 161
Marces, Gaby, 80
Martin, Gordon, 212n2
Martin, Kent, 210n3
Marx, Groucho, 171
*The Mask* (Roffman), 205n24
Mason, James, 169
Max, John, 67, 131, 136, 139-41, 143, 158, 187-89
May, Derek, 102
McCarthy, Joe, 174
McCarty, Robert, 40
McCulloch, Warren, 4, 58, 63, 67, 72-73, 95, 109, 133, 165, 167-68, 170, 172, 175-76, 178, 180-81
McKinny's Cotton Pickers, 98

McLain, George, 99
McLaren, Norman, 14, 16-18, 22, 28, 39-40, 42-44, 47-48, 52, 75, 82, 85, 88, 108, 163, 207-8n6, 212n25
McLean, Grant, 211n15
McLuhan, Marshall, 211n15
McManus, George, 120
McNamara, Robert, 98
Mead, Margaret, 58
Mead, Taylor, 195n4
Mekas, Jonas, 41-42, 47, 51, 205-6n5, 207-8n6
*Memorandum* (Brittain and Spotton), 89
Memphis Jug Band, 62
*Men Against the Ice* (Bairstow), 19
Menken, Marie, 207-8n6
Merz, Bob, 145
Meyrink, Gustav, 221n56
Mickey Mouse, 51
*A Midsummer Night's Dream* (Shakespeare), 99
Milestone, Lewis, 36
Millar, David, 43-44, 50-52, 116, 124, 214n24
Miller, Glenn, 19
Milton, John, 72
Mingus, Charles, 214n30
Molotov, Vyacheslav, 82, 97
Monroe, Marilyn, 34
Montreal International Film Festival, 21-22, 185
Monty Python, 204n16
*Mondo Cane* (Cavara, Jacopetti and Prosperi), 100-101
Moneo, Cameron, 196n11
Montparnasse, Kiki de, 209n24
Moore, Linda, 182
Morris, Michael, 170
Moskowitz, Sam, 63
*A Movie* (Conner), 50-51
*Mundane vs. Nirvana* (posterboard collage), 131
Munro, Grant, 82, 207-8n6
Musée des beaux-arts de Montreal, 11-12
musique concrète, 26, 200n44
Mussolini, Benito, 95-96

*N-Zone* (Lipsett), 127, 129–51, 153–55, 158, 162, 191
Nancarrow, Conlon, 5
*Nancy* (comic strip), 166–67
National Aeronautics and Space Administration, USA (NASA), 95, 101, 111, 121
National Film Act, Canada (1939), 1
National Film Act, Canada (1950), 16
National Film Board of Canada (NFB), 1–6, 14–19, 21–23, 26–27, 30–32, 36–37, 39–44, 47, 51–53, 56, 67, 74–75, 78, 82–83, 86, 88–89, 92, 100, 102, 104, 107–8, 110–11, 115, 124–25, 128–29, 133, 136, 148-51, 153–55, 157–58, 162–63, 177–78, 182–87, 190–92
*Neighbours* (McLaren), 17, 207–8n6
Neo-Dada, 2, 50–51, 78, 109, 183, 216–17n24
*New Film* (working title), 53, 57. See also 21-87
*The Nine Billion Names of God* (Clarke), 121
Nixon, Richard, 34, 99
*No Reason to Stay* (Ransen), 188
Nolan, Brian, 210n3
Nolan, Roy, 200n46
*North* (Reeve), 151–52
*Notes from the Underground* (Dostoyevsky), 90
Nutter, Christopher, 187–88, 190, 192, 198n12, 223–24n29

Oakes, Russell E. ('The Wacky Wizard of Waukesha'), 111–13
*The Occult Wars* (working title), 158–59. See also Strange Codes
*Ocean's 11* (Milestone), 36
October Crisis, 154–55
*Odds & Ends* (Conger Belson), 37
Olson, Charles, 202–3n30
*Olympic with Returned Soldiers* (Lismer), 12
Omnism, 4, 69, 72, 158, 174, 210n2, 215–16n13
Ono, Yoko, 212–13n9
*Opening Speech* (McLaren), 22

Orff, Carl, 80
Osborn, Robert, 40

Paik, Nam June, 212–13n9
*Paradise Lost* (Milton), 72
Parker, Morten, 78, 188
Parti de l'Unité Nationale, 9
Parti Rhincéros, 142–43
*Pas de deux* (McLaren), 75
Patry, Pierre, 22
*Paul Tomkowicz: Street-railway Switchman* (Kroitor), 37
Paul Whiteman Orchestra, 93
Pearson, Lester B., 119
Peking Opera, 144, 164–65, 167–68, 170, 180
*Pen Point Percussion* (McLaren), 204n11
Perry, Sam, 207n23
Peterson, Sidney, 2
Piaget, Jean, 86
Pilon, Jean-Claude, 72
Pindal, Kaj, 19, 28, 31, 52, 84, 115
*Pines of Rome* (Respighi), 50
Pius XII, 97
Plato, 114
*Poen* (Reeve), 104
*Police* (Macartney-Filgate), 32, 34, 82
Poolman, Willem, 204n4
Porteous, Timothy, 220n35
Potterton, Gerald, 19, 52, 82
*Prayers* (working title), 123. See also The Search
*The Praying Jew (Rabbi of Vitebsk)* (Chagall), 147
*Print-Out* (working title), 108. See also Fluxes
*Processional* (proposed title), 57–58, 61–62. See also 21-87
Project Mercury (NASA), 95
Prosperi, Franco E., 100
*Pull My Daisy* (Leslie and Frank), 37
*The Puzzle of Pain* (Lipsett), 102
Pynchon, Thomas, 220n38

Radio-Canada, 13, 21
*Ralph 124C 41+* (Gernsback), 63

Ransen, Mort, 188
Rathburn, Eldon, 32, 34, 36, 82
Raxlen, Rick, 136
Ray, Man, 209n24
Read, Herbert, 86
*Reason Over Passion* (Wieland), 216n20
*The Red Lantern with Piano Accompaniment*, 144, 147
Reeve, Josef, 103–4, 151–52
*Regards sur l'occultisme* (Coté), 101–2, 104, 123
*Remembering Arthur* (Lavut), 191–92, 205n25, 215n6
Rennick, Donald, 124
Respighi, Ottorino, 50
*Restricted Dogs* (Zemel), 102, 128, 135
*Revelation* (proposed title), 27. See also *Very Nice, Very Nice*
Rexroth, Kenneth, 197n14
Rhee, Syngman, 98
*Rhinocéros* (Ionesco), 217n31
Rice, Ron, 2
Richards, I.A., 196–97n13
Richie, Donald, 39
Ridley, Charles A., 195n5
Riefenstahl, Leni, 195n5
Rimbaud, Arthur, 159
Rockefeller, John D., 94
Roffman, Julian, 205n24
Rohmer, Sax, 173
*Rooftops of New York* (McCarty), 40
Roosevelt, Eleanor, 119
Roussel, Raymond, 159, 164
Royal Canadian Mounted Police, 9
Rubin, Barbara, 218n49
Rubin, Jerry, 174
Ruttmann, Walter, 26
Ryan, Terry, 52, 150, 183–84, 187
Rysanek, Leonie, 114

Sagan, Carl, 101
Sammartino, Bruno, 31
Sanders, Ed, 174
Sandiford, Judith, 11, 52–53, 56, 82, 84, 140, 143, 152–57, 162, 181, 183–84, 187–88, 190, 192, 197n3, 198n14, 202n28, 206n18, 211–12n22, 215n2, 216n23
Schaeffer, Pierre, 26
*Schichlegruber—Doing the Lambeth Walk* (Ridley), 195n5
schizophrenia, 1, 7, 154, 189
Schliemann, Heinrich, 159, 164, 166
Schneider, Eddie August, 93, 97
Schnurmacher, Thomas, 186–87
School of Art and Design (Montreal), 11–14, 17, 22, 84, 157. See also Art Association of Montreal
Schultz-Reichel, Fritz (Crazy Otto), 19–20, 30–31, 59, 83, 148
Schwitters, Kurt, 131–32, 138
*Science Friction* (VanDerBeek), 49–50
*The Search* (proposal), 123
*A Season in Hell* (Rimbaud), 159
*Seawards the Great Ships* (Harris), 40
*Secret Codes and Decoding* (Alexander), 166
*The Secret Museum of Mankind*, 130
*September Five at Saint-Henri* (Aquin), 22, 215n4
Shakery, Karin, 205n25
Shakery, Neil, 52, 84, 202n18, 205n25
Shepard, Alan, 58–59, 65
Siegel, Lois, 184, 187–90, 212n2
*Silence* (Cage), 74
Skinner, B.F., 210n10, 211–12n22
Slade, Mark, 123–24, 152, 179, 183, 187, 192, 213–14n22, 214n24
*The Sleep of Endymion* (Girodet de Roussy-Trioson), 78
Smith, Jack, 2
Smith, W. Eugene, 211n17
Sons of the South, 61
Southern, Terry, 159
Sparks, John B., 4, 105, 160
*Spartacus* (Kubrick), 40
Spiller, Frank, 111, 133, 152
Spotton, John, 89
*Sprockets* (series), 177–78
Sputnik (Soviet Union satellite), 116
*The Squeeze* (Harris), 203n36
*Star Wars* (franchise), 191

*Star Wars: A New Hope* (Lucas), 224n43
Stauffacher, Frank, 43
*Steppenwolf* (Hesse), 159, 179, 221n50
Sterne, Laurence, 159
Stettinius Jr., Edward, 97
Stone, Noel, 78
*Strange Codes* (Lipsett), 159–80, 182–83, 191
*Strangely Elated* (working title), 27–28, 57. *See also* Very Nice, Very Nice
Studio d'Essai, 26
Surrealism (movement), 2, 46, 48–51, 162

Taylor, Maxwell, 98
Telstar (AT&T satellite), 121
Tenney, James, 196n10
Theatre of the Absurd, 2–3
theatre of cruelty, 161, 220n32
Thelema, 101
Thich Quang Duc, 65, 213–14n22
*The Things I Cannot Change* (Ballantyne), 215n4
Thomas, Dylan, 71–72, 76, 115, 197n14, 207–8n6, 219n20
Thomson, Tom, 12
*THX 1138* (Lucas), 224n43
*Tibetan Yoga and Secret Doctrines* (Evans-Wentz), 130
*Time-Capsule* (proposed title), 90–91. *See also* A Trip Down Memory Lane
Tojo, Hideki, 80
Toynbee, Arnold, 116
*Traffic Flow* (Lipsett), 185–86, 215n4
Trasov, Vincent, 170
*A Trip Down Memory Lane* (Lipsett), 91–101, 103–4, 108–9, 117, 124, 130–31, 133, 145, 155, 167, 211–12n22
*Tristram Shandy* (Sterne), 159
*Triumph of the Will* (Riefenstahl), 195n5
Trudeau, Pierre, 129, 154, 183
Truman, Harry, 98
*A Trumpet for the Combo* (Parker), 188
*Tschaikovsky Pas de Deux* (Balanchine), 75
Tudor, David, 73
TV Ontario, 192–93
*Two Bagatelles* (McLaren and Munro), 207–8n6

*Two Films by Lipsett* (Rennick), 124–25, 155. *See also* Free Fall *and* A Trip Down Memory Lane
*The Two Hands of God* (Watts), 216n19

Urban Holiness Service, 76–77, 83
Ushev, Theodore, 224n45

Valentin, Karl, 161
Van Vliet, Don (Captain Beefheart), 220n38
VanDerBeek, Stan, 44, 48–51, 169
Vaucanson, Jacques de, 60
Verdi, Giuseppe, 114
Verrall, Robert, 19, 22, 27, 38, 40, 124, 129, 154, 163, 174, 185–86, 199n39
*Very Nice, Very Nice* (Lipsett), 25–40, 44, 46, 50–53, 55–57, 59, 65, 69, 79, 82–83, 91, 101, 103–4, 112, 117, 129–30, 134, 145, 148, 164, 185, 187–88, 190
Viet Nam war, 65, 98, 129, 192
Vineberg, Dusty, 198n17, 100
*Viridiana* (Buñuel), 39
Vlachos, Constantinos, 94
Vogel, Amos, 203–4n3
Vostell, Wolf, 78. *See also* décollage
Voyager (NASA), 101

*Walden* (Mekas), 207–8n6
Walker, Stuart, 113
*The Wardrobe* (Dunning, Hayward and Williams), 44–45
Warhol, Andy, 48
Washington, George, 34
Watson, Patricia, 103
Watts, Alan, 4, 124, 133
*Weekend* (Ruttman), 26
Wees, William, 196–97n13
Weinberg, Herman G., 44, 46–48
Weiss, Peter, 161
Weiss, Sabine, 209n23, 211n17
*Werewolf of London* (Walker), 113, 122
West, Adam, 121
Whalley, George, 32
*What on Earth!* (Pindal and Drew), 115
*Wide Angle Saxon* (Land), 221n50

Wieland, Joyce, 216n20
Wilhelm II, 94
Williams, Dick, 44–45
Williams, Evan, 94
*Winky Dink and You* (series), 48
*The Wisdom of Insecurity* (Watts), 124
Woloshen, Steven, 201n7
*The Women Among Us* (series), 22
World War I, 92, 132
World War II, 13, 16, 139, 166, 217n31
Wright, Basil, 14

Yin Cheng-Tsung, 144
Young, La Monte, 108n9

Zemel, Carol, 134, 140
Zemel, Henry, 102, 112, 114, 127–29, 131, 134–39, 141–45, 147, 149–51, 162–63, 172, 175, 220n43, 222n2, 223n16